**Real-Resumes for Auto Industry Jobs...**
including real resumes used to change careers
and resumes used to gain federal employment

Anne McKinney, Editor

PREP PUBLISHING

FAYETTEVILLE, NC

**PREP Publishing**
1110½ Hay Street
Fayetteville, NC 28305
(910) 483-6611

Copyright © 2003 by Anne McKinney

All rights reserved under International and Pan-American Copyright Conventions. No part of this book may be reproduced or copied in any form or by any means–graphic, electronic, or mechanical, including photocopying, taping, or information storage and retrieval systems–without written permission from the publisher, except by a reviewer, who may quote brief passages in a review. Published in the United States by PREP Publishing.

Library of Congress Cataloging-in-Publication Data

Real-resumes for auto industry jobs : including real resumes used to change careers and resumes used to gain federal employment / Anne McKinney [editor].
     p. cm. -- (Real-resumes series)
  ISBN 1-885288-33-6
  1. Resumes (Employment)  2. Automobile industry and trade. I. McKinney, Anne, 1948- II. Series.

  HF5383.R3953 2003
  650.14'2--dc21                                                    2003042946
                                                                                                      CIP

Printed in the United States of America

## By PREP Publishing

*Business and Career Series:*

RESUMES AND COVER LETTERS THAT HAVE WORKED

RESUMES AND COVER LETTERS THAT HAVE WORKED FOR MILITARY PROFESSIONALS

GOVERNMENT JOB APPLICATIONS AND FEDERAL RESUMES

COVER LETTERS THAT BLOW DOORS OPEN

LETTERS FOR SPECIAL SITUATIONS

RESUMES AND COVER LETTERS FOR MANAGERS

REAL-RESUMES FOR COMPUTER JOBS

REAL-RESUMES FOR MEDICAL JOBS

REAL-RESUMES FOR FINANCIAL JOBS

REAL-RESUMES FOR TEACHERS

REAL-RESUMES FOR STUDENTS

REAL-RESUMES FOR CAREER CHANGERS

REAL-RESUMES FOR SALES

REAL ESSAYS FOR COLLEGE & GRADUATE SCHOOL

REAL-RESUMES FOR AVIATION & TRAVEL JOBS

REAL-RESUMES FOR POLICE, LAW ENFORCEMENT & SECURITY JOBS

REAL-RESUMES FOR SOCIAL WORK & COUNSELING JOBS

REAL-RESUMES FOR CONSTRUCTION JOBS

REAL-RESUMES FOR MANUFACTURING JOBS

REAL-RESUMES FOR RESTAURANT, FOOD SERVICE & HOTEL JOBS

REAL-RESUMES FOR MEDIA, NEWSPAPER, BROADCASTING & PUBLIC AFFAIRS JOBS

REAL-RESUMES FOR RETAILING, MODELING, FASHION & BEAUTY JOBS

REAL-RESUMES FOR HUMAN RESOURCES & PERSONNEL JOBS

REAL-RESUMES FOR NURSING JOBS

REAL-RESUMES FOR AUTO INDUSTRY JOBS

REAL RESUMIX AND OTHER RESUMES FOR FEDERAL GOVERNMENT JOBS

REAL KSAS--KNOWLEDGE, SKILLS & ABILITIES--FOR GOVERNMENT JOBS

REAL BUSINESS PLANS AND MARKETING TOOLS

*Judeo-Christian Ethics Series:*

SECOND TIME AROUND

BACK IN TIME

WHAT THE BIBLE SAYS ABOUT...Words that can lead to success and happiness

A GENTLE BREEZE FROM GOSSAMER WINGS

BIBLE STORIES FROM THE OLD TESTAMENT

# Contents

Introduction ............................................................................................. 1

**PART ONE: SOME ADVICE ABOUT YOUR JOB HUNT** ........................................ 1
Step One: Planning Your Career Change and Assembling the Right Tools ......................... 4
Step Two: Using Your Resume and Cover Letter ............................................................... 6
Step Three: Preparing for Interviews ................................................................................ 9
Company Information Available at Libraries .................................................................. 10
Step Four: Handling the Interview and Negotiating Salary ............................................. 11
Looking Closer: The Anatomy of a Cover Letter ............................................................. 14

**PART TWO: REAL-RESUMES FOR AUTO INDUSTRY JOBS** ................................ 17
Account Manager, Corporate Car Rentals ....................................................................... 18
Account Sales Representative ......................................................................................... 20
Auto and Truck Repairman .............................................................................................. 22
Auto Damage Adjuster .................................................................................................... 24
Auto Dealer Business Manager ....................................................................................... 26
Auto Store Manager ........................................................................................................ 28
Auto Store Manager ........................................................................................................ 30
Auto Supply Store Manager ............................................................................................ 32
Automobile Business Manager ....................................................................................... 34
Automobile Dealership Business Manager ..................................................................... 36
Automobile Sales Consultant .......................................................................................... 38
Automotive Restorer ....................................................................................................... 40
BMW Technician ............................................................................................................. 42
Business Manager ........................................................................................................... 44
Business Office Manager ................................................................................................. 46
Car Wash Operations Manager ....................................................................................... 48
Certified Sales and Leasing Consultant ........................................................................... 50
Chief of Maintenance ...................................................................................................... 52
Claims Representative and Insurance Adjuster .............................................................. 54
Communications Maintenance Supervisor .................................................................... 56
Company President and Sales Manager ......................................................................... 58
Consultant with experience as a used car dealer ........................................................... 60
Controller for a trucking company .................................................................................. 62
Division General Manager ............................................................................................... 64
Driver & Vehicle Maintenance Supervisor ..................................................................... 66
Engineering Equipment Repairman and Heavy Truck and Equipment Repairman ............... 68
Finance Manager ............................................................................................................. 70
Fleet Maintenance Supervisor ........................................................................................ 72
Freight Coordinator ......................................................................................................... 74
Freight Terminal Manager ............................................................................................... 76
Gas Station Owner (Career Change) ............................................................................... 78
General Auto Sales Manager ........................................................................................... 80
General Manager for an auto auction business .............................................................. 82
General Manager and Founder ....................................................................................... 84
General Manager and Owner .......................................................................................... 86
Generator Mechanic ........................................................................................................ 88
Inspector .......................................................................................................................... 90
Long-Haul Truck Driver .................................................................................................... 92

Maintenance and Operations Supervisor .................................................. 94
Maintenance Director ............................................................................... 96
Maintenance Manager .............................................................................. 98
Manager Trainee ..................................................................................... 100
Mechanic and Shop Foreman .................................................................. 102
Owner and Founder of an Auto Audio Store (Career Change) ................. 104
Parts Department Manager ..................................................................... 106
President and General Manager .............................................................. 108
Power Plant Mechanic ............................................................................. 110
Public Relations Specialist and Sales Manager ....................................... 112
Purchasing Manager of Industrial Materials ........................................... 114
Quality Control Inspector ........................................................................ 116
Regional Marketing Representative ........................................................ 118
Rental Agent Supervisor ......................................................................... 120
Sales Consultant ..................................................................................... 122
Sales Representative .............................................................................. 124
Sales Representative and European Delivery Manager .......................... 126
Sales Manager for an automobile dealership ......................................... 128
Senior Advisor & Logistician (Career Change) ........................................ 130
Senior Claims Representative ................................................................. 132
Senior Mechanic ...................................................................................... 134
Senior Power Production Specialist ........................................................ 136
Senior Purchasing Manager .................................................................... 138
Service Manager ..................................................................................... 140
Service Station Manager ......................................................................... 142
Store Manager ........................................................................................ 144
Store Manager, Bikes and Motorcyles Shop ........................................... 146
Superintendent of Maintenance (Career Change) .................................. 148
Transportation Company Manager (Career Change) .............................. 150
Vehicle Maintenance Mechanic .............................................................. 152
Vehicle Maintenance Shop Foreman ...................................................... 154
Vehicle Maintenance Supervisor ............................................................ 156
Vehicle Maintenance Supervisor ............................................................ 158
Wheeled Vehicle Mechanic ..................................................................... 160

## PART THREE: APPLYING FOR FEDERAL GOVERNMENT JOBS ............ 163
Senior Transportation Terminal Manager (Resumix) .............................. 164
About 612s and KSAs with Continuation Sheets .................................... 167
Automotive Worker (KSAs) ..................................................................... 172
Maintenance Technician (KSAs) ............................................................. 175

# A WORD FROM THE EDITOR: ABOUT THE REAL-RESUMES SERIES

Welcome to the Real-Resumes Series. The Real-Resumes Series is a series of books which have been developed based on the experiences of real job hunters and which target specialized fields or types of resumes. As the editor of the series, I have carefully selected resumes and cover letters (with names and other key data disguised, of course) which have been used successfully in real job hunts. That's what we mean by "Real-Resumes." What you see in this book are *real* resumes and cover letters which helped real people get ahead in their careers.

The Real-Resumes Series is based on the work of the country's oldest resume-preparation company known as PREP Resumes. If you would like a free information packet describing the company's resume preparation services, call 910-483-6611 or write to PREP at 1110½ Hay Street, Fayetteville, NC 28305. If you have a job hunting experience you would like to share with our staff at the Real-Resumes Series, please contact us at preppub@aol.com or visit our website at http://www.prep-pub.com.

*We hope the superior samples will help you manage your current job campaign and your career so that you will find work aligned to your career interests.*

The resumes and cover letters in this book are designed to be of most value to people already in a job hunt or contemplating a career change. If we could give you one word of advice about your career, here's what we would say: Manage your career and don't stumble from job to job in an incoherent pattern. Try to find work that interests you, and then identify prosperous industries which need work performed of the type you want to do. Learn early in your working life that a great resume and cover letter can blow doors open for you and help you maximize your salary.

**Real-Resumes for Auto Industry Jobs..**
including real resumes used to change careers
and resumes used to gain federal employment

Anne McKinney, Editor

# Introduction: The Art of Changing Jobs... and Finding New Careers

As the editor of this book, I would like to give you some tips on how to make the best use of the information you will find here. Because you are considering a career change, you already understand the concept of managing your career for maximum enjoyment and self-fulfillment. The purpose of this book is to provide expert tools and advice so that you *can* manage your career. Inside these pages you will find resumes and cover letters that will help you find not just a job but the type of work you want to do.

**Overview of the Book**
Every resume and cover letter in this book actually worked. And most of the resumes and cover letters have common features: most are one-page, most are in the chronological format, and most resumes are accompanied by a companion cover letter. In this section you will find helpful advice about job hunting. Step One begins with a discussion of why employers prefer the one-page, chronological resume. In Step Two you are introduced to the direct approach and to the proper format for a cover letter. In Step Three you learn the 14 main reasons why job hunters are not offered the jobs they want, and you learn the six key areas employers focus on when they interview you. Step Four gives nuts-and-bolts advice on how to handle the interview, send a follow-up letter after an interview, and negotiate your salary.

The cover letter plays such a critical role in a career change. You will learn from the experts how to format your cover letters and you will see suggested language to use in particular career-change situations. It has been said that "A picture is worth a thousand words" and, for that reason, you will see numerous examples of effective cover letters used by real individuals to change fields, functions, and industries.

The most important part of the book is the Real-Resumes section. Some of the individuals whose resumes and cover letters you see spent a lengthy career in an industry they loved. Then there are resumes and cover letters of people who wanted a change but who probably wanted to remain in their industry. Many of you will be especially interested by the resumes and cover letters of individuals who knew they definitely wanted a career change but had no idea what they wanted to do next. Other resumes and cover letters show individuals who knew they wanted to change fields and had a pretty good idea of what they wanted to do next.

Whatever your field, and whatever your circumstances, you'll find resumes and cover letters that will "show you the ropes" in terms of successfully changing jobs and switching careers.

Before you proceed further, think about why you picked up this book.
- Are you dissatisfied with the type of work you are now doing?
- Would you like to change careers, change companies, or change industries?
- Are you satisfied with your industry but not with your niche or function within it?
- Do you want to transfer your skills to a new product or service?
- Even if you have excelled in your field, have you "had enough"? Would you like the stimulation of a new challenge?
- Are you aware of the importance of a great cover letter but unsure of how to write one?
- Are you preparing to launch a second career after retirement?
- Have you been downsized, or do you anticipate becoming a victim of downsizing?
- Do you need expert advice on how to plan and implement a job campaign that will open the maximum number of doors?
- Do you want to make sure you handle an interview to your maximum advantage?

- Would you like to master the techniques of negotiating salary and benefits?
- Do you want to learn the secrets and shortcuts of professional resume writers?

### Using the Direct Approach

As you consider the possibility of a job hunt or career change, you need to be aware that most people end up having at least three distinctly different careers in their working lifetimes, and often those careers are different from each other. Yet people usually stumble through each job campaign, unsure of what they should be doing. Whether you find yourself voluntarily or unexpectedly in a job hunt, the direct approach is the job hunting strategy most likely to yield a full-time permanent job. The direct approach is an active, take-the-initiative style of job hunting in which you choose your next employer rather than relying on responding to ads, using employment agencies, or depending on other methods of finding jobs. You will learn how to use the direct approach in this book, and you will see that an effective cover letter is a critical ingredient in using the direct approach.

*The "direct approach" is the style of job hunting most likely to yield the maximum number of job interviews.*

### Lack of Industry Experience Not a Major Barrier to Entering New Field

"Lack of experience" is often the last reason people are not offered jobs, according to the companies who do the hiring. If you are changing careers, you will be glad to learn that experienced professionals often are selling "potential" rather than experience in a job hunt. Companies look for personal qualities that they know tend to be present in their most effective professionals, such as communication skills, initiative, persistence, organizational and time management skills, and creativity. Frequently companies are trying to discover "personality type," "talent," "ability," "aptitude," and "potential" rather than seeking actual hands-on experience, so your resume should be designed to aggressively present your accomplishments. Attitude, enthusiasm, personality, and a track record of achievements in any type of work are the primary "indicators of success" which employers are seeking, and you will see numerous examples in this book of resumes written in an all-purpose fashion so that the professional can approach various industries and companies.

*Using references in a skillful fashion in your job hunt will inspire confidence in prospective employers and help you "close the sale" after interviews.*

### The Art of Using References in a Job Hunt

You probably already know that you need to provide references during a job hunt, but you may not be sure of how and when to use references for maximum advantage. You can use references very creatively during a job hunt to call attention to your strengths and make yourself "stand out." Your references will rarely get you a job, no matter how impressive the names, but the way you use references can boost the employer's confidence in you and lead to a job offer in the least time.

You should ask from three to five people, including people who have supervised you, if you can use them as a reference during your job hunt. You may not be able to ask your current boss since your job hunt is probably confidential.

A common question in resume preparation is: "Do I need to put my references on my resume?" No, you don't. Even if you create a references page at the same time you prepare your resume, you don't need to mail, e-mail, or fax your references page with the resume and cover letter. Usually the potential employer is not interested in references until he meets you, so the earliest you need to have references ready is at the first interview. Obviously there are exceptions to this standard rule of thumb; sometimes an ad will ask you to send references with your first response. Wait until the employer requests references before providing them.

An excellent attention-getting technique is to take to the first interview not just a page of references (giving names, addresses, and telephone numbers) but an actual letter of reference written by someone who knows you well and who preferably has supervised or employed you. A professional way to close the first interview is to thank the interviewer, shake his or her hand, and then say you'd like to give him or her a copy of a letter of reference from a previous employer. Hopefully you already made a good impression during the interview, but you'll "close the sale" in a dynamic fashion if you leave a letter praising you and your accomplishments. For that reason, it's a good idea to ask supervisors during your final weeks in a job if they will provide you with a written letter of recommendation which you can use in future job hunts. Most employers will oblige, and you will have a letter that has a useful "shelf life" of many years. Such a letter often gives the prospective employer enough confidence in his opinion of you that he may forego checking out other references and decide to offer you the job on the spot or in the next few days.

With regard to references, it's best to provide the names and addresses of people who have supervised you or observed you in a work situation.

Whom should you ask to serve as references? References should be people who have known or supervised you in a professional, academic, or work situation. References with big titles, like school superintendent or congressman, are fine, but remind busy people when you get to the interview stage that they may be contacted soon. Make sure the busy official recognizes your name and has instant positive recall of you! If you're asked to provide references on a formal company application, you can simply transcribe names from your references list. In summary, follow this rule in using references: If you've got them, flaunt them! If you've obtained well-written letters of reference, make sure you find a polite way to push those references under the nose of the interviewer so he or she can hear someone other than you describing your strengths. Your references probably won't ever get you a job, but glowing letters of reference can give you credibility and visibility that can make you stand out among candidates with similar credentials and potential!

The approach taken by this book is to (1) help you master the proven best techniques of conducting a job hunt and (2) show you how to stand out in a job hunt through your resume, cover letter, interviewing skills, as well as the way in which you present your references and follow up on interviews. Now, the best way to "get in the mood" for writing your own resume and cover letter is to select samples from the Table of Contents that interest you and then read them. A great resume is a "photograph," usually on one page, of an individual. If you wish to seek professional advice in preparing your resume, you may contact one of the professional writers at Professional Resume & Employment Publishing (PREP) for a brief free consultation by calling 1-910-483-6611.

## Part One: Some Advice About Your Job Hunt

**STEP ONE: Planning Your Career Change and Assembling the Tools**

**What if you don't know what you want to do?**
Your job hunt will be more comfortable if you can figure out what type of work you want to do. But you are not alone if you have no idea what you want to do next! You may have knowledge and skills in certain areas but want to get into another type of work. What *The Wall Street Journal* has discovered in its research on careers is that most of us end up having at least three distinctly different careers in our working lives; it seems that, even if we really like a particular kind of activity, twenty years of doing it is enough for most of us and we want to move on to something else!

That's why we strongly believe that you need to spend some time figuring out *what interests you* rather than taking an inventory of the skills you have. You may have skills that you simply don't want to use, but if you can build your career on the things that interest you, you will be more likely to be happy and satisfied in your job. Realize, too, that interests can change over time; the activities that interest you now may not be the ones that interested you years ago. For example, some professionals may decide that they've had enough of retail sales and want a job selling another product or service, even though they have earned a reputation for being an excellent retail manager. We strongly believe that interests rather than skills should be the determining factor in deciding what types of jobs you want to apply for and what directions you explore in your job hunt. Obviously one cannot be a lawyer without a law degree or a secretary without secretarial skills; but a professional can embark on a next career as a financial consultant, property manager, plant manager, production supervisor, retail manager, or other occupation if he/she has a strong interest in that type of work and can provide a resume that clearly demonstrates past excellent performance in *any* field and *potential* to excel in another field. As you will see later in this book, "lack of exact experience" is the last reason why people are turned down for the jobs they apply for.

**How can you have a resume prepared if you don't know what you want to do?**
You may be wondering how you can have a resume prepared if you don't know what you want to do next. The approach to resume writing which PREP, the country's oldest resume-preparation company, has used successfully for many years is to develop an "all-purpose" resume that translates your skills, experience, and accomplishments into language employers can understand. What most people need in a job hunt is a versatile resume that will allow them to apply for numerous types of jobs. For example, you may want to apply for a job in pharmaceutical sales but you may also want to have a resume that will be versatile enough for you to apply for jobs in the construction, financial services, or automotive industries.

Based on more than 20 years of serving job hunters, we at PREP have found that your best approach to job hunting is **an all-purpose resume** and **specific cover letters tailored to specific fields** rather than using the approach of trying to create different resumes for every job. If you are remaining in your field, you may not even need more than one "all-purpose" cover letter, although the cover letter rather than the resume is the place to communicate your interest in a narrow or specific field. An all-purpose resume and cover letter that translate your experience and accomplishments into plain English are the tools that will maximize the number of doors which open for you while permitting you to "fish" in the widest range of job areas.

*Figure out what interests you and you will hold the key to a successful job hunt and working career. (And be prepared for your interests to change over time!)*

*"Lack of exact experience" is the last reason people are turned down for the jobs for which they apply.*

**Your resume will provide the script for your job interview.**
When you get down to it, your resume has a simple job to do: Its purpose is to blow as many doors open as possible and to make as many people as possible want to meet you. So a well-written resume that really "sells" you is a key that will create opportunities for you in a job hunt.

This statistic explains why: The typical newspaper advertisement for a job opening receives more than 245 replies. And normally only 10 or 12 will be invited to an interview.

But here's another purpose of the resume: it provides the "script" the employer uses when he interviews you. If your resume has been written in such a way that your strengths and achievements are revealed, that's what you'll end up talking about at the job interview. Since the resume will govern what you get asked about at your interviews, you can't overestimate the importance of making sure your resume makes you look and sound as good as you are.

Your resume is the "script" for your job interviews. Make sure you put on your resume what you want to talk about or be asked about at the job interview.

**So what is a "good" resume?**
Very literally, your resume should motivate the person reading it to dial the phone number or e-mail the screen name you have put on the resume. When you are relocating, you should put a local phone number on your resume if your physical address is several states away; employers are more likely to dial a local telephone number than a long-distance number when they're looking for potential employees.

If you have a resume already, look at it objectively. Is it a limp, colorless "laundry list" of your job titles and duties? Or does it "paint a picture" of your skills, abilities, and accomplishments in a way that would make someone want to meet you? Can people understand what you're saying? If you are attempting to change fields or industries, can potential employers see that your skills and knowledge are transferable to other environments? For example, have you described accomplishments which reveal your problem-solving abilities or communication skills?

The one-page resume in chronological format is the format preferred by most employers.

**How long should your resume be?**
One page, maybe two. Usually only people in the academic community have a resume (which they usually call a *curriculum vitae*) longer than one or two pages. Remember that your resume is almost always accompanied by a cover letter, and a potential employer does not want to read more than two or three pages about a total stranger in order to decide if he wants to meet that person! Besides, don't forget that the more you tell someone about yourself, the more opportunity you are providing for the employer to screen you out at the "first-cut" stage. A resume should be concise and exciting and designed to make the reader want to meet you in person!

**Should resumes be functional or chronological?**
Employers almost always prefer a chronological resume; in other words, an employer will find a resume easier to read if it is immediately apparent what your current or most recent job is, what you did before that, and so forth, in reverse chronological order. A resume that goes back in detail for the last ten years of employment will generally satisfy the employer's curiosity about your background. Employment more than ten years old can be shown even more briefly in an "Other Experience" section at the end of your "Experience" section. Remember that your intention is not to tell everything you've done but to "hit the high points" and especially impress the employer with what you learned, contributed, or accomplished in each job you describe.

Real-Resumes Series edited by Anne McKinney

### STEP TWO: Using Your Resume and Cover Letter

**Once you get your resume, what do you do with it?**
You will be using your resume to answer ads, as a tool to use in talking with friends and relatives about your job search, and, most importantly, in using the "direct approach" described in this book.

*When you mail your resume, always send a "cover letter."*
A "cover letter," sometimes called a "resume letter" or "letter of interest," is a letter that accompanies and introduces your resume. Your cover letter is a way of personalizing the resume by sending it to the specific person you think you might want to work for at each company. Your cover letter should contain a few highlights from your resume—just enough to make someone want to meet you. Cover letters should always be typed or word processed on a computer—never handwritten.

> Never mail or fax your resume without a cover letter.

**1. Learn the art of answering ads.**
There is an "art," part of which can be learned, in using your "bestselling" resume to reply to advertisements.

Sometimes an exciting job lurks behind a boring ad that someone dictated in a hurry, so reply to any ad that interests you. Don't worry that you aren't "25 years old with an MBA" like the ad asks for. Employers will always make compromises in their requirements if they think you're the "best fit" overall.

*What about ads that ask for "salary requirements?"*
What if the ad you're answering asks for "salary requirements?" The first rule is to avoid committing yourself in writing at that point to a specific salary. You don't want to "lock yourself in."

> What if the ad asks for your "salary requirements?"

*There are two ways to handle the ad that asks for "salary requirements."*
First, you can ignore that part of the ad and accompany your resume with a cover letter that focuses on "selling" you, your abilities, and even some of your philosophy about work or your field. You may include a sentence in your cover letter like this: "I can provide excellent personal and professional references at your request, and I would be delighted to share the private details of my salary history with you in person."

Second, if you feel you must give some kind of number, just state a range in your cover letter that includes your medical, dental, other benefits, and expected bonuses. You might state, for example, "My current compensation, including benefits and bonuses, is in the range of $30,000-$40,000."

*Analyze the ad and "tailor" yourself to it.*
When you're replying to ads, a finely tailored cover letter is an important tool in getting your resume noticed and read. On the next page is a cover letter which has been "tailored to fit" a specific ad. Notice the "art" used by PREP writers of analyzing the ad's main requirements and then writing the letter so that the person's background, work habits, and interests seem "tailor-made" to the company's needs. Use this cover letter as a model when you prepare your own reply to ads.

**6** Part One: Some Advice About Your Job Hunt

Date

Exact Name of Person
Title or Position
Name of Company
Address (number and street)
Address (city, state, and zip)

Dear Exact Name of Person (or Sir or Madam if answering a blind ad):

With the enclosed resume, I would like to express my interest in exploring employment opportunities with your organization.

With 20 years in the automotive industry, I am a management professional experienced in all phases of the industry, including used car sales and financing as well as general sales management. Originally recruited by my present employer for a newly created position, I have advanced with Hank Wallace of Flagstaff, AZ, and am highly valued as a resourceful and effective General Sales Manager. Although I am held in high regard by the executives of this large dual dealership, I have made the decision to selectively explore other opportunities and would ask that my interest in your organization be kept in confidence at this time.

Recruited as the dealership's first Outside Buyer, I was promoted to Used Car General Sales Manager. Soon after, I enjoyed a further promotion to General Sales Manager. In the first job I took the store from a losing operation to a multimillion-dollar producer and then advanced to oversee a sales staff which increased from 28 to 36 and led them in building a 30% increase in sales—the highest rate of growth of any dealership in the region. My accomplishments include earning a prestigious recognition award from Toyota and being one of only three people in the region to earn the "Toyota Professional Used Car Manager Recognition Award" in consecutive years. Because of my reputation and expertise, I was the only General Sales Manager once invited to be a member of an automotive team comprised of only General Managers except for myself.

If you can use an astute manager who excels in finding solutions for the tough problems while leading the way to increased sales, profitability, and customer satisfaction, I hope you will contact me to suggest a time when we might meet to discuss your needs. I can provide outstanding references at the appropriate time.

Sincerely,

Molly Sue Bickford

*Employers are trying to identify the individual who wants the job they are filling. Don't be afraid to express your enthusiasm in the cover letter!*

**2. Talk to friends and relatives.**
Don't be shy about telling your friends and relatives the kind of job you're looking for. Looking for the job you want involves using your network of contacts, so tell people what you're looking for. They may be able to make introductions and help set up interviews.

About 25% of all interviews are set up through "who you know," so don't ignore this approach.

**3. Finally, and most importantly, use the "direct approach."**
More than 50% of all job interviews are set up by the "direct approach." That means you actually mail, e-mail, or fax a resume and a cover letter to a company you think might be interesting to work for.

> The "direct approach" is a strategy in which you choose your next employer.

*To whom do you write?*
In general, you should write directly to the *exact name* of the person who would be hiring you: say, the vice-president of marketing or data processing. If you're in doubt about to whom to address the letter, address it to the president by name and he or she will make sure it gets forwarded to the right person within the company who has hiring authority in your area.

*How do you find the names of potential employers?*
You're not alone if you feel that the biggest problem in your job search is finding the right names at the companies you want to contact. But you can usually figure out the names of companies you want to approach by deciding first if your job hunt is primarily geography-driven or industry-driven.

In a **geography-driven job hunt,** you could select a list of, say, 50 companies you want to contact **by location** from the lists that the U.S. Chambers of Commerce publish yearly of their "major area employers." There are hundreds of local Chambers of Commerce across America, and most of them will have an 800 number which you can find through 1-800-555-1212. If you and your family think Atlanta, Dallas, Ft. Lauderdale, and Virginia Beach might be nice places to live, for example, you could contact the Chamber of Commerce in those cities and ask how you can obtain a copy of their list of major employers. Your nearest library will have the book which lists the addresses of all chambers.

In an **industry-driven job hunt,** and if you are willing to relocate, you will be identifying the companies which you find most attractive in the industry in which you want to work. When you select a list of companies to contact **by industry,** you can find the right person to write and the address of firms by industrial category in *Standard and Poor's, Moody's,* and other excellent books in public libraries. Many Web sites also provide contact information.

Many people feel it's a good investment to actually call the company to either find out or double-check the name of the person to whom they want to send a resume and cover letter. It's important to do as much as you feasibly can to assure that the letter gets to the right person in the company.

**On-line research** will be the best way for many people to locate organizations to which they wish to send their resume. It is outside the scope of this book to teach Internet research skills, but librarians are often useful in this area.

*What's the correct way to follow up on a resume you send?*
There is a polite way to be aggressively interested in a company during your job hunt. It is ideal to end the cover letter accompanying your resume by saying, "I hope you'll welcome my call next week when I try to arrange a brief meeting at your convenience to discuss your current and future needs and how I might serve them." Keep it low key, and just ask for a "brief meeting," not an interview. Employers want people who show a determined interest in working with them, so don't be shy about following up on the resume and cover letter you've mailed.

## STEP THREE: Preparing for Interviews

It pays to be aware of the 14 most common pitfalls for job hunters.

But a resume and cover letter by themselves can't get you the job you want. You need to "prep" yourself before the interview. Step Three in your job campaign is "Preparing for Interviews." First, let's look at interviewing from the hiring organization's point of view.

*What are the biggest "turnoffs" for potential employers?*
One of the ways to help yourself perform well at an interview is to look at the main reasons why organizations *don't* hire the people they interview, according to those who do the interviewing.

Notice that "lack of appropriate background" (or lack of experience) is the *last* reason for not being offered the job.

***The 14 Most Common Reasons Job Hunters Are Not Offered Jobs*** *(according to the companies who do the interviewing and hiring):*

1. Low level of accomplishment
2. Poor attitude, lack of self-confidence
3. Lack of goals/objectives
4. Lack of enthusiasm
5. Lack of interest in the company's business
6. Inability to sell or express yourself
7. Unrealistic salary demands
8. Poor appearance
9. Lack of maturity, no leadership potential
10. Lack of extracurricular activities
11. Lack of preparation for the interview, no knowledge about company
12. Objecting to travel
13. Excessive interest in security and benefits
14. Inappropriate background

Department of Labor studies have proven that smart, "prepared" job hunters can increase their beginning salary while getting a job in *half* the time it normally takes. (4½ months is the average national length of a job search.) Here, from PREP, are some questions that can prepare you to find a job faster.

*Are you in the "right" frame of mind?*
It seems unfair that we have to look for a job just when we're lowest in morale. Don't worry *too* much if you're nervous before interviews. You're supposed to be a little nervous, especially if the job means a lot to you. But the best way to kill unnecessary

fears about job hunting is through 1) making sure you have a great resume and 2) preparing yourself for the interview. Here are three main areas you need to think about before each interview.

### *Do you know what the company does?*
Don't walk into an interview giving the impression that, "If this is Tuesday, this must be General Motors."

*Research the company before you go to interviews.*

Find out before the interview what the company's main product or service is. Where is the company heading? Is it in a "growth" or declining industry? (Answers to these questions may influence whether or not you want to work there!)

Information about what the company does is in annual reports, in newspaper and magazine articles, and on the Internet. If you're not yet skilled at Internet research, just visit your nearest library and ask the reference librarian to guide you to printed materials on the company.

### *Do you know what you want to do for the company?*
Before the interview, try to decide how you see yourself fitting into the company. Remember, "lack of exact background" the company wants is usually the last reason people are not offered jobs.

Understand before you go to each interview that the burden will be on you to "sell" the interviewer on why you're the best person for the job and the company.

### *How will you answer the critical interview questions?*
Put yourself in the interviewer's position and think about the questions you're most likely to be asked. Here are some of the most commonly asked interview questions:

*Anticipate the questions you will be asked at the interview, and prepare your responses in advance.*

**Q:** *"What are your greatest strengths?"*
**A:** Don't say you've never thought about it! Go into an interview knowing the three main impressions you want to leave about yourself, such as "I'm hard-working, loyal, and an imaginative cost-cutter."

**Q:** *"What are your greatest weaknesses?"*
**A:** Don't confess that you're lazy or have trouble meeting deadlines! Confessing that you tend to be a "workaholic" or "tend to be a perfectionist and sometimes get frustrated when others don't share my high standards" will make your prospective employer see a "weakness" that he likes. Name a weakness that your interviewer will perceive as a strength.

**Q:** *"What are your long-range goals?"*
**A:** If you're interviewing with Microsoft, don't say you want to work for IBM in five years! Say your long-range goal is to be *with* the company, contributing to its goals and success.

**Q:** *"What motivates you to do your best work?"*
**A:** Don't get dollar signs in your eyes here! "A challenge" is not a bad answer, but it's a little cliched. Saying something like "troubleshooting" or "solving a tough problem" is more interesting and specific. Give an example if you can.

*Q: "What do you know about this organization?"*
A: Don't say you never heard of it until they asked you to the interview! Name an interesting, positive thing you learned about the company recently from your research. Remember, company executives can sometimes feel rather "maternal" about the company they serve. Don't get onto a negative area of the company if you can think of positive facts you can bring up. Of course, if you learned in your research that the company's sales seem to be taking a nose-dive, or that the company president is being prosecuted for taking bribes, you might politely ask your interviewer to tell you something that could help you better understand what you've been reading. Those are the kinds of company facts that can help you determine whether or not you want to work there.

> Go to an interview prepared to tell the company why it should hire you.

*Q: "Why should I hire you?"*
A: "I'm unemployed and available" is the wrong answer here! Get back to your strengths and say that you believe the organization could benefit by a loyal, hard-working cost-cutter like yourself.

In conclusion, you should decide in advance, before you go to the interview, how you will answer each of these commonly asked questions. Have some practice interviews with a friend to role-play and build your confidence.

## STEP FOUR: Handling the Interview and Negotiating Salary

Now you're ready for Step Four: actually handling the interview successfully and effectively. Remember, the purpose of an interview is to get a job offer.

> A smile at an interview makes the employer perceive of you as intelligent!

**Eight "do's" for the interview**
According to leading U.S. companies, there are eight key areas in interviewing success. You can fail at an interview if you mishandle just one area.

1. **Do wear appropriate clothes.**
   You can never go wrong by wearing a suit to an interview.

2. **Do be well groomed.**
   Don't overlook the obvious things like having clean hair, clothes, and fingernails for the interview.

3. **Do give a firm handshake.**
   You'll have to shake hands twice in most interviews: first, before you sit down, and second, when you leave the interview. Limp handshakes turn most people off.

4. **Do smile and show a sense of humor.**
   Interviewers are looking for people who would be nice to work with, so don't be so somber that you don't smile. In fact, research shows that people who smile at interviews are perceived as more intelligent. So, smile!

5. **Do be enthusiastic.**
   Employers say they are "turned off" by lifeless, unenthusiastic job hunters who show no special interest in that company. The best way to show some enthusiasm for the employer's operation is to find out about the business beforehand.

6. **Do show you are flexible and adaptable.**
   An employer is looking for someone who can contribute to his organization in a flexible, adaptable way. No matter what skills and training you have, employers know every new employee must go through initiation and training on the company's turf. Certainly show pride in your past accomplishments in a specific, factual way ("I saved my last employer $50.00 a week by a new cost-cutting measure I developed"). But don't come across as though there's nothing about the job you couldn't easily handle.

7. **Do ask intelligent questions about the employer's business.**
   An employer is hiring someone because of certain business needs. Show interest in those needs. Asking questions to get a better idea of the employer's needs will help you "stand out" from other candidates interviewing for the job.

8. **Do "take charge" when the interviewer "falls down" on the job.**
   Go into every interview knowing the three or four points about yourself you want the interviewer to remember. And be prepared to take an active part in leading the discussion if the interviewer's "canned approach" does not permit you to display your "strong suit." You can't always depend on the interviewer's asking you the "right" questions so you can stress your strengths and accomplishments.

*Employers are seeking people with good attitudes whom they can train and coach to do things their way.*

**An important "don't": Don't ask questions about salary or benefits at the first interview.**
Employers don't take warmly to people who look at their organization as just a place to satisfy salary and benefit needs. Don't risk making a negative impression by appearing greedy or self-serving. The place to discuss salary and benefits is normally at the second interview, and the employer will bring it up. Then you can ask questions without appearing excessively interested in what the organization can do for you.

**Now...negotiating your salary**
Even if an ad requests that you communicate your "salary requirement" or "salary history," you should avoid providing those numbers in your initial cover letter. You can usually say something like this: "I would be delighted to discuss the private details of my salary history with you in person."

Once you're at the interview, you must avoid even appearing *interested* in salary before you are offered the job. Make sure you've "sold" yourself before talking salary. First show you're the "best fit" for the employer and then you'll be in a stronger position from which to negotiate salary. **Never** bring up the subject of salary yourself. Employers say there's no way you can avoid looking greedy if you bring up the issue of salary and benefits before the company has identified you as its "best fit."

*Don't appear excessively interested in salary and benefits at the interview.*

Interviewers sometimes throw out a salary figure at the first interview to see if you'll accept it. You may not want to commit yourself if you think you will be able to negotiate a better deal later on. Get back to finding out more about the job. This lets the interviewer know you're interested primarily in the job and not the salary.

When the organization brings up salary, it may say something like this: "Well, Mary, we think you'd make a good candidate for this job. What kind of salary are we talking about?" You may not want to name a number here, either. Give the ball back to the interviewer. Act as though you hadn't given the subject of salary much thought and respond something like this: "Ah, Mr. Jones, I wonder if you'd be kind enough to tell me what salary you had in mind when you advertised the job?" Or ... "What is the range you have in mind?"

Don't worry, if the interviewer names a figure that you think is too low, you can say so without turning down the job or locking yourself into a rigid position. The point here is to negotiate for yourself as well as you can. You might reply to a number named by the interviewer that you think is low by saying something like this: "Well, Mr. Lee, the job interests me very much, and I think I'd certainly enjoy working with you. But, frankly, I was thinking of something a little higher than that." That leaves the ball in your interviewer's court again, and you haven't turned down the job either, in case it turns out that the interviewer can't increase the offer and you still want the job.

*Salary negotiation can be tricky.*

**Last, send a follow-up letter.**
Mail, e-mail, or fax a letter right after the interview telling your interviewer you enjoyed the meeting and are certain (if you are) that you are the "best fit" for the job. The people interviewing you will probably have an attitude described as either "professionally loyal" to their companies, or "maternal and proprietary" if the interviewer also owns the company. In either case, they are looking for people who want to work for *that* company in particular. The follow-up letter you send might be just the deciding factor in your favor if the employer is trying to choose between you and someone else. You will see an example of a follow-up letter on page 16.

*A follow-up letter can help the employer choose between you and another qualified candidate.*

**A cover letter is an essential part of a job hunt or career change.**
Many people are aware of the importance of having a great resume, but most people in a job hunt don't realize just how important a cover letter can be. The purpose of the cover letter, sometimes called a **"letter of interest,"** is to introduce your resume to prospective employers. The cover letter is often the critical ingredient in a job hunt because the cover letter allows you to say a lot of things that just don't "fit" on the resume. For example, you can emphasize your commitment to a new field and stress your related talents. The cover letter also gives you a chance to stress outstanding character and personal values. On the next two pages you will see examples of very effective cover letters.

**A cover letter is an essential part of a career change.**

*Please do not attempt to implement a career change without a cover letter. A cover letter is the first impression of you, and you can influence the way an employer views you by the language and style of your letter.*

**Special help for those in career change**
We want to emphasize again that, especially in a career change, the cover letter is very important and can help you "build a bridge" to a new career. A creative and appealing cover letter can begin the process of encouraging the potential employer to imagine you in an industry other than the one in which you have worked.

As a special help to those in career change, there are resumes and cover letters included in this book which show valuable techniques and tips you should use when changing fields or industries. The resumes and cover letters of career changers are identified in the table of contents as "Career Change" and you will see the "Career Change" label on cover letters in Part Two where the individuals are changing careers.

## Looking Closer: The ANATOMY OF A COVER LETTER

**Addressing the Cover Letter:** Get the exact name of the person to whom you are writing. This makes your approach personal.

**First Paragraph:** This explains why you are writing.

**Second Paragraph:** You have a chance to talk about whatever you feel is your most distinguishing feature.

**Third Paragraph:** You bring up your next most distinguishing qualities and try to sell yourself.

**Fourth Paragraph:** Here you have another opportunity to reveal qualities or achievements which will impress your future employer.

**Final Paragraph:** She asks the employer to contact her. Make sure your reader knows what the "next step" is.

**Alternate Final Paragraph:** It's more aggressive (but not too aggressive) to let the employer know that you will be calling him or her. Don't be afraid to be persistent. Employers are looking for people who know what they want to do.

Date

Exact Name of Person
Title or Position
Name of Company
Address (number and street)
Address (city, state, and zip)

Dear Exact Name of Person (or Sir or Madam if answering a blind ad):

I would appreciate an opportunity to talk with you soon about how I could contribute to your organization through the application of my expertise in the field of fleet maintenance supervision as well as through my reputation as a self-motivated, articulate, and honest professional.

While serving as Vehicle Maintenance Supervisor at Towson Ford-Lincoln, Towson, MD, I have earned a reputation as a professional who can be depended on for personal integrity, resourcefulness, and dedication to excellence in everything I attempt. I train and supervise 18 people involved in automobile repair as well as maintain an inventory of spare parts and tools.

Throughout my career I have excelled in building productive teams of mechanically adept and knowledgeable professionals and have always achieved excellent safety records. I have emphasized compliance with EPA guidelines and all safety regulations and led one organization to a two-year accident-free record and another to three years of accident-free operations.

I am confident that through my ability to meet challenges head on and exceed expectations in all operational areas, I can contribute to any organization in need of a mature knowledgeable professional. With a reputation for high personal standards of integrity, self-confidence, and superior leadership and team building skills I can make important contributions to any organization.

I hope you will welcome my call soon to arrange a brief meeting to discuss your current and future needs and how I might serve them. Thank you in advance for your time.

Sincerely,

Federico M. Munoz

(Alternate last paragraph:
I hope you will call or write me soon to suggest a time convenient for us to meet and discuss your current and future needs and how I might serve them. Thank you in advance for your time.)

**Semi-blocked Letter**

Date

Date

Three blank spaces

Exact Name of Person
Title or Position
Name of Company
Address (number and street)
Address (city, state, and ZIP)

Address

Dear Exact Name of Person: (or Dear Sir or Madam if answering a blind ad.)

Salutation

    With the enclosed resume, I would like to make you aware of my interest in the job of Sales Manager in the Columbus, OH area. As you know, we had the pleasure of working together when you were Events Coordinator. I can also provide an outstanding reference from Nathan Johnson. I believe you are already aware of my track record of outstanding performance as well as my demonstrated abilities related to operations management, sales management, customer service, and inventory control.

One blank space

    As you know, I have excelled as Store Manager in Kansas City. I began with Western as a Parts Clerk and gained expertise in that aspect of the business. I believe you are aware that I have excelled in my positions at Western while also working a full-time job as a Military Policeman. As an MP, I worked in jobs which included Investigator and United Nations Body Guard.

    It is my desire to continue working to advance the profitability and growth of Western, and I wanted to formally ask you to consider me for the job of Sales Manager. I offer proven sales abilities and have trained employees at the Kansas City store in effective sales techniques. I believe solid product knowledge is a key to effectiveness in sales, and I certainly offer expert understanding of bikes and motorcycles. I am proud of the fact that I have hired and developed employees in the Kansas City store whom I have trained to utilize strong selling skills.

Body

    Let me know if you need any information other than what I have provided. I would enjoy the opportunity to talk with you by phone or in person about this position, and I feel certain I would further contribute to the company in that capacity. I send best wishes.

One blank space

                          Sincerely,

Signature

                          Grif Wadleigh

CC: Nathan Johnson

cc: Indicates you are sending a copy of the letter to someone

Date

Exact Name of Person
Title or Position
Name of Company
Address (number and street)
Address (city, state, and zip)

**Follow-up Letter**

Dear Exact Name:

A great follow-up letter can motivate the employer to make the job offer, and the salary offer may be influenced by the style and tone of your follow-up letter, too!

I am writing to express my appreciation for the time you spent with me on 9 December, and I want to let you know that I am sincerely interested in the position of Controller which we discussed.

I feel confident that I could skillfully interact with your 60-person work force, and I would cheerfully travel as your needs require. I want you to know, too, that I would not consider relocating to Salt Lake City to be a hardship! It is certainly one of the most beautiful areas I have ever seen.

As you described to me what you are looking for in the person who fills this position, I had a sense of "déjà vu" because my current boss was in a similar position when I went to work for him. He needed someone to come in and be his "right arm" and take on an increasing amount of his management responsibilities so that he could be freed up to do other things. I have played a key role in the growth and profitability of his multiunit business, and he has come to depend on my sound financial and business advice as much as my day-to-day management skills. Since this is the busiest time of the year in the automotive business, I feel that I could not leave him during that time. I could certainly make myself available by mid-January.

It would be a pleasure to work for a successful individual such as yourself, and I feel I could contribute significantly to your hotel chain not only through my accounting and business background but also through my strong qualities of loyalty, reliability, and trustworthiness. I am confident that I could learn Quick Books rapidly, and I would welcome being trained to do things your way.

Yours sincerely,

Jacob Evangelisto

**16** Real-Resumes Series

# PART TWO: REAL-RESUMES FOR AUTO INDUSTRY JOBS

In this section, you will find resumes and cover letters of auto industry professionals—and of people who want to work in those fields. How do they differ from other job hunters? Why should there be a book dedicated to people seeking jobs in this field? Based on more than 20 years of experience in working with job hunters, this editor is convinced that resumes and cover letters which "speak the lingo" of the field you wish to enter will communicate more effectively than language which is not industry specific. This book is designed to help people (1) who are seeking to prepare their own resumes and (2) who wish to use as models "real" resumes of individuals who have successfully launched careers in the human resources and personnel field or who have advanced in the field. You will see a wide range of experience levels reflected in the resumes in this book. Some of the resumes and cover letters were used by individuals seeking to enter the field; others were used successfully by senior professionals to advance in the field.

**Newcomers to an industry sometimes have advantages over more experienced professionals.** In a job hunt, junior professionals can have an advantage over their more experienced counterparts. Prospective employers often view the less experienced workers as "more trainable" and "more coachable" than their seniors. This means that the mature professional who has already excelled in a first career can, with credibility, "change careers" and transfer skills to other industries.

**Newcomers to the field may have disadvantages compared to their seniors.** Almost by definition, the inexperienced professional—the young person who has recently earned a college degree, or the individual who has recently received certifications respected by the industry—is less tested and less experienced than senior managers, so the resume and cover letter of the inexperienced professional may often have to "sell" his or her potential to do something he or she has never done before. Lack of experience in the field she wants to enter can be a stumbling block to the junior manager, but remember that many employers believe that someone who has excelled in anything—academics, for example—can excel in many other fields.

**Some advice to inexperienced professionals...**
If senior professionals could give junior professionals a piece of advice about careers, here's what they would say: Manage your career and don't stumble from job to job in an incoherent pattern. Try to find work that interests you, and then identify prosperous industries which need work performed of the type you want to do. Learn early in your working life that a great resume and cover letter can blow doors open for you and help you maximize your salary.

**Special help for career changers...**
For those changing careers, you will find useful the resumes and cover letters marked "Career Change" on the following pages. Consult the Table of Contents for page numbers showing career changers.

*Auto industry professionals might be said to "talk funny." They talk in lingo specific to their field, and you will find helpful examples throughout this book.*

Date

Exact Name of Person
Exact Title
Exact Name of Company
Address
City, State, Zip

**ACCOUNT MANAGER CORPORATE CAR RENTALS**

Notice the fourth paragraph. In a gracious way, this junior professional is announcing her desire to become a part of an organization which will use her in sales management roles. Here's a tip about employers: they like people who know what they want to do, because if you are in a job doing what you want to do, you are more likely to excel — and make money for the company.

Dear Exact Name of Person (or Dear Sir or Madam if answering a blind ad):

I would appreciate an opportunity to talk with you soon about how I could contribute to your organization through my demonstrated skills in sales management as well as my exceptional communication, organizational, and time management abilities.

As you will see from my enclosed resume, I am presently excelling as a Corporate Account Manager with Quality Rent-a-Car. When I assumed responsibility for corporate accounts, monthly sales were an average of $27,000. Due to my initiative in developing new accounts and maximizing existing accounts, sales have risen to $98,000 per month, and I have received numerous awards for sales excellence.

Joining this national company three weeks after graduating from college, I quickly mastered all aspects of branch management, customer service, sales, and administration during the management training program. As Assistant Branch Manager, I was the top seller in the region in both outside and inside sales, and my branch was the top office in the region in Customer Satisfaction scores. In addition, two employees whom I trained were promoted through two levels of advancement, to Assistant Branch Manager positions. Since joining this company, I have earned a reputation as a talented and articulate sales professional with strong managerial abilities.

Although I am highly respected in my present job and achieving results in all areas of performance, I feel that my abilities would be better utilized in a sales management role than in the administrative positions for which Quality is grooming me.

If you can use an intelligent, enthusiastic, and results-oriented professional, I hope you will contact me to suggest a time when we might meet to discuss your needs. I can assure you in advance that I could rapidly become an asset to your organization.

Sincerely,

Elizabeth Hyland

# ELIZABETH HYLAND

1110½ Hay Street, Fayetteville, NC 28305 • preppub@aol.com • (910) 483-6611

---

**OBJECTIVE**  To benefit an organization that can use an articulate young sales and management professional with exceptional communication, time management, and organizational skills and a background in multiunit sales management and staff development.

**EDUCATION**  **B.S., Psychology and Business Administration,** University of Las Vegas, 1994.
- Maintained a cumulative 3.5 GPA while working 30 hours per week and completing this rigorous degree program in three years.
- Was elected Panhellenic Chairwoman (1993) and Pledge Class Vice President (1991), Psi Alpha chapter of Chi Omega Sorority.
- Played first-string goalie on women's water polo team (1992-94); participated on the women's cross country team (1993); counseled a special needs child with Tourette's Syndrome (1992); placed 2nd in a scholarship pageant.

**EXPERIENCE**  *Am advancing in a track record of promotion with Quality Rent-a-Car:*
**2002-present: CORPORATE ACCOUNT MANAGER.** Las Vegas, NV. Design and sell corporate account programs to business and government clients; increased monthly sales to $160,000 from $45,000 since taking over corporate accounts for this 12-store area.
- Provide government and private industry representatives with information on the advantages of a corporate rental car program in their travel plans.
- Generate business through a combination of client visits and employee referrals.
- Prepare and submit bids used in obtaining federal, state, and local government contracted business from 12 rental car offices throughout Nevada.
- Created and implemented a corporate business training manual; responsible for all corporate training for 52 current employees and new hires.
- Organize and coordinate corporate presence at events such as corporate trade shows, business expos, and career fairs.
- Was recognized with the **Employee Excellence Award** in December 2003.
- Received the **#1 Corporate Class Performance Award** for the western region in 2003.

**2000-02: ASSISTANT BRANCH MANAGER.** Tempe, AZ. Set sales records in several areas while also supervising a staff of four full-time and three part-time employees.
- Earned recognition as "Top Seller" in both inside and outside sales for the Arizona region and established the highest number of corporate accounts of any manager in the area.
- Trained and motivated manager trainees in daily branch rental business.
- Managed and collected branch receivables and vehicle repossessions.
- Devised a new method for the reservations process which streamlined branch operations and increased productivity.
- Provided exceptional customer service which enabled the branch to place first in customer satisfaction scores for the region in 2001.

**MANAGEMENT TRAINEE.** Monterey, CA (1999-00). Mastered all aspects of branch office management, customer service, sales, and administration; achieved sales in the top 5% of my training groups.
- Orchestrated a branch delivery service project which involved a staff of 12 and 225 vehicles.

**PERSONAL**  Affiliations and professional memberships include the Las Vegas Chamber of Commerce, Las Vegas Business Network, and National Defense Transportation Association. Excellent personal and professional references on request.

Date

Exact Name of Person
Title or Position
Name of Company
Address (number and street)
Address (city, state, and ZIP)

**ACCOUNT SALES REPRESENTATIVE**

Dear Exact Name of Person (or Dear Sir or Madam if answering a blind ad):

I would appreciate an opportunity to talk with you soon about how I could contribute to your organization through my sales experience with both wholesale and retail automotive parts suppliers with an emphasis on providing strong customer service support.

From my enclosed resume you will gain a sense of my accomplishments, skills, and abilities. After joining the Universal Automotive Aftermarket team as a Service Representative in 2000, I earned a 2002 promotion to Account Sales Representative. While providing eight automotive warehouses scattered throughout Illinois with high-quality support, I increased my 2002 sales figures 8% over the 2001 figures for this territory. As part of an eight-person team working in the three-state area of Illinois, Iowa, and Wisconsin, I contributed to an $11 million record in sales for fiscal 2002 and was singled out by my peers as the team's "Most Valuable Player" for both 2002 and 2003.

In addition to experience as a Parts Manager and Service Writer, I earned ASE certification in seven areas (suspension and steering, heating and air conditioning, engine repair, electrical systems, engine performance, brakes, and parts specialist) and attended the antilock brake clinic and school. I am very proud of achieving this Automotive Service Excellence certification in very difficult testing, a rare accomplishment for someone who is not involved on a daily basis in car and light truck repair.

With strong mechanical abilities and technical skills, I offer a proven understanding of the aftermarket business and can relate to people at all levels — from the small garage owner/operator, to service center managers, to mechanics, to warehouse distributors and retail sales personnel. Accustomed to travel, I feel that my approximately 15 years in the vehicle service and automotive aftermarket industries would be of value to an organization in need of a dependable and knowledgeable professional with outstanding sales and marketing skills. During this time I have seen many changes in the industry and have kept up with the latest trends and most efficient methods of transacting business.

I hope you will welcome my call soon to arrange a brief meeting at your convenience to discuss your current and future needs and how I might serve them. Thank you in advance for your time.

Sincerely yours,

Harry S. Burkingberg

# HAROLD SOL BURKINGBERG ("Harry")

1110½ Hay Street, Fayetteville, NC 28305  •  preppub@aol.com  •  (910) 483-6611

---

**OBJECTIVE**  To apply my sales and service experience to an organization that can use a dedicated and loyal hard worker who has earned a reputation as a talented sales professional with strong technical and mechanical skills as well as a genuine customer-service orientation.

**EXPERIENCE**  *Set numerous sales records, earned promotion on the basis of my accomplishments, and gained considerable knowledge in this track record with the Universal Automotive Aftermarket sales team based in Moline, IL:*

**2002-present: ACCOUNT SALES REPRESENTATIVE.** Excel in providing quality sales support to eight automotive warehouse distributors who handled Fram, Autolite, and Bendix parts within the state of Illinois and as a member of an eight-person team which enjoyed $11 million in sales during the most recent fiscal year.
- Increased 2002 sales an impressive 8% over 2001 sales while supporting such major accounts as Allied Automotive in Springfield and BDB in Deerfield.
- Was singled out as "Most Valuable Player" in the region in both 2002 and 2003.
- Contributed to the success of a team which called on a total of 55 warehouses in the three-state region of Illinois, Iowa, and Wisconsin; the team's major accounts included the following:

| | | |
|---|---|---|
| Dixie Tool – Deerfield, IL | U.C.I. — Harrisburg, IL | P.D.I. — Decatur, IL |
| Tidewater Battery — Wausau, WI | C.R.W. – De Pere, WI | U.C.I. – Fort Dodge, IA |

**2000-02: SERVICE REPRESENTATIVE.** Traveled extensively throughout the Southern and Midwestern states as a member of a team of specialists involved in major product line changeovers as well as providing the merchandising and support to large warehouses.

**PARTS MANAGER** and **SERVICE WRITER.** Laine Automotive Shop, Urbana, IL (1992-99). Supervised three people in a 10-bay service center with 20 employees: handled the purchase and resale of automotive and light truck parts to customers and company mechanics.
- Was persistent in locating sources for hard-to-find parts for repairs as well as custom and high-performance parts.
- Advised customers on what repairs were needed on their vehicles and coordinated the arrangements for scheduling and making the repairs.
- Gained in-depth knowledge of automotive and light truck troubleshooting and mechanical repairs along with the operating aspects of running the auto parts section.

**TRAINING, CERTIFICATIONS & SPECIAL SKILLS**  Earned a certificate in **Electrical Installation and Maintenance**, Elgin Community College, Elgin, IL.
Received ASE (Automotive Service Excellence) certification after completing very difficult technical training despite not being involved on a regular basis with mechanical work:

| | | |
|---|---|---|
| suspension and steering | brakes | engine repair |
| heating and air conditioning | electrical systems | parts specialist |
| antilock brake school and clinic | engine performance | |

Attended additional corporate-sponsored training courses emphasizing the areas of sales skills and understanding the automotive aftermarket; excelled in Quality Leadership School.
Offer computer knowledge and experience in using Word and Excel.
Am experienced in the use of various automotive repair test equipment including basic Sun diagnostic machine features and engine-building tools.

**PERSONAL**  Enjoy applying technical and mechanical skills while making high-performance automobile engine repairs as well as working on antique radios. Am available for frequent travel.

Date

Exact Name of Person
Title or Position
Name of Company
Address (no., street)
Address (city, state, zip)

**AUTO AND TRUCK REPAIRMAN**

Dear Exact Name of Person: (if answering a blind ad, Dear Sir or Madam:)

I would enjoy an opportunity to talk with you soon, in person, about how my cost-effectiveness and expertise with heavy equipment and repair could substantially benefit your organization.

As you will see from my resume, my dedication and attention to detail has often resulted in significant savings. Most recently at Schultz Equipment Repair, LTD., I was responsible for reducing the cost of a bulldozer engine by repairing the engine instead of replacing it, saving approximately $40,000 at one time. My expertise in heavy mobile equipment has saved thousands of dollars in many other instances.

I have developed a reputation for doing the work right the first time and am proud of my solid record. My experience in employment with Dade County Industrial Development in a civil service positions has permitted me to gain a wide variety of hands-on expertise with industrial equipment. This extensive training prepared me well for my supervisory experience overseas. In addition, I have learned to work harmoniously with many different types of people and also enjoy taking the initiative in situations where repairs are warranted.

I am certain I could make valuable contributions to your organization, too, and I am sure, realize cost-effective savings with repairs.

I hope you will call or write me soon to suggest a time convenient for us to meet and discuss your current and future needs and how I might serve them. Thank you in advance for your time.

Yours sincerely,

Frank E. Cunningham

# FRANK E. CUNNINGHAM

1110½ Hay Street, Fayetteville, NC 28305 • preppub@aol.com • (910) 483-6611

___

**OBJECTIVE**       I want to benefit an organization that can profit from an experienced mechanic, repairman, trainer, and inspector whose troubleshooting skills and expert knowledge routinely result in valuable cost savings.

**EXPERIENCE**       **AUTO AND TRUCK REPAIRMAN.** Schultz Equipment Repair Ltd., Miami, FL (2004-present). Successfully completed two contracts (one 18-month, one 7-month) inspecting and performing repairs on diesel trucks as well as a full range of construction equipment, including forklifts, cranes, and bulldozers.
- Determine nature and extent of repairs.
- Interpret instructions and specifications; read blueprints.
- Work closely with the Dade County Corps of Engineers.
- Established maintenance procedures and standards.
- Maintain these and other truck models: 953, AM2, AM5, AM8 Kenworth.
- Repair Paulson Inc. engines, power trains, and chassis components.
- Minimize downtime and saved $40,000 by repairing instead of replacing a bulldozer engine.
- Saved $2,000 by repairing a Paulson Inc. engine exhaust system instead of replacing the turbocharger. Reduced by $8,000 the total cost of an Ellis automatic transmission through repairing the turbocharger instead.
- Trained my Schultz counterparts to be self-sufficient mechanics with engineering and heavy truck equipment.

**MAINTENANCE ASSISTANT.** Radlink Inc., Miami, FL (2001-2004). Reduced the total cost of a textile machinery operation by 20% by properly maintaining machinery at correct specifications.

**HEAVY EQUIPMENT MECHANIC.** Dade County Industrial Development, Miami, FL (1997-2001). Performed mechanical maintenance on city transport vehicles and industrial equipment.
- Received "Outstanding Performance Award" for work on diesel engines and reducing overall manhours by making repairs.
- Gained skills and experience on diesel engines while advancing from helper to full mechanic in a very competitive system.

Other experience:
**MECHANIC.** Gerald Tires and Brakes, Miami, FL (1996-1997). Learned valuable skills in doing an excellent job on repairing front-end brakes and alignments under tight deadlines with limited resources while providing customer service.

**TRAINING**       Completed training in vehicle air-conditioning and electrical systems, Manater Community College, Miami, FL.
Completed mechanics in repair and operation of heavy equipment engines and systems courses.
Acquired extensive "on-the-job" training with engineer company, Bellman Engineering Corp.

**PERSONAL**       Take great pride in my work and in training coworkers to attain efficient production. Am cost-conscious and hard-working. Enjoy international travel; am flexible about living and working conditions. Willing to relocate.

Date

Exact Name of Person
Title or Position
Name of Company
Address (no., street)
Address (city, state, zip)

**AUTO DAMAGE ADJUSTER**

Dear Exact Name of Person (or Dear Sir or Madam if answering a blind ad):

I would appreciate an opportunity to talk with you soon about how I could contribute to your organization through my expertise as an automobile damage adjuster.

As you will note on my resume, I am working for the Allstate Insurance Company and was instrumental in helping the company develop territories throughout New Jersey prior to being transferred to South Carolina in 2002. As the first adjuster sent into South Carolina, I opened the Florence office, which now includes two drive-in locations as well as a guaranteed repair shop which I monitor while also averaging up to 125 claims monthly as the only Allstate adjuster within a 50-mile area.

In previous assignments with Allstate, I was instrumental in training new adjusters, and I am proud to have played a key role in developing some of the industry's most capable appraisers. I offer a reputation for unquestioned honesty, high productivity, strong negotiating skills, and technical knowledge.

I am highly regarded within the Allstate organization and can offer outstanding personal and professional references not only from Allstate but also from satisfied customers, regulators, and others with whom I have worked. Although my future within Allstate is very secure, I am writing to you because I am aware of your company's fine reputation and believe there might be a good fit between your strategic goals and my extensive expertise.

I hope you will call or write me soon to suggest a time convenient for us to meet and discuss your current and future needs and how I might serve them. Thank you in advance for you time.

Sincerely yours,

Richard C. MacDuff

(Alternate last paragraph:
I hope you will welcome my call soon to arrange a brief meeting at your convenience to discuss your current and future needs and how I might serve them. Thank you in advance for your time.)

# RICHARD C. MACDUFF

1110½ Hay Street, Fayetteville, NC 28305 • preppub@aol.com • (910) 483-6611

---

**OBJECTIVE**      To benefit a company that can use an expert automobile appraiser and licensed insurance adjuster who offers a proven commitment to outstanding customer service along with a reputation for unquestioned honesty, strong negotiating skills, and technical knowledge.

**LICENSE**      Licensed by the state of South Carolina as an Auto Damage Adjuster and Auto Appraiser.
- Was previously licensed in New Jersey as an Automobile Damage Adjuster/Appraiser.
- Hold a valid South Carolina Driver's License with a violation-free record.

**EXPERIENCE**      **AUTO DAMAGE ADJUSTER.** Allstate Insurance Company, Florence, SC (2002-present) and New Jersey State (2000-01). Began with Allstate as a part-time security guard on weekends, and was offered a chance to train as an adjuster; excelled in all schools and training programs, and have exceeded corporate goals in every job I have held within Allstate.
- *2002-present*: Am the first adjuster sent into South Carolina, and have played a key role in implementing the company's strategic plan to do more business inland selling auto policies; in a highly competitive market, opened the Florence office "from scratch," which now includes two drive-in locations as well as a guaranteed repair shop which I monitor while averaging 100-125 claims monthly as the only adjuster within a 50-mile area.
- *2000-01:* After initial training as an adjuster, worked in Jersey City and Trenton, NJ: averaged five claims per day while helping the company earn a reputation for outstanding customer service.
- Relocated to Newark, where I trained new adjusters.
- Worked in Wainscot County, a huge territory 30 miles wide and 100 miles long, where I made a significant contribution to building the territory; when I left as the only adjuster in Wainscot County, I was replaced with four adjusters in this rapidly expanding territory where I had helped Allstate earn a name for excellent service.
- Built a six-adjuster territory into a 14-adjuster territory in Somerville.

*Technical knowledge*: Skilled at utilizing Mitchell Estimate Systems and CCC Total Loss Evaluation as well as guidebooks, including NADA and the Red Book; routinely use equipment including a CRT and personal computer.
- Known for my excellent negotiating skills and ability to settle claims quickly and fairly.
- In the Florence area, have improved customer relations and reduced loss ratio 15%.
- Skilled at evaluating total losses, coordinating removal of salvage, and handling motor vehicle titles.

**Other experience**:
**AUTO & FURNITURE UPHOLSTERER.** Unique Furniture of Trenton, Trenton, NJ (1990-99). Worked in upholstery of auto seats, vinyl tops, convertible tops, and interior trim while customizing automobile and boat interiors.
**NAVAL PETTY OFFICER.** (1985-89). After joining the Navy, advanced rapidly through the ranks to E-5 in four years while managing people as well as inventories of ammunition, missiles, and nuclear fuel; was strongly urged to make a career out of the Navy.

**EDUCATION & TRAINING**      Completed college course work in Business Administration and Management, Mercer County Community College, Trenton, NJ, 1990-92.
Completed technical training in Risk & Insurance and Insurance Law as well as numerous courses conducted by companies such as General Motors and Honda pertaining to refinishing, principles of four-wheel steering, transmission repair, computer operation, and other areas.

**PERSONAL**      Offer an unusual combination of exceptional organizational and communication skills.

Date

Exact Name of Person
Title or Position
Name of Company
Address (no., street)
Address (city, state, zip)

**AUTO DEALER BUSINESS MANAGER**

Dear Exact Name of Person (or Dear Sir or Madam if answering a blind ad):

Can your organization use a result-oriented sales executive with a track record of success? Are you interested in hiring a self-motivated, mature, enthusiastic sales professional with excellent organizational and communication skills?

My experience includes personal selling to the industrial and consumer products markets, with hands-on experience in the areas of market research, sales forecasting, sales training and personnel development, financial statement analysis, and tangible and conceptual product presentations. I have a strong work ethic and a "can do" approach to setting and accomplishing personal and corporate objectives. Currently, I am Business Manager at Miami Toyota, where I have increased company gross profits 20% in one year.

May I meet with you soon to explore how my extensive sales background and abilities can assist your organization in furthering its objectives?

Thank you for your time and consideration. I look forward to hearing from you once you have completed your review of my qualifications.

Sincerely yours,

Larry M. Morrow

# LARRY M. MORROW

1110½ Hay Street, Fayetteville, NC 28305 • preppub@aol.com • (910) 483-6611

---

**OBJECTIVE**  To offer my leadership, problem-solving ability, and public relations skills to an organization that can use a dynamic motivator with a track record of accomplishments in sales and sales management at the retail level and as a manufacturers' sales representative.

**EXPERIENCE**  **AUTO DEALER BUSINESS MANAGER.** Miami Toyota, Inc., Miami, FL (2003-present). Direct all aspects of administration operations in automotive product sales, including retail sales, vehicle leasing, and sales of insurance products at this high-volume car dealership.
- Apply my analytical skills and financial expertise in selling insurance products such as accident and health, credit life, physical damage, and extended service agreements.
- Prepare profit-and-loss statements and monitor cash flow.
- Cost effectively manage the purchasing, receipt, and utilization of inventory.
- Hire personnel and oversee training on selling techniques, presentation skills, and the use of electronic data entry equipment.
- Have increased company gross profits 20% in one year.
- Was recognized by manufacturer for outstanding overall sales performance with all-expense-paid trips to Hawaii and Puerto Rico.

**DISTRICT MANAGER.** Chrysler Corporation, North and South Dakota (2000-02). Acted as point-of-contact in supplying wholesale Chrysler Motors products to more than 20 direct franchise dealers; monitored the retail sales activity of these dealerships.
- Assist Chrysler/Jeep/Eagle franchises with advertising and promotion.
- Analyzed dealers' financial statements and counseled the dealerships' principal(s) to ensure a positive financial position.
- Organized and conducted training of personnel, assisting dealers with merchandising, distribution allocation, operational and sales forecasting, trade show participation, and use of the Chrysler computer system.
- Played instrumental role in my district achieving 100+% accomplishment of objectives and outstanding sales performance, market penetration, and consumer satisfaction.
- Increased sales 28% in 1988 versus prior year sales with fewer dealers.

**SALES REPRESENTATIVE.** R.J. Reynolds Tobacco, Atlanta, GA (1995-99). Became a highly valuable member of this organization's sales force, making numerous contributions to the "bottom line."
- Sold tobacco products via retail independents, chain accounts, direct accounts, wholesalers, jobbers, and government agencies.
- Was ranked #1 in my zone for sales and account development in 1996 and 1997.

*Highlights of other experience:*
**Area Sales Representative.** Faberware Corporation. Commended for my exceptional sales and service of 30 direct accounts producing more than $10 million dollars annually in retail sales of ventilation products, intercom systems, hardware, and fixtures.
**General Manager.** SoundZone Stores. Hired, supervised, and trained a sales staff of 19 while managing all facets of operation for a key consumer audio/video/appliance outlet; was consistently ranked #1 in my division in annual sales and profits.

**EDUCATION**  **B.A. degree** in **Business Administration,** Dalton College, Dalton, GA, 1993.

**PERSONAL**  Demonstrate a positive ability to increase sales and motivate others through persistence, dedication, and unflagging enthusiasm. Rapidly master new software.

Date

Exact Name of Person
Title or Position
Name of Company
Address (no., street)
Address (city, state, zip)

**AUTO STORE MANAGER**

Dear Exact Name of Person (or Dear Sir or Madam if answering a blind ad):

I would appreciate an opportunity to talk with you soon about how I could contribute to your organization through my experience in all aspects of management/auto advisor, including shouldering the full responsibility for profit and loss and for market share.

My management career began with AutoZone, Inc., Ada, OK. After only seven months as a sales representative, I was promoted to manage the store and, in my first year as a manager, took sales from $800,000 to $1,100,000 without any increase in payroll. I was selected Manager of the Year in 2000.

Most recently while managing a "superstore," Parts Plus Automotive in Tulsa, OK, with four assistant managers and more than 30 employees, I produced dramatic increases in sales, increased profit as a percentage of sales, and cut payroll as a percentage of the operating budget. I became known for "setting the standard" for customer service and was even featured in written articles because of my commitment to outstanding customer service.

As requested in your ad, my salary history for the past three years has been in the $45,000 range. You would find me to be an innovative and resourceful professional who has a congenial style of dealing with people. I am skilled at simultaneously coordinating numerous functional areas ranging from sales, to personnel training, to inventory control. I can provide exceptional personal and professional references upon request.

I hope you will call or write me soon to suggest a time convenient for us to meet and discuss your current and future needs and how I might serve them. Thank you in advance for your time.

Sincerely yours,

Harriet G. Barrington

# HARRIET GRACE BARRINGTON

1110½ Hay Street, Fayetteville, NC 28305 • preppub@aol.com • (910) 483-6611

---

**OBJECTIVE**  To contribute to an organization that can use a store manager with a proven ability to manage multiunit operations and start up new stores using my award-winning talents related to sales, customer service, financial control, employee supervision, and quality control.

**EXPERIENCE**  **AUTO STORE MANAGER.** Parts Plus Automotive, Tulsa, OK (2002-present). Became known for "setting the standard" for customer service in this company, and was featured in publications because of my commitment to outstanding service; have come to believe that superior customer service is the key to competing in today's marketplace.
- Have excelled in customer service as well as these key management areas:
  *profit*           *inventory control*      *personnel development*
  *sales*           *store appearance*       *gross markup*
- In a unit which has two different sections — automotive retail and automotive repair — supervise four assistant managers and more than 30 employees.
- With a customer base of 150,000 customers per year, posted 2003 retail sales of $4.2 million.
- From 2002 to 2003, steadily increased profit from 9% to 16% as a percentage of sales.
- Cut payroll from 10.5% to 8.5% of the store's total budget.
- Produced a 26% increase in sales in 2002 compared to 2001.

**STORE MANAGER.** AutoZone, Inc., Ada, OK (2000-02). Began as a Sales Representative and, after only seven months, was promoted to manage the store; in my first year as a manager, took sales from $800,000 to $1,100,000 without any increase in payroll!
- Supervised a unit with more than 10 employees producing $1.2 million in annual sales on a customer base of 100,000 people a year.
- Was selected as ***Manager of the Year, 2000***, a selection made from among 15 other managers based on personnel development, shrinkage, sales, and profits.
- Was handpicked as ***Training Coordinator*** for Division Seven; oversaw the training of 150 people and was responsible for orienting/training all new employees.
- Was named to the company's ***Advisory Council*** in charge of long-range planning.
- Operated the company's 6th highest-volume store, and led it to consistently rank first out of 100 stores in the volume of special orders placed.

**SALESPERSON.** Arrow Auto Parts, Edmond, OK (1995-00). Learned the auto parts business and became an expert in consulting technical manuals related to parts; learned the terminology of the automotive/automotive parts business.

**EDUCATION**  Excelled in extensive sales and management training sponsored by:
  Fred Pryor Seminars          AutoZone
  Tulsa Community College      Parts Plus
- Through formal course work, have become knowledgeable about numerous aspects of automotive service including engine repair, brakes, manual drive trains/axles, suspension and steering, and heating and air conditioning.
- Hold an Automotive Service Certificate, Tulsa Community College.

**PERSONAL**  Offer the ability to get along with others. Am self-motivated and flexible. Will provide outstanding personal and professional references upon request.

Date

Exact Name of Person
Title or Position
Name of Company
Address (number and street)
Address (city, state, and zip)

## AUTO STORE MANAGER

The Objective of the resume is a blend of all-purpose and specific. He mentions his specialized knowledge of the automotive industry as well as his management skills which are transferable to any field.

Dear Exact Name of Person: (or Dear Sir or Madam if answering a blind ad.)

I would appreciate an opportunity to talk with you soon about how I could benefit your organization through my outstanding abilities gained in a multifunctional business where I oversaw activities including training and supervision, merchandising and promotion, sales and customer service, as well as administrative and fiscal operations.

As the Store Manager of a Southern Auto location which had $2.5 million in sales its last fiscal year, I have become very efficient at managing my time while dealing with three different operational areas — parts, tires and service, and automotive accessories. This store averages from 1,500 to 1,700 transactions a week with average weekly sales in the $40-60,000 range. In my five years as Store Manager I have achieved consistently high levels of productivity, sales, and customer satisfaction.

As you will see from my enclosed resume, before joining Southern Auto I earned rapid advancement with Quality Auto Parts. In my five years with this organization I was promoted to Store Manager after starting as a part-time sales person and then becoming a Merchandiser, a Parts Specialist, and Assistant Manager. As Store Manager I was involved in making decisions concerning merchandising, computer operations and fiscal control, inventory control, and public relations as well as internal employee counseling and supervision.

A dedicated and hard-working professional, I can be counted on to find ways to ensure customer satisfaction and productivity while always impacting favorably on the organization's bottom line.

I hope you will welcome my call soon to arrange a brief meeting at your convenience to discuss your current and future needs and how I might serve them. Thank you in advance for your time.

Sincerely yours,


Eugene Lobato

# EUGENE LOBATO

1110½ Hay Street, Fayetteville, NC 28305 • preppub@aol.com • (910) 483-6611

---

**OBJECTIVE**  To benefit an organization in need of an experienced manager with a strong background in inventory control/parts ordering, merchandising and sales, public relations, and fiscal operations along with specialized knowledge of the automotive parts business.

**EXPERIENCE**  **AUTO STORE MANAGER.** Southern Auto, Atlanta, GA (2001-present). Direct and oversee all phases of daily operations in an established store with 28 employees and with average weekly sales of from $40,000 to $60,000; motivate employees to achieve high levels of productivity, sales, and customer satisfaction.
- Played an important role in the success of a location with $2.5 million in annual sales and from 1,500 to 1,700 transactions a week.
- Received an Award of Excellence as an Auto Parts Specialist in recognition of my professionalism and knowledge of the inventory control aspect of the business (2003).
- Received Customer Service Award Pin for my exceptional customer relations.
- Earned certification in tires and parts in recognition of my expertise in providing customer service in these areas (2002).
- Was chosen to attend a corporate training program for store managers in 2002.
- Participated in setting up and running a job fair booth in order to recruit management trainees for Southern Auto at technical colleges throughout the southeast (2001).
- Carried out interesting sales merchandising and promotional activities which helped to increase sales of additional services once customers entered the store.
- Became skilled in time management while overseeing the operation of distinctly different areas within one location — parts, tires and service, and automotive accessories.

**STORE MANAGER.** Quality Auto Parts, Macon, GA (1997-01). Earned rapid promotion with this business and was placed in charge of overseeing all aspects of store operations from personnel, to sales, to inventory control.
- Advanced from a part-time sales position to Merchandiser, then to Parts Specialist and Assistant Manager, and in 1999 was promoted to Store Manager.
- Became familiar with management unique to the automotive parts industry involving public relations, computer operations/fiscal controls, and parts and inventory control.
- Supervised as many as 14 employees in a location which averaged from $15,000 to $18,000 in sales a week.

**EDUCATION**  Completed one semester of Business Administration, Priory College, Atlanta, GA.
Studied Electronic Engineering and Business Management, Atlanta Technical Community College, GA.

**TRAINING**  Was selected for corporate-sponsored training including:
"Introduction to Management" — a part of the Southern Auto Management School
Technical Electronic Ignition Course — Wells Manufacturing Corp.

**CERTIFICATIONS**  Received ASE (Automotive Service Excellence) certification as a Parts Specialist and Western Auto certification as a Master Tire Specialist and Parts Specialist.

**PERSONAL**  Am a well-rounded professional with excellent communication skills in all areas — dealing with the public and with employees. Have a pleasant and friendly personality.

Date

Exact Name of Person
Title or Position
Name of Company
Address (no., street)
Address (city, state, zip)

**AUTO SUPPLY STORE MANAGER**

Dear Exact Name of Person: (if answering a blind ad, Dear Sir or Madam:)

With the enclosed resume, I would like to confidentially express my interest in exploring management opportunities in your organization. I can provide outstanding references at the appropriate time, and I am held in the highest regard and am considered to be on the "fast track" by my current employer. However, I would ask that you treat my interest in your organization in confidence until we have a chance to talk in person.

As you will see from my enclosed resume, I began my retail management career with Champs in Tucson, AZ, where I was a Manager in Training and Assistant Manager. I developed excellent retail management skills while working for one of the largest athletic footwear retailers in the country.

Currently, I was recruited by Parts Plus, and I have been promoted from Sales Associate, to Commercial Specialist and Assistant Manager, to Store Manager. I am presently being groomed for promotion into higher management levels.

As a Store Manager, I have made numerous contributions to several stores. At the Parts Plus store in Tempe, I manage 20 employees and a $1.5 million annual sales volume while transforming that store into a model operation which hosted the district's Leadership Training seminars. On my own initiative, I prospected for outside commercial accounts and brought the commercial accounts up to a sufficient volume that I managed a Commercial Specialist to handle and grow that segment of Part Plus's business. I personally have won numerous sales awards within Parts Plus, and I have trained employees in techniques designed to boost sales and maximize profitability.

One of my strong abilities is the ability to troubleshoot problems, and recently I have been selected to take over the management of a troubled store in Tucson. I am already correcting numerous problems related to inventory and shrink, personnel and staffing, store standards, as well as sales and profitability.

If you can use a top producer to join your management team, I hope you will contact me to suggest a time when we might meet to discuss your needs. Thank you in advance for your time.

Sincerely,

Evan Charles Goliath

# EVAN CHARLES GOLIATH

1110½ Hay Street, Fayetteville, NC 28305  •  preppub@aol.com  •  (910) 483-6611

---

**OBJECTIVE**  To benefit a company that can use an experienced retail manager who has enjoyed a track record of rapid promotion based on my ability to troubleshoot problems, select and train quality employees, control inventory and reduce shrink, and increase sales.

**EDUCATION**  **Bachelor of Arts Degree** in **Business Administration** with concentration in **Marketing and Finance** and a **Minor in Economics**, The University of Arizona, Tucson, AZ, 1995.
- Computer-related coursework included PASCAL, BASIC, and RPG languages.

Was selected for intensive leadership training sponsored by Parts Plus.
- Only the top store managers across the U.S. were chosen for this elite training in Savannah emphasizing recruiting, interviewing, and hiring of employees as well as other topics.

Completed extensive management training sponsored by Parts Plus.

**EXPERIENCE**  **AUTO SUPPLY STORE MANAGER.** Parts Plus, locations in Tempe, Phoenix, and Tucson, AZ (2002-present). Began with Parts Plus as a Sales Associate, then advanced to Commercial Specialist and Assistant Manager, and then was promoted to Store Manager; am being groomed for further promotion to higher management levels.
- At the Tempe store, manage 20 employees and a store with sales of $1.5 million yearly; established many commercial accounts and manage a Commercial Specialist to prospect for and serve large outside commercial accounts.
- After we transformed the Phoenix store into what was considered a "model" operation, we created and hosted Leadership Training seminars for management in the district.
- Recently was handpicked to troubleshoot and correct a wide variety of problems at the Tucson store, which has 18 employees producing $1.75 million yearly in sales; corrected numerous problems related to plan-o-grams, staffing, loss prevention, as well as overall store profitability and store standards.
- Have distinguished myself within Parts Plus for excellent skills related to inventory control; while the district goal is 1.4% shrink, I have averaged 1.1% shrink. At the store in Phoenix, reduced shrink from 2.3% to .97%. Achieved this change through rigorous analyzing paperwork, conducting physical audits to assess truck shortages, and performing intensive follow-through of inventory credits.
- Have become skilled at recruiting, hiring, training, and managing employees as well as retraining employees in sales, store standards, and other areas which has led to winning sales contests. Have won District Crime Buster Award for catching shoplifters and warehouse shortages as well as paperwork errors.

**MANAGER-IN-TRAINING.** Champs, Tucson, AZ (1996-01). Developed excellent retail management skills while working for this large athletic footwear retailer.
- Developed excellent retail selling and customer service skills; fine-tuned my retail management skills in a $3 million per year store. Served as Assistant Manager; opened and closed the store, handled shipping and receiving, and managed store operations.

**Highlights of other experience:**
**DIE CASTING OPERATOR.** Hurley Manufacturing. Began as a temporary Assembly Line Worker and was hired full-time because of my excellent performance in meeting or exceeding production goals. Developed excellent troubleshooting skills, and trained new operators.

**PERSONAL**  Am a highly motivated self starter and go-getter who enjoys making a difference. Can provide outstanding personal and professional references upon request.

Date

Exact Name of Person
Title or Position
Name of Company
Address (no., street)
Address (city, state, zip)

**AUTOMOBILE BUSINESS MANAGER**

Dear Exact Name of Person (or Dear Sir or Madam if answering a blind ad):

I would appreciate an opportunity to talk with you soon about how I could contribute to your organization through my well-rounded experience related to automobile dealership business office and support department operations.

In my position as the Business Manager for Kennesaw Subaru in Kennesaw, GA, I have become very adept at handling the details which ensure that everything is done correctly and on time in order to complete sales and deliver the vehicle to the customer. Some of my main areas of responsibility include running credit checks, negotiating loan agreements, seeing that sales personnel complete proper documentation, and selling warranties and additional products.

As you will see from my resume, my prior experience has included jobs which called for strong sales and customer service skills as well as a base of knowledge in all phases of automobile dealership operations.

With a degree in Marketing (concentrating in Retail Business), I have earned a reputation as a dependable and honest professional. I enjoy the challenge of learning new methods and procedures. With a high degree of self motivation, I offer a strong ability to motivate others through my enthusiasm and dedication.

I believe that through my enthusiasm, motivational abilities, empathy, and compassion for others, I can make valuable contributions to an organization that seeks a professional with these qualities.

I hope you will welcome my call soon to arrange a brief meeting at your convenience to discuss your current and future needs and how I might serve them. Thank you in advance for your time.

Sincerely yours,

Dahlia S. McOwens

(Alternate last paragraph:
I hope you will call or write me soon to suggest a time convenient for us to meet and discuss your current and future needs and how I might serve them. Thank you in advance for your time.)

# DAHLIA S. McOWENS

1110½ Hay Street, Fayetteville, NC 28305 • preppub@aol.com • (910) 483-6611

---

**OBJECTIVE**  To offer my experience as a professional with a broad base of knowledge of automobile dealerships and of what must be done to ensure the smooth operation of the business department and supporting areas in order to make the greatest impact on the bottom line.

**EXPERIENCE**  **AUTOMOBILE BUSINESS MANAGER.** Kennesaw Subaru, Kennesaw, GA (2002-present). In a busy dealership, oversee a wide range of behind-the-scenes activities which guarantee support for the sales force as well as completion of contracts after automobiles are sold.
- Handle sales support functions ranging from running credit checks, to assisting the sales personnel in completing documents necessary for bank approval and ultimate vehicle delivery, to completing all paperwork needed to get contract cashed.
- Use my communication skills and knowledge to negotiate with lending institutions, find the best rates, and secure loan approval.
- Deal closely with customers while selling them additional services such as extended warranties, credit life insurance, A & H, and security systems. Prepare documentation in case of warranty cancellations; research problems and see that corrections are made.

*Advanced to a position of increased responsibility based on my accomplishments and performance with Liberty Ford, Inc., Columbus, GA:*
**BUSINESS MANAGER.** (2000-02). Advanced to this position after displaying an aptitude for quickly learning new aspects of dealership support operations.
- Gained experience in daily activities ranging from running credit checks, to assisting the sales personnel in document preparation, negotiating with lending institutions, selling extended warranties and other services, and preparing regular reports.

**GENERAL OFFICE CLERK.** (1997-99). Was cross-trained in a wide range of areas including cashier for the parts and service departments, service dispatcher, and receptionist as well as assisting with warranty claims processing and inventory control.

**SALES ASSOCIATE.** Clothes Galore, Columbus, GA (1995-96). Consistently set sales records for these popular clothing stores which have different types of clientele; helped customers make decisions on styles and colors as well as on accessories to complement the items they selected.
- Placed on the "Rising Star" list for six consecutive months for having the top volume of sales. Gained additional experience in inventory control and stocking.

**CASHIER/CLERK.** Wellington Ford, Columbus, GA (1992-94). Became familiar with the background support needed to keep an automobile dealership running smoothly.

*Highlights of other experience:* Gained sales and customer experience in a jewelry store and fast food restaurant.

**EDUCATION & TRAINING**  **A.A. degree in Marketing,** Columbus State University, Columbus, GA, 1992.
Completed corporate training seminars on the following topics: Ford Motor Company's leasing programs and a Heritage Insurance program on management techniques.

**PROFESSIONAL AFFILIATION**  Hold membership in the Ford ESP Professional Sales Guild — maintained a warranty penetration rate above 50% and passed an examination.

**PERSONAL**  Am a very hard-working individual with a reputation for dependability, honesty, and integrity.

Date

Exact Name of Person
Exact Title
Exact Name of Company
Address
City, State, Zip

Dear Exact Name of Person (or Dear Sir or Madam if answering a blind ad):

With the enclosed resume, I would like to make you aware of my background as an experienced professional with exceptional supervisory, communication, and analytical skills as well as a strong bottom-line orientation and a proven ability to maximize profits and sales.

I was recruited by AutoMax for my present position as Business Manager, and my rapid success in that position resulted in my being entrusted with the responsibility for overseeing the finance departments at both of their locations. I supervise three finance managers as well as a sales force of 15 automotive sales representatives. Through my efforts in promoting finance and warranty products, the dealership's average aftermarket profit has increased from $300 per vehicle to $500 per vehicle.

In my previous position with Virginia Bank & Trust, I was promoted rapidly, achieving a position as Assistant Vice President after only 33 months. I began with the company as a Credit Analyst and was promoted to Commercial Relationship Manager at the end of seven months of service. In this position, I actively recruited new commercial accounts and serviced existing accounts. During my tenure, my commercial accounts portfolio grew from $15 million to $25 million, and I doubled non-interest (fee-based) income from $20,000 per year to $40,000 per year.

I have earned Master of Business Administration and Bachelor of Science in Business Administration degrees from Virginia University.

If you can use a hard-working young manager with proven business savvy, I would enjoy an opportunity to meet with you in person to discuss your needs. Although I can provide outstanding references at the appropriate time, I would appreciate your holding my interest in your company in confidence at this point. I can assure you in advance that I have an exceptional reputation and could become a valuable asset to your company.

Sincerely,

William Wright

---

**AUTOMOBILE DEALERSHIP BUSINESS MANAGER**

Sometimes a detour in our career makes us realize what we really like to do! This "middle manager" on the fast track was recruited for a business management position in the automobile industry. Although he excelled in the work, he didn't find it as satisfying and stimulating as the work he'd done in banking and financial institutions. Hence, this resume and cover letter are designed to help him change industries.

# WILLIAM WRIGHT

1110½ Hay Street, Fayetteville, NC 28305 • preppub@aol.com • (910) 483-6611

---

**OBJECTIVE**     To benefit an organization that can use an enthusiastic, experienced manager with exceptional supervisory, communication, and analytical skills who offers a track record of success in maximizing profitability and increasing sales.

**EDUCATION**     **Master of Business Administration,** Virginia University, Greenville, VA, 1993 — GPA 3.6.
**Bachelor of Science in Business Administration** concentration in **Finance,** Virginia University, 1992.

**EXPERIENCE**     **AUTOMOBILE DEALERSHIP BUSINESS MANAGER.** Somerville AutoMax, Somerville, VA (2003-present). Was recruited for this position by this automotive dealership; oversee sales force of 15 employees.
- After excelling as Business Manager at one of AutoMax's locations, was entrusted with the additional responsibility of managing the finance departments at both locations.
- Supervise three finance managers, ensuring accurate and efficient preparation, processing, and completion of loan documentation.
- Communicate directly with lenders by phone and fax to obtain financing for customers; process loan applications for nearly 200 customers per month.
- Maximize the dealership's profit by selling and promoting the sale of aftermarket products such as extended warranties and credit life insurance.
- Established a secondary finance program for customers with past credit problems.
- Increased the dealership's average profit on aftermarket sales from $300 per vehicle to more than $500 per vehicle.

**At Virginia Bank & Trust, was promoted in the following "track record" of increasing responsibility by this large national bank:**
*1999-03:* **COMMERCIAL RELATIONSHIP MANAGER.** Greenville, VA. Was rapidly promoted within the organization; advanced to Commercial Relationship Manager after seven months with Virginia Bank & Trust, and to Assistant Vice President after only 33 months.
- Actively recruited new commercial accounts while providing the highest level of customer service to established accounts.
- Communicated the advantages of Virginia Bank & Trust and promoted our products and services to new and existing customers.
- Through my efforts, my commercial accounts portfolio grew from $15 million to $25 million during my tenure.
- Doubled fee-based (non-interest) income from $20,000 per year to $40,000 per year for accounts that I managed.

*1998-99:* **CREDIT ANALYST.** Various locations in VA. Started with Virginia Bank & Trust upon completion of my MBA program; quickly mastered skills related to loan pricing and the making of credit decisions.
- Underwrote loan requests for Relationship Managers throughout VA.
- Analyzed financial statements including balance sheets and income statements; gained valuable knowledge related to cash flow management.
- Completed Relationship Manager Development Course, November, 1998.

**AFFILIATIONS**     Rotary International — Finance Committee Chairperson
Member, Chamber of Commerce

**PERSONAL**     Excellent personal and professional references are available upon request.

Date

Exact Name of Person
Title or Position
Name of Company
Address (no., street)
Address (city, state, zip)

**AUTOMOBILE SALES CONSULTANT**

Dear Exact Name of Person (or Dear Sir or Madam if answering a blind ad):

Can you use a hard-working young professional with versatile skills related to sales and marketing, computer operations, operations management, and employee supervision?

I offer a reputation for adaptability, the ability to relate easily to others, and a knack for creative and innovative thinking. As you will see from my resume, I also have had the experience of living and working abroad while serving my country in the U.S. Air Force. During this period I became very skilled in reading, writing, and speaking German and also very familiar with German culture and customs.

When you read my attached resume I believe you will become convinced of my ability to adapt quickly to and excel in new environments. Most recently I have excelled in a sales position and, with no prior industry experience, I was selected as top sales consultant within only months of being in the job. Previously I demonstrated my ability to "juggle" numerous simultaneous activities as general manager of a small business. I have my B.S. degree in Business Administration, and I pride myself on my ability to creatively apply my diversified knowledge in ways that will profit my employer.

You would find me to be a results-oriented professional who believes that one of the keys to success in business is treating customers graciously and building relationships that last. I pride myself on loyalty to my employer, and I think that building and cementing the employer's customer base for future repeat business is probably the most important contribution an employee can make to his employer.

I hope you will welcome my call soon to arrange a brief meeting at your convenience to discuss your current and future needs and how I might serve them. Thank you in advance for your time.

Sincerely yours,

Dion C. Leland

(Alternate last paragraph:
I hope you will call or write me soon to suggest a time convenient for us to meet and discuss your current and future needs and how I might serve them. Thank you in advance for your time.)

# DION CHARLES LELAND

1110½ Hay Street, Fayetteville, NC 28305 • preppub@aol.com • (910) 483-6611

---

**OBJECTIVE**  To benefit an organization that can use a results-oriented young professional with versatile skills related to sales and marketing, computer operations, and operations management and employee supervision.

**EDUCATION**  **Bachelor of Science degree in Business Administration,** University of Kentucky, Lexington, KY, 1991.

**EXPERIENCE**  **AUTOMOBILE SALES CONSULTANT.** BMW of Louisville, Louisville, KY (2002-present). Am very skilled in "selling" customers on the quality of these new automobiles while ensuring they are fully informed on the features of the different models, the company's history, warranty terms, and maintenance agreements.
- Honored as the "Sales Consultant of the Quarter" for May through July 2002, was recognized for my high sales volume and value as a team member and professional.
- Apply my excellent communication and interpersonal skills while "prospecting" for new customers and conducting phone and mail follow-ups after sales were completed.
- Handle the details of preparing all the precontract paperwork.
- Learned effective techniques which are transferable to successfully complete sales of any quality product; received 46 hours of specialized corporate sales training.

**GENERAL MANAGER.** Dunford Enterprises, Frankfort, KY (1999-01). Learned all aspects of developing and running a small business by starting "from scratch" and operating a novelty/toy wholesale distribution company.
- Controlled all functional areas ranging from advertising, to bookkeeping, to making sales presentations, to pricing, to inventory control, to customer service.
- Developed leads and made sales presentations to large and small grocery store chains, convenience stores, drugstore chains, and department stores.

*Advanced in supervisory roles while developing my technical skills working with state-of-the-art data processing and communications systems, U.S. Air Force, McGuire AFB, NJ:*
**DATA PROCESSING OPERATIONS SUPERVISOR.** (1998-99). Trained and supervised specialists who collected and inputted data into a Sperry 1100/60 mainframe computer.
- Provided quality control while ensuring data from offices throughout the military community were correctly entered and output was complete and of a high quality.

**COMMUNICATIONS SECURITY SPECIALIST.** (1996-97). Ensured that classified communications equipment and materials were safeguarded and secure as the Air Force base's only specialist in this role.

**SUPERVISORY TELECOMMUNICATIONS SPECIALIST.** USAF, Germany (1991-94). Trained technical personnel in the operation of various types of communications equipment while handling day-to-day functions including: typing/preparing/routing/transmitting outgoing messages, operating cryptographic equipment, and operating a tactical switchboard.
- Was selected to supervise and train American and German personnel operating a switchboard system which provided telephone service to NATO military forces from the U.S., Germany, France, Belgium, Holland, Italy, and the United Kingdom.

**PERSONAL**  Speak, read, and write German; am very familiar with German customs and culture. Was honored with two commendation medals for "meritorious service." Held a Top Secret security clearance. Am very creative and have a reputation for thoroughness and loyalty.

Date

Exact Name of Person
Title or Position
Name of Company
Address (no., street)
Address (city, state, zip)

**AUTOMOTIVE RESTORER**

Dear Exact Name of Person (or Dear Sir or Madam if answering a blind ad):

I would appreciate an opportunity to talk with you soon about the contributions I could make to your organization through my expertise in the installation, maintenance, repair, and operation of a wide range of electrical and mechanical systems, along with my experience in shop management and employee training and supervision.

As you can see from my resume, I have had extensive experience not only in first-line repair and maintenance of a wide range of systems and engines, but also in the setup and management of repair and maintenance operations, including controlling parts and supply inventories. I also have a talent for effective motivation and for "jump-starting" the initiative of employees.

You would find me to be a highly qualified master of my trade who is a loyal, flexible self-starter who enjoys challenges and problem-solving.

I hope you will welcome my call soon to arrange a brief meeting at your convenience to discuss your current and future needs and how I might serve them. Thank you in advance for your time.

Sincerely,

Sean V. Lockwood, Jr.

(Alternate last paragraph:
I hope you will call or write me soon to suggest a time convenient for us to meet and discuss your current and future needs and how I might serve them. Thank you in advance for your time.)

# SEAN V. LOCKWOOD, JR.

1110½ Hay Street, Fayetteville, NC 28305 • preppub@aol.com • (910) 483-6611

---

**OBJECTIVE**  To benefit an organization that can use a talented and safety-conscious mechanic who offers hands-on technical expertise in the installation, maintenance, repair, operation, and troubleshooting of a wide range of electrical and mechanical systems, as well as excellent personnel supervision, project management, motivational, and planning skills.

**EXPERIENCE**  **AUTOMOTIVE RESTORER.** Ready Auto Paint & Body Repair, Fresno, CA (2003-present). Own and operate a business repairing and restoring damaged motor vehicles in addition to hiring, training, and supervising a staff of 3 mechanics.

**SYSTEMS REPAIR MANAGER.** John Deere Co., Waterloo, IA (2000-02). Refined general mechanic and electrical skills supervising a shop of 9 mechanics assembling, repairing, and troubleshooting tracked vehicles.
- Repaired and overhauled transmissions, engines, firing systems, undercarriages, electrical/hydraulic systems, torque converters, and dividers.
- Conducted calibration, operational, and diagnostic tests to determine performance levels of all systems.
- Instructed and supervised mechanic specialists in repair work to tracked and heavy-wheeled vehicles. Successfully worked with a broad range of technical specialists.

**SENIOR SYSTEMS MECHANIC.** Jackson Ford-Lincoln-Mercury, Brainerd, MN (1998-00). Wore many hats acting as shop leader, quality assurance specialist, and mechanic for an automotive repair shop.
- Trained, supervised, evaluated, and directed the technical staff.
- Controlled all departmental inventory management and parts ordering.
- Recognized by top-level management for excellent decision-making.

**MECHANIC SUPERVISOR.** Chandler's Automotive Shop, Brainerd, MN (1994-97). Directed a crew of 6 mechanics in the repair of customers' vehicles.
- Sharpened ability to accurately predict needed supplies of repair parts.
- Acted as Shop Manager in his absence. Planned work so that all repairs and maintenance were completed with accuracy and either on or before schedule.

**PERSONNEL PROJECT MANAGER.** U.S. Army, Aberdeen Proving Ground, MD (1991-93). Handpicked to coordinate the compilation and analyses of individual tasks to develop and implement an innovative training program for tank systems mechanics.
- Designed and developed all program lesson plans, training manuals, extension courses, skills qualification tests, and technical competence tests.

**TANK SYSTEMS MECHANIC.** U.S. Army, Ft. Riley, KS (1987-90). Refined technical expertise while providing support as a tank systems mechanic repairing and reconditioning M60 tanks. Commended for quick and accurate completion of repairs.

**EDUCATION**  Completed a wide range of technical training and professional development courses, including classes in leadership, management, hull repair, automotive electrical and suspension systems, automotive electrical/turbine/diesel engines, automotive maintenance, and business.

**PERSONAL**  Am an enthusiastic, hard-working professional who believes in always giving 100%. Work well independently or as a contributing member of a team. Have received numerous outstanding performance evaluations.

Date

Exact Name of Person
Exact Title of Position
Exact Name of Company
Address (no., street)
Address (city, state, zip)

**BMW TECHNICIAN**

Dear Exact Name of Person (or Dear Sir or Madam if answering a blind ad):

At the recommendation of Mr. Harold Cochran, I am sending you a resume to indicate my interest in the position of Instructor at the BMW Performance Center.

As you will see from my resume, I offer an extensive background in the automotive industry and have specialized in BMW maintenance, service, and repair for the past few years. I became associated with BMW because after I bought a BMW when I was vacationing Germany, I quickly became acquainted with the superior abilities of this driving machine, and I decided that I would pursue employment with the BMW organization.

In my current position as a BMW Technician with Highland BMW in Oakdale, NY, I have been recognized as one of BMW's most skilled technicians. I received a letter from the General Manager of BMW of the Eastern Region commending me for achieving one of the company's highest Customer Satisfaction Index (CSI) scores in the Eastern Region.

Although I am excelling in my current position, I feel I could make significant contributions to BMW in some capacity in which I am involved in training other technicians to "do it right, the first time." Prior to joining the BMW organization, I also gained extensive experience as a Technical Instructor while serving at Caterpillar, where I provided formal classroom instruction as well as hands-on training to personnel at multiple sites. While earning numerous awards for technical expertise as well as safety achievements, I excelled in extensive technical training which included the U.S. Army Engineer School and the Heavy Equipment Mechanic School.

I would appreciate your advising me about the next step I should take in exploring the possibility of becoming an Instructor at the BMW Performance Center. I can provide outstanding references at the appropriate time.

Sincerely,

Adrian B. Jansen II

# ADRIAN B. JANSEN II

1110½ Hay Street, Fayetteville, NC 28305 • preppub@aol.com • (910) 483-6611

---

**OBJECTIVE**  To contribute to an organization that can use a highly skilled automotive troubleshooter and problem solver with specialized expertise related to BMW along with experience in training others in classroom and field settings.

**CERTIFICATIONS & BMW TRAINING**  ACT Certified BMW Master Technician; ASE Certified Master Technician.
Completed BMW of North America Service Training at the BMW Eastern Region Training Center and the Southern Region Training Center, 2000-present.
- Programs included classroom instruction in BMW theory and computer systems as well as hands-on experience in diagnosis, repair, and programming of BMW systems.

**EDUCATION**  Excelled academically (4.0 GPA) while completing **more than two years of college course work** at North Central Texas College, Gainesville, TX.
Completed **Associate of Science degree equivalent in Automotive Service and Repair,** Miami University Hamilton Campus, Hamilton, OH, 1990.
- Two-year program included instruction in automotive theory and systems repair as well as hands-on experience in troubleshooting, repair, and rebuilding of automotive systems.

Completed **extensive technical training** sponsored by the U.S. Army including **U.S. Army Engineer School and Heavy Equipment Mechanic School;** gained skills related to performing general support-level repairs on military equipment including combustion-powered vehicles such as 1¼ ton thru 22½ ton trucks, truck tractors, semi trailers; combat and combat-support vehicles including personnel carriers and armored vehicle bridge launchers (AVLB).
- Became skilled in troubleshooting brakes, steering, fuel injection, and hydraulics using test measurement and diagnostic equipment (TMDE) such as pressure gauges, dial indicators, and specialized test equipment (STE/ICE).

**EXPERIENCE**  **BMW TECHNICIAN.** Oakdale, NY (2000-present). Have been recognized as one of BMW's most skilled technicians in the following work history:
- Received a letter in 2003, from the General Manager of BMW of the Eastern Region recognizing me in the "top 20% of all technicians in the Eastern Region based on Customer Satisfaction Index (CSI) scores." Routinely serve as Acting Shop Foreman in the foreman's absence. Troubleshoot the most complex problems.

**Reputation as a technical expert:** Have become skilled at all aspects of troubleshooting, servicing, and repairing BMWs as well as diagnosing, servicing, and repairing rear-wheel drive systems. Utilize DIS/TIS tester to aid in diagnosis process. Analyze, repair, and adjust two- and four-wheel alignment systems.

**While serving at Caterpillar, Inc., Hamilton, OH, refined my automotive skills:**
**AUTOMOTIVE MECHANIC & HEAVY EQUIPMENT MECHANIC SUPERVISOR.** (1995-99). At this major manufacturer of heavy equipment, trained and supervised mechanics in performing the full range of overhaul, repair, and rebuild of vehicles and generators. Also delivered prepositioned equipment to customers throughout the United States.
- Directed maintenance and inspection programs; performed repairs, overhauls, and rebuilds of 12-cylinder, 2000-hp engines requiring unusually precise repairing, fitting, and adjusting of moving parts. Maintained a perfect safety record.
- Experienced in repairing/maintaining brake, hydraulic, pneumatic, and electrical systems as well as the clutch and transmission.

**PERSONAL**  Resourceful problem solver. Strong personal initiative. Excellent references. Have been evaluated as a highly motivated leader whose technical competence surpasses expectations.

Date

Exact Name of Person
Exact Title
Exact Name of Company
Address
City, State, Zip

**BUSINESS MANAGER**

The cover letter is designed to be versatile, so that she can explore employment options inside and outside the auto industry.

Dear Exact Name of Person (or Dear Sir or Madam if answering a blind ad):

With the enclosed resume, I would like to make you aware of my interest in exploring employment opportunities with your organization. As you will see from my resume, I have worked as a Business Manager for the past 5 years, and I am held in the highest regard by my current employer. I can provide outstanding references at the appropriate time, but I would ask that you not contact my current employer until after we speak.

I give credit for much of my success as a Business Manager to the outstanding training I received in my first job as an Assistant Business Manager. From there, I was recruited for my first full-time job as a Business Manager, and in that job I negotiated and closed more than 80 contracts monthly while single-handedly managing my employer's finance and insurance business. In my current position, I am one of three full-time Business Managers, and I consistently lead the other managers in the amount of income generated.

I am committed to excellence in all I do, and that is why I worked hard to earn my C.B.I.F. Certification which designates me as a certified member of the Connecticut Board of Insurance and Finance. I am skilled at negotiating the details of loan closings, and I have become skilled in selling extended warranties, life insurance, total loss protection, accident and health protection, and other products. My customers know that my concern for their well-being is genuine, and I derive one of my greatest satisfactions in life from creating happy customers.

I am an outgoing individual who is known for my cheerful disposition as well as my reputation as a congenial coworker. I pride myself on my ability to establish warm working relationships with sales professionals and customers as well as with government agencies and business organizations. I believe my attention to detail and commitment to excellence in all I do are qualities transferable to any industry.

If you are interested in discussing the possibility of joining your organization, I hope you will contact me to suggest a time when we might meet in person.

Yours sincerely,

Miriam Nicholls

# MIRIAM NICHOLLS

1110½ Hay Street, Fayetteville, NC 28305 • preppub@aol.com • (910) 483-6611

---

**OBJECTIVE**     I want to contribute to an organization that can use an experienced and hard-working young business manager who offers a proven ability to increase profit, satisfy customers, sell and explain financial services, and establish congenial working relationships with others.

**EDUCATION**     **Bachelor of Arts Degree in Communicative Arts and Literature,** Eastern Connecticut State University, Willimantic CT, 1999.

**CERTIFICATION & TRAINING**     C.B.I.F. Certified by the Connecticut Board of Insurance and Finance, 2000. Certified Notary Public.
Completed numerous training programs related to areas including Marketing Concepts, Business Management, Principles of Loans and Finance, Automobile Financing, Extended Warranty Protection, Life Insurance, Total Loss Protection, and Accident/ Health Insurance.

**EXPERIENCE**     **Have derived great satisfaction in life from establishing strong customer relationships and by helping customers finance and protect one of the largest purchases in their lives:**
**BUSINESS MANAGER.** Ed Vader Cadillac, Inc., Hamden, CT (2003-present). Was recruited for this position because of my strong industry reputation. Have consistently achieved the highest "Sales Per Vehicle" income of the three business managers at this auto dealership.
- Assist customers in obtaining credit approval for vehicle purchases; work closely with loan officers at financial institutions. Determine various rate structures which balance consumer needs and company profit goals.
- At the closing of the loan, I achieve additional profit for the dealership of $45,000-$75,000 monthly by selling "add-on" products such as extended service contracts, warranties, total loss protection, and other services which protect the consumer's investment.
- Complete and turn the Department of Motor Vehicles (DMV) and insurance paperwork.
- Have established an atmosphere of "friendly competition" with the other two business managers which has led to a significant increase in finance and insurance income.

**BUSINESS MANAGER.** Taylor Toyota Dealers of Hamden, Hamden, CT (2001-04). Was specially recruited to become this established Toyota dealership's first full-time Business Manager; produced a significant increase in finance and insurance income through my ability to close the sale and satisfy customers.
- Established cordial working relationships with the dealership's 6-8 sales representatives.
- Became known for my skill in accurately and quickly completing detailed paperwork for financial institutions, DMV, and other organizations. While working as the dealership's only Business Manager, became skilled in multi-tasking.

**ASSISTANT BUSINESS MANAGER.** New Haven Chrysler/Dodge, New Haven, CT (1999-01). In my first job in the car business, was trained in every aspect of automobile financing and related insurance sales. Was trained by an outstanding industry professional in the importance of preparing perfect paperwork. I believe my subsequent success as a Business Manager was due to the excellent training I received in this job.

**ADVERTISING REPRESENTATIVE.** New Trends Enterprises, Willimantic, CT (1996-99). In my first job after graduating from college, created effective advertisements for customers who included middle schools, local hotels, and businesses.
- Was the company's first advertising representative, and boosted sales significantly.

**PERSONAL**     Outstanding references. Strong computer skills including experience with Word.

Date

Exact Name of Person
Title or Position
Name of Company
Address (number and street)
Address (city, state, and zip)

**BUSINESS OFFICE MANAGER**

Dear Exact Name of Person (or Sir or Madam if answering a blind ad):

I would appreciate an opportunity to talk with you soon about how I could contribute to your organization through my versatile experience and the application of my analytical, financial, and organizational skills.

In my current position as Business Manager for Thomason Chevrolet-Geo, Wichita, KS, I am in charge of all financial contracting on car purchases and an administrative representative to bank sources. The company has sent me to extensive financial and insurance schooling.

Previously, I was Loan Originator and Financial Consultant for Norris Financial Services in Kansas City, KS. I contacted pre-screened candidates to discuss/propose refinancing packages designed to lower mortgage payments or interest amounts.

I feel my well-rounded experience and financial expertise could be an asset to your organization. I hope you will welcome my call soon to arrange a brief meeting at your convenience to discuss your current and future needs and how I might serve them. Thank you in advance for your time.

Sincerely yours,

Kevin A. Levinski

# KEVIN A. LEVINSKI

1110½ Hay Street, Fayetteville, NC 28305 • preppub@aol.com • (910) 483-6611

---

**OBJECTIVE**  I want to contribute to an organization that can use an accomplished salesman, communicator, negotiator, and problem-solver who has excelled in selling services and products in highly competitive markets.

**SUMMARY OF EXPERIENCE**  Offer outstanding personal and professional references, based on my "track record" as a loyal and hard-working producer who can be counted on to make continuous contributions to the "bottom line."

**EXPERIENCE**  **BUSINESS OFFICE MANAGER.** Thomason Chevrolet-Geo, Wichita, KS (2003-present). Am in charge of all financial contracting on car purchases and administrative representative to bank sources. Attended extensive financial and insurance schooling.

**LOAN ORIGINATOR** and **FINANCIAL CONSULTANT.** Norris Financial Services, Kansas City, KS (2000-02). Have worked with the top management of this national company to pioneer exciting new canvassing methods and statistical evaluation techniques while personally remaining in the top 10% of all corporate sales professionals.
- As a loan originator, contacted pre-screened candidates to discuss/propose refinancing packages designed to lower mortgage payments or interest amounts.
- As a financial consultant and broker, coordinated proposals with a wide range of mortgage lenders; found the lender that was the "best fit" for the borrower.
- Through extensive telephone work which involved transmitting hundreds of details, became skilled in creating "pictures in words" to sell concepts effectively.
- Became highly respected as a wise decision-maker who could make prudent business judgements under pressure.

**AUTOMOBILE SALESMAN.** Lawrence, KS (1995-99). Excelled in selling automobiles for two prominent dealerships:
- At M & O Chevrolet Company (1997-99), learned that the customer always turns to his salesman for help if a problem occurs after the sale; was named "Salesman of the Month."
- At Bryan Automotive Center (1995-96), consistently ranked in the top third of sales professionals while selling "high ticket" items and providing excellent customer service.

**MAINTENANCE SUPERVISOR** and **EXPANSION PROGRAM MANAGER.** Warren Hospital, Wichita, KS (1991-94). Managed a complex operation involving all types of building maintenance while hiring, training, and managing a four-person staff.
- Directed a $2 million expansion program.
- Was commended for my management ability in directing two tough inspections related to hospital accreditation.

**GENERAL MANAGER.** Skyline Furniture Company, Topeka, KS (1990-91). Managed all store employees, marketing, bookkeeping, and inventory control for a furniture business.

**EDUCATION & TRAINING LICENSES**  Completed extensive formal and on-the-job training in sales, marketing, finance, and management.
Licensed as an insurance agent with the Kansas State Department of Insurance.
Licensed as a Notary Public.

**PERSONAL**  Have become a valuable employee and respected decision maker in every job I have held. Have an inner drive to excel and improve business operations.

Date

Exact Name of Person
Title or Position
Name of Company
Address (no., street)
Address (city, state, zip)

**CAR WASH OPERATIONS MANAGER**

Dear Exact Name of Person (or Dear Sir or Madam if answering a blind ad):

Can you use an experienced, knowledgeable, and energetic professional who offers experience in managing a diversified facility with car wash, express lube, detailing, and gift shop as well as previous experience in office management, sales, and customer service?

In my present position as the General Manager of Convenient Auto Wash (San Diego and El Cajon, CA), I have been successful in building sales and for the past two fiscal years — 2002 and 2003 — produced 20% increases in sales volume! During this period I also played a key role in a "start-up" operation in both locations from construction and equipment installation, through landscaping and set-up, to full operation.

As you will see from my resume, I offer a broad base of experience in office management, personnel supervision, sales, and customer service. I have always been commended for my ability to ensure smooth and efficient service in a courteous and concerned manner.

I feel that my ability to maximize employee performance, reduce costs, and increase profits combines with my practical computer, office administration, and sales experience to make me a professional with valuable skills to offer your organization.

I hope you will welcome my call soon to arrange a brief meeting at your convenience to discuss your current and future needs and how I might serve them. Thank you in advance for your time.

Sincerely yours,


Elena M. Perkins

(Alternate last paragraph:
I hope you will call or write soon to suggest a time convenient for us to meet and discuss your current and future needs and how I might serve them. Thank you in advance for your time.)

# ELENA M. PERKINS

1110½ Hay Street, Fayetteville, NC 28305 • preppub@aol.com • (910) 483-6611

---

**OBJECTIVE** To contribute to an organization that can benefit from my managerial experience as well as my talents related to providing customer service, increasing sales and profitability, reducing expenses, guaranteeing efficient work flow, and maximizing employee potential.

**SPECIAL KNOWLEDGE**
- Offer experience in the operation of specialized cloth, conveyer, and full-service car wash systems manufactured by Hanna.
- Operate DRB CarWatch system as well as computer systems; am familiar with software including Word, Excel, and Access.

**EDUCATION/ TRAINING**
Studied **Business Administration,** Cypress College, El Cajon, CA, campus.
Earned certification in Express Lube Management, Texaco Training Center, Houston, TX.

**EXPERIENCE** **CAR WASH OPERATIONS MANAGER.** Convenient AutoWash, San Diego and El Cajon, CA (2002-present). Contribute to the "bottom line" through my ability to handle the details of managing a multifaceted business which includes a car wash, express lube service, gift shop, and auto detail shop with approximately 60 employees in four departments in two locations.
- Lead efforts resulting in 20% sales increases for two consecutive years — 2002 and 2003.
- Participate in all phases of opening the facilities in San Diego and El Cajon — from construction and equipment installation, to landscaping, to actual operations.
- Polish my skills in many areas including overseeing office operations such as accounts payable and receivable, labor control, payroll, expense controls, and managing fleet accounts.
- Became familiar with equipment repair and maintenance. Hire, train, counsel, and fire employees. Prepare advertising materials; develop sales and promotional ideas.

*Gained experience in office & retail sales management, U.S. Government, Berlin, Germany*:
**OFFICE MANAGER.** U.S. Army (1999-01). Supervised five employees while ensuring customer satisfaction and the smooth operation of a customer service facility.
- Acted as General Manager in his absence: made decisions which required "discretion and sound judgment" in determining and acting on the seriousness of situations.
- Prepared written reports and correspondence for executives and staff members.
- Ensured Equal Opportunity and Affirmative Action Plans requirements were applied.

**ADMINISTRATIVE ASSISTANT.** U.S. Army (1997-98). Assisted an average of more than 100 customers a day in a personnel actions center while answering phone and in-person inquiries and making referrals to other agencies when appropriate.
- Gained experience in using automated systems to maintain correspondence and records files and ensure they were complete, accurate, and up to date at all times.

**SUPERVISORY RETAIL SALES SPECIALIST.** AAFES (Army and Air Force Exchange Service) (1995-96). Supervised at least three sales clerks and provided customer assistance in the women's and children's clothing departments of a busy retail sales facility.
- Prepared regular performance reports, scheduled employees, and made decisions on vacation and sick leave approval.

**PERSONAL** Was entrusted with a Top Secret security clearance. Am highly skilled in ensuring optimum manpower utilization and high levels of employee performance. Will relocate.

Date

Exact Name of Person
Exact Name of Company
Address
City, state zip

**CERTIFIED SALES & LEASING CONSULTANT**

Dear Exact Name (or Dear Sir or Madam if answering a "blind ad"):

With the enclosed resume, I would like to enquire about sales, credit, or collections positions available within your organization.

As you will see from my resume, I offer a track record of outstanding performance in sales and customer service as well as in credit and collections. In my most recent job with Revere Ford-Lincoln, South Bend, IN, I assist customers in making one of the largest consumer purchases most people ever make, and I have become known for my skill in negotiating the best deal for the company while satisfying customers with the characteristics of their product and loan package.

In previous jobs I managed credit and collections activities, and I am very knowledgeable about collections laws and procedures. In addition to managing accounts receivable while also managing other employees involved in accounts payable/receivable, I have personally performed both inside and outside collections and have handled bankruptcies and small claims court actions. I am skilled at handling loan processing and in making decisions about loan approvals.

After working in sales and finance for the past several years, I have come to strongly believe that persistent follow-up is vital to customer satisfaction, loyalty, and repeat business. I also believe that repeat business and referrals are the key to the success of any business, and I pride myself on my ability to provide such an outstanding experience for the customer that he/she will want to come back and deal with me in the future. I can provide outstanding personal and professional references.

If you feel you can use my versatile skills and extensive experience in dealing with people in both sales and credit/collections situations, I hope you will contact me to suggest a time when we might meet in person to discuss your needs. Thank you in advance for your time.

Yours sincerely,

Jackson W. Friendly

# JACKSON W. FRIENDLY

1110½ Hay Street, Fayetteville, NC 28305 • preppub@aol.com • (910) 483-6611

---

**OBJECTIVE**  To contribute to an organization that can use an experienced professional who offers expertise related to sales, credit management, and loan origination/loan processing and who is known as a hard worker with outstanding customer service and public relations skills.

**EXPERIENCE**  **CERTIFIED SALES & LEASING CONSULTANT.** Revere Ford-Lincoln, South Bend, IN (2002-present). In customer surveys, am always singled out for special mention because of my outstanding customer service skills combined with my expert handling of loan processing.
- Learned a great deal about consumer psychology and consumer behavior while helping people make one of the most expensive purchasing decisions in their lives.
- Became known for my skill in negotiating the best deal for the company while assuring that the customer was very satisfied with product as well as loan features.
- Have become skilled in all aspects of sales and customer service: maintain a loyal customer base of satisfied customers and enjoy an extremely high rate of referrals of new customers from previous satisfied clients.
- Create and implement creative marketing campaigns using direct mail.
- Became skilled at listening "between the lines" to customer needs and desires and figuring out appropriate products for their budgets and tastes.
- Learned how to analyze various loan features and variables and how to tailor a loan package that best fit customer needs. Developed a highly satisfied customer base who would trust me to handle their financial affairs in any professional situation.

**GENERAL MANAGER.** Better Lawn Maintenance, Inc., Muncie, IN (1995-01). Managed a privately owned company which provided landscaping and lawn maintenance services to commercial and residential accounts.
- Oversaw marketing and advertising. Negotiated contracts, hired and trained employees, administered payroll, and oversaw the financial management of the company.

**CREDIT & COLLECTIONS MANAGER.** Manhattan Spa Health Club, Inc., Manhattan, KS (1991-95). Handled all aspects of credit and collections for a stylish spa and health club facility with multiple locations catering to an upscale clientele.
- Managed accounts receivable. Prepared collections letters and performed collections activities, including taking delinquent accounts to small claims court.
- Handled bankruptcies and small claims actions for various facility locations.
- Prepared numerous reports and written operational analyses used for decision making.

**ASSISTANT CREDIT MANAGER.** Franklin's Furniture, Manhattan, KS (1990-91). In my first job in the credit and loan management field, worked for a large furniture company and learned the nuts and bolts of the credit and collections function.
- Handled loan approvals; administered billing and accounts receivable.

**EDUCATION**  Studied Business Accounting, Wake Technical Community College, Manhattan, KS, 1988-90.

**TRAINING**  Excelled in courses sponsored by Ford Motor Company and other companies related to sales, customer service, financial management, credit and collections, and leasing.

**PERSONAL**  Whether in sales or customer service, I have come to believe that follow-up is vital to customer satisfaction, loyalty, and repeat business. I believe that repeat business and referrals are the key to the success of businesses, and I excel in providing such a great first-time experience for the customer that he/she always wants to come back and deal with me in the future.

Date

Exact Name of Person
Title or Position
Name of Company
Address (no., street)
Address (city, state, zip)

**CHIEF OF MAINTENANCE**

Dear Exact Name of Person (or Dear Sir or Madam if answering a blind ad):

I would appreciate an opportunity to talk with you soon about how I could contribute to your organization through my expertise in large fleet maintenance management along with my experience in managing assets and personnel.

In my present position as Chief of Maintenance, All Pro Automotive, Bloomington, IN, I direct a general support maintenance shop while overseeing activities including automotive, fuel, and electric component repair and rebuild operations. As Senior Maintenance Manager, City of Evansville Fleet Maintenance, IL, I trained and supervised more than 100 mechanics. I "turned around" a facility which had officially been classified as "below average" and transformed it into one with a reputation as highly efficient." As Maintenance Manager, I received an "honor roll award" for seven consecutive months after "turning around" a program with a reputation for very poor performance.

My technical abilities, insistence on high-quality performance from my employees, and enthusiastic and energetic personality have enabled me to succeed while serving in every position held. As you will see from my resume, I excelled in more than 1,000 hours of training programs emphasizing leadership, time management, and communication skills in addition to a five-month Warrant Officer Technical Course leading to certification as a Maintenance Manager.

I feel certain that you would find me to be an articulate and persuasive leader with a "track record" of success in building teams, increasing productivity and efficiency, and managing multimillion-dollar assets.

I hope you will welcome my call soon to arrange a brief meeting at your convenience to discuss your current and future needs and how I might serve them. Thank you in advance for your time.

Sincerely yours,


Larry E. Ohrman

# LARRY EDWARD OHRMAN

1110½ Hay Street, Fayetteville, NC 28305  •  preppub@aol.com  •  (910) 483-6611

---

**OBJECTIVE**  To contribute my enthusiastic leadership style to an organization that can use an articulate communicator, tested and proven manager of multimillion-dollar assets, and authoritative decision maker with specialized experience in automotive fleet maintenance management.

**EXPERIENCE**  **CHIEF OF MAINTENANCE.** All Pro Automotive, Bloomington, IN (2002-present). Direct a functional reorganization from a backup repair shop to a "stand-alone" general support maintenance shop while planning, organizing, and overseeing activities including automotive, fuel, and electric component repair and rebuild operations.
- Develop and train a team of 40 mechanics in a variety of functional areas ranging from proper troubleshooting procedures to repair methods and shop operational policy.
- Control more than 30 major vehicle refurbishment projects.
- Provided the leadership which resulted in reducing the backlog by an impressive 30%.
- Was handpicked to manage a team involved in a new equipment testing project.

**SENIOR MAINTENANCE MANAGER.** Fleet Maintenance, City of Evansville, IL (2000-02). Trained and supervised more than 100 mechanics in an organization maintaining in excess of 400 items of automotive equipment.
- "Turned around" a facility which had officially been classified as "below average" and transformed it into one with a reputation as "highly efficient."
- Received an "honor roll award" for seven consecutive months.

**SENIOR MAINTENANCE MANAGER.** Volkswagen, Berlin, Germany (1998-00). Refined my leadership skills planning and managing operation of a 20-bay facility supporting more than 450 items of automotive equipment.
- Gained supervisory experience while overseeing in-house training for more than 70 mechanics in proper troubleshooting procedures, repair techniques, and shop policy.

**Refined my supervisory skills in this "track record" of accomplishments. U.S. Army:**
**MAINTENANCE SUPERVISOR.** Saudi Arabia (1995-97). Received a prestigious Department of Defense Commendation Medal for my "leadership and professionalism" managing a 70-person department involved in the war in the Middle East.

**MAINTENANCE SUPERVISOR.** Ft. Lewis, WA (1993-94). Credited with providing leadership and direction, guided an operation which had been operating at extremely low efficiency levels and developed it into a stable facility with a reputation for providing high-quality maintenance services.

**PERSONNEL RECRUITER.** Boston, MA (1990-92). Polished my verbal and written communication skills while interviewing qualified young people and "selling" them on the advantages of a military career, teaching seminars on civics and government, and making presentations to community and government leaders.

**EDUCATION & TRAINING**  **Associate of Science degree** in Automotive Maintenance, Wheaton College, Wheaton, IL, 1989. Completed more than 1,000 hours of training in advanced leadership, communications, and time management in addition to the five-month Warrant Officer Technical Course leading to certification in maintenance management. Was the honor graduate of these programs.

**PERSONAL**  Earned eight Army Commendation Medals for "outstanding achievements" as a technician, leader, and maintenance manager. Am a persuasive speaker. Secret security clearance.

Date

Exact Name of Person
Title or Position
Name of Company
Address (no., street)
Address (city, state, zip)

**CLAIMS REPRESENTATIVE & INSURANCE ADJUSTER**

Dear Exact Name of Person (or Dear Sir or Madam if answering a blind ad):

With the attached resume, I would like to make you aware of my interest in the position as Claims Manager – Field in MD. Nancy Riverdale suggested that I fax this resume to you, and she feels that my expertise and skills would be assets for Aetna in the MD Claims Manager position in Annapolis, MD.

### Extensive claims expertise
Shortly after receiving my college degree from Bowie State University, I embarked upon a career as a Claims Representative and I have been promoted to Senior Claims Representative and Office Team Leader within GMAC. While excelling in all aspects of my job, I have contributed significantly to numerous task forces designed to improve the efficiency of claims processing and customer satisfaction. I have trained and mentored numerous junior adjusters, and I have set an example for them to follow in my positive attitude, work ethic, and aggressive pursuit of advanced training and professional development courses. In GMAC's 13-adjuster office, I function as the Litigation Adjuster and have acquired much experience in settling disputes through mediation.

### Proven management and communication skills
In addition to the numerous management courses I took while earning my college degree, I have refined my management and communication skills in jobs as an assistant manager for a shoe store, small business manager, and district sales representative. I offer a proven ability to establish effective working relationships, and I enjoy the responsibility of training, coaching, and developing junior employees.

### Outstanding track record
I recently completed my annual performance appraisal and received exemplary scores on all performance areas. GMAC has recognized my management abilities: the company offered me a management position in Georgia, and GMAC has also identified me as the individual it wants to build and manage the company's force of adjusters in Montana if business volume grows to a level where field adjusters are justified.

I am well acquainted with Aetna's reputation for excellence, and I would appreciate an opportunity to discuss the MD–Claims Manager position in Annapolis with you. Although I can provide outstanding references from GMAC at the appropriate time, I would appreciate your holding my expression of interest in your company in confidence until we discuss the position. Thank you in advance for your time and professional courtesies.

Yours sincerely,

Edward R. Stickman

# EDWARD R. STICKMAN

1110½ Hay Street, Fayetteville, NC 28305 • preppub@aol.com • (910) 483-6611

---

**OBJECTIVE**      To benefit an organization that can use a resourceful problem solver with strong analytical, communication, and management skills who has excelled as a claims adjuster in all aspects of automobile and homeowners property/claims settlement including material damage (MD).

**EDUCATION**      **Bachelor of Science in Leisure Science,** Bowie State University, Bowie, MD, 2001.
- Played varsity football, 1998-99; was active in intramural sport including softball, basketball, co-ed football, and football.
- Placed on Honor Roll in 1997, Dean's List in 1999, and Athletic Dean's List in 1999.
- Completed numerous courses in management and excelled in internships which tested my ability to plan, program, manage, and evaluate recreational programs and activities.

**LICENSE**      Maryland Property & Casualty (P&C) license
Licensed as a Notary Public through 2005
Completed AIC 33 designation; planning to pursue further AIC courses.

**EXPERIENCE**      **SENIOR CLAIMS REPRESENTATIVE & INSURANCE ADJUSTER.** GMAC Insurance, Baltimore, MD (2001-present). Have become respected for my material damage (MD) expertise in an office with 13 adjusters; function as the Litigation Adjuster and have acquired vast experience in settling disputes through mediation.
- Handle daily office claims management responsibilities including the disbursement of claims load to adjusters in Baltimore and Montgomery counties.
- As the Office Team Leader, I examine files, provide direction toward claim settlement, and handle external and internal complaints.
- Assume responsibilities as office supervisor in the office manager's absence.
- Approve authority requests and all extended hours scheduling.
- Have trained many adjusters, and continuously set an example for other adjusters through my positive attitude, work ethic, and aggressive pursuit of advanced training.
- Have played a key role on numerous company task forces designed to streamline claims performance, improve cross-claims coordination, and increase the contact percentage as well as customer satisfaction of loss participants.
- Coordinated the company's local Catastrophe (CAT) Team, and was a quarterly award winner within GMAC for my contributions to the CAT Team.

**Prior management and sales experience (mostly summer and part-time jobs while earning my college degree): ASSISTANT MANAGER.** Foot Locker, Largo, MD. Was involved in hiring, training, and managing retail associates at this store which employed six people; continuously provided training designed to refine the customer service, communication, and problem solving skills of associates.

**TRAINING & CONTINUING EDUCATION**      **I-Car Certifications, 2001-present:**

| | |
|---|---|
| Advanced Vehicle Systems | Aluminum Repair |
| Steering and Suspension | Electronics 1 and 2 |
| Electronics 3 and 4 | Collision Repair 2000 |
| Plastic Repair | Finish Matching |
| Finish Matching Combo | Detailing Update |
| Aluminum Repair, Replacement, and Welding | |

**PERSONAL**      Can provide outstanding references from all employers. Pride myself on my dedication to physical fitness. Offer experience in automobile and homeowners property/claims settlement.

Date

Exact Name of Person
Title or Position
Name of Company
Address (number and street)
Address (city, state, and zip)

**COMMUNICATIONS MAINTENANCE SUPERVISOR**

Dear Exact Name of Person (or Sir or Madam if answering a blind ad):

I would appreciate an opportunity to talk with you soon about how I could contribute to your organization through my versatile supervisory and managerial abilities as well as through my reputation as a professional who can be counted on for personal integrity, resourcefulness, and dedication to excellence in everything I attempt.

You will see from my enclosed resume that in all the positions I have held, I have consistently developed and implemented programs and changes in functional operations which resulted in outstanding results in all measurable areas of operations. I have had direct supervision over as many as 35 employees as well as inventories of state-of-the-art vehicles, weapons systems, and communications equipment worth as much as $33 million. I have developed and implemented a variety of training, inventory control, and maintenance programs which have been accepted and held up as the standard for other similar units.

I am confident that through my track record of achieving results, building teams, and bringing about needed improvements, I am the type of mature professional who would be of benefit to any organization which values initiative, drive, and self-confidence.

I hope you will welcome my call soon to arrange a brief meeting to discuss your current and future needs and how I might serve them. Thank you in advance for your time.

Sincerely,

Walter E. Hollins

(Alternate last paragraph:
I hope you will call or write me soon to suggest a time convenient for us to meet and discuss your current and future needs and how I might serve them. Thank you in advance for your time.)

# WALTER ERVIN HOLLINS

1110½ Hay Street, Fayetteville, NC 28305 • preppub@aol.com • (910) 483-6611

**OBJECTIVE**  To offer my proven management skills to an organization that can use a well-rounded mature professional with expertise in supervising maintenance operations, maximizing human potential, and conducting training which produces skilled personnel.

**EXPERIENCE**  **MAINTENANCE SUPERVISOR.** Rent-A-Car, Bonn, Germany (2002-present). Quickly brought about changes which increased productivity and customer service capabilities while supervising six mechanics and a clerk in an operation which performed all maintenance on a fleet of 27 vehicles and accompanying support equipment valued in excess of $500,000.
- Control repair/service parts inventories and a $160,000 annual operating budget.
- Increased the lines of repair parts from 52 to over 225 without exceeding the budget.
- Implemented a certification program for the company's maintenance operators.

**COMMUNICATIONS MAINTENANCE SUPERVISOR.** Alliant Food Services, Lansing, MI (1999-01). Directed support for 452 pieces of equipment valued in excess of $12 million; equipment included vehicles, trailers, generator sets, and communications-electronics systems.
- As the advisor on procedures and quality control measures for four subordinate units and their maintenance programs, made recommendations on improvements.
- Developed and implemented programs including a Unit Level Logistics class and a maintenance indoctrination program for managers as well as a drivers training program which earned acceptance as the standard for the parent organization.
- Maintained an impressive 98% operational readiness rate.

**MAINTENANCE SUPERVISOR.** City of Lexington, KY (1995-98). Provided leadership and expertise which allowed this support facility with 35 employees to receive high evaluations in every performance area while maintaining 48 vehicles/28 generator sets worth $33 million.
- Oversaw a functional reorganization during which all old equipment was removed and totally new state-of-the-art communications equipment was installed and set up.
- Displayed initiative while actively overseeing a repair parts recovery program which saved the city $65,000.
- Achieved equipment readiness rates consistently at least 5% above the standard and achieved vehicle readiness rates at least 13% above the average for the parent organization as a whole.
- Organized and conducted a maintenance orientation program which so impressed one senior executive that he requested my plan be put into writing as a guideline for others.

**MAINTENANCE SUPERVISOR.** Ace Construction Co., Berlin, Germany (1992-94). Supervised 15 mechanics/clerks in a maintenance support department of an organization with 13 tracked vehicles and 69 wheeled vehicles and trailers while providing sound management for human resources. Controlled a $7 million inventory of repair parts.

**EDUCATION & TRAINING**  Completed approximately 80 semester hours of college course work with an emphasis on the field of management, Northeast Louisiana University, Monroe, LA.
Excelled in more than a year of training emphasizing management, maintenance, and leadership development; took a 40-hour course in federal and state environmental practices.

**COMPUTERS**  Knowledgeable of computer applications to include using Excel and PowerPoint software.

**PERSONAL**  Top Secret security clearance. Face challenges head on and work well under pressure.

Date

Exact Name of Person
Title or Position
Name of Company
Address (number and street)
Address (city, state, and zip)

## COMPANY PRESIDENT & SALES MANAGER

Employers are *very* inquisitive about why an entrepreneur wants to make a change. This accomplished individual uses his cover letter to emphasize that he has worked in a big company as well as in the small company which he founded, and he makes it clear that he now wishes to be involved in sales. (Employers are looking for people who know what they want to do; entrepreneurs are usually definite in their preferences about what they want to do next.)

Dear Exact Name of Person (or Sir or Madam if answering a blind ad):

With the enclosed resume, I would like to introduce you to the sales expertise, leadership ability, and management skills which I could put to work for your organization.

I am in the process of selling a company which I built "from scratch" and which, through my strong sales and management skills, I have grown into a profitable and respected small company in only two years. Although I have been successful in this entrepreneurial venture, I have decided that I wish to devote most of my energies to sales rather than to the day-to-day management details of a small business.

As you will see from my resume, I also offer a track record of proven results in managing a large company. In my first job after leaving the University of North Carolina at Chapel Hill, I went to work for a company in the oil industry and I advanced into the General Manager position. During the 20 years which I spent managing this large, diversified business with wholesale and retail operations, I took the initiative in building the first 10-minute oil change unit in VA. After acting as sales manager and developing the commercial fleet business, I sold the business to the Jiffy Lube franchise for a profit.

I can assure you that I am a tireless hard worker who thoroughly enjoys selling and developing a new marketing program as well as a great product/service. Although much of my experience has been in petroleum operations/sales and in automotive parts/sales with specialized knowledge of lubricants sales, I have proven my ability to sell products in other industries. As a Sales Representative of insurance products, I exceeded all quotas and was named a National Quick Start winner.

A naturally outgoing individual with a proven ability to lead and motivate others, I have been active in numerous leadership capacities in my community. I am a former past president of the Rotary Club and former director of the Chamber of Commerce. If you can use my considerable sales and management abilities, I hope you will write or call me to suggest a time when we could meet in person.

Sincerely,

Wallace Jackson

# WALLACE JACKSON

1110½ Hay Street, Fayetteville, NC 28305 • preppub@aol.com • (910) 483-6611

---

**OBJECTIVE**  To benefit an organization which can use a dynamic communicator and creative sales professional with outstanding negotiating and management skills along with a proven ability to transform ideas into operating realties while maximizing profit and market share.

**EXPERIENCE**  **COMPANY PRESIDENT and SALES MANAGER.** Tidewater Sales & Rentals, Richmond, VA (2002-present). Utilized my entrepreneurial ability, aggressive sales orientation, strategic planning capabilities, and management skills to start a pre-owned car business "from scratch."
- Although I have been successful in starting up and managing a profitable business, I have decided to sell the company and seek a full-time sales situation.

**SALES REPRESENTATIVE.** State Farm Insurance, Richmond, VA (1998-02). As a Property and Casualty Insurance Sales Professional for State Farm, handled "Family Insurance Checkups" and personal lines.
- Excelled in my first sales experience outside the automotive and petroleum industry; was selected as a National Quick Start winner in 1999; received a company-paid excursion to Los Angeles, CA, for advanced training.
- Exceeded quotas and boosted insurance sales by introducing a unique insurance concept: a membership benefits package for independent business owners which provided clients with maximum insurance coverage through membership in the National Association for the Self-Employed (NASE) or other association programs.

**GENERAL MANAGER.** Jackson Oil Company Inc., Tidewater, VA (1995-98). In my first job out of college, began with Mayfield Oil Company and advanced into the General Manager position; provided leadership in turning around a marginally profitable company and then helped it to achieve higher levels of sales and profitability each year; negotiated the buyout of key assets of Mayfield Oil Company by Jackson Oil Company in 1997 and continued as the corporation's chief executive officer.
- At the head of a diversified multiplex consisting of an oil company and a chain of convenience stores, worked at the wholesale buying level of the petroleum industry while gaining experience in managing a chain of retail convenience stores.
- Oversaw staffing, sales, purchasing, bookkeeping, financial management including accounts receivable/payable, vendor relations, and inventory control.
- Transformed a business with only 5 employees into a leading competitor in the region with a 40+ work force and profits which multiplied sevenfold.
- Took the initiative in building the first 10-minute oil change unit in VA and developed the operation from start-up to 35 cars a day; developed the commercial fleet accounts and then sold the business to the Fast Lube franchise for a profit in 1995!
- Established and managed a profitable automatic car wash business.

**EDUCATION**  Completed two years of college coursework, University of North Carolina at Chapel Hill, 1991-93.
**Sales Training**: Completed extensive sales and management seminars since 1993 including Dale Carnegie and A.L. Williams Management Seminars.
**Technical Training:** Completed numerous petroleum industry seminars and training programs sponsored by automotive and oil industry giants

**AFFILIATIONS**  Former President, Rotary Club of the Tidewater Region. Membership Chairman, Social Chairman, and Chairman of the Board.
**Other:** Chairman of Miss Tidewater Pageant; Chairman of Tidewater Christmas Parade for five years; Chairman, Tidewater Centennial Parade; Co-Chairman of Tidewater Heart Fund.

**PERSONAL**  Enjoy hunting, saltwater fishing, golf, and UNC athletic events. Outstanding references.

Date

Exact Name of Person
Exact Title of Person
Exact Name of Organization
Exact Address
City, State zip

**CONSULTANT WITH EXPERIENCE AS A USED CAR DEALER**

Dear Exact Name: (or Dear Sir or Madam if answering a blind ad):

With the enclosed resume, I would like to enquire about sales positions available within your organization. I am confident that I could rapidly become a valuable asset in whatever capacity you feel you could most benefit from my unique talents and abilities.

Although most of my business savvy has come from "real-world" experience, I do hold a Master of Science degree in Business Administration, a Master's degree in Guidance and Counseling, and a B.S. degree. After earning my college degree, I worked for several years as a High School Guidance Counselor, and then economics forced me to seek a simultaneous part-time job as a Salesman for used with a prominent Stokes KIA dealership in Winter Park. That part-time job opened my eyes to my talent for selling cars and motivating others, and thus began an impressive career in the automotive industry.

After completing a two year Dealer Trainee Program with Mitsubishi Motor Company, I became a General Manager of Mitsubishi Motors in Gainesville, FL. I was successful in turning around that dealership which had experienced multimillion-dollar losses in three previous years, and I led it to show a profit of $375,000 – its first profit in four years. Subsequently, I served as a Consultant to start-up dealerships and to mature dealerships in need of a strong manager to resolve sales and profitability problems.

As the General Sales Manager for Stokes KIA I played a major role in increasing market penetration by 49%. I was then recruited by the Jeep Corporation to serve as President and General Manager for Southern Automotives Jeep Dealers. I led the company to achieve gross sales of 19.5 a year along with a $970,000 profit-before-tax income for two consecutive years. We received the Dealer of the Year Award from Stokes for two consecutive years, and we were recognized as a five-star dealer – the ultimate achievement in customer service - for two years.

Most recently, I have managed a successful start-up of a used car dealership, which became a major force in the market in less than two years. I feel certain that my experience and skills could complement your management team, and I would enjoy the opportunity to talk with you in person about your needs and how I might serve them. I can provide excellent personal and professional references at the appropriate time, and I can assure you that I am a dynamic individual with an outstanding reputation within the industry along with an aggressive bottom-line orientation and a results-oriented style of interacting with others. Thank you in advance for your time.

Sincerely,

Henry K. Lattimore

# HENRY K. LATTIMORE

1110½ Hay Street, Fayetteville, NC 28305 • preppub@aol.com • (910) 483-6611

---

**OBJECTIVE**  I want to contribute to an organization that can use a dynamic leader who has excelled in recruiting and training personnel, developing and implementing effective human resources policies, as well as troubleshooting difficult problems and identifying creative solutions.

**EDUCATION**  **Master of Science** in **Guidance and Counseling Degree,** University of Florida, Gainesville, FL.
**Bachelor of Science Degree,** Rollins College, Winter Park, FL.
Completed two-year Dealer Trainee Program of Mitsubishi Motor Company, Gainesville, FL, 2002.

**EXPERIENCE**  **CONSULTANT.** Mitsubishi Motor Company, Gainesville, FL (2002-present). Sent in by Mitsubishi Motor Company to provide consultation to troubled operations and dealerships suffering severe financial losses nationwide.
- Work with the existing management, drawing on my years of industry expertise to develop effective solutions to management, sales, and operational problems.

**PRESIDENT & GENERAL MANAGER.** Quality Autos, Gainesville, FL (2000-02). Supervised 12 individuals including five sales professionals, four finance specialists, one manager, two assistant sales manager, office personnel, and the Service Department.
- Founded a company which rapidly became a major competitor.

**PRESIDENT & GENERAL MANAGER.** Southern Automotives Jeep Dealers, Winter Park, FL (1998-00). Supervised 53 individuals who included 14 sales professionals, three finance specialists, the Used Car Manager, the New Car Manager, the Service and Parts Manager, the Service Department, the Recon Department, and the office personnel.
- Led the company to achieve gross sales of $24.5 million a year, and achieved a $970,000 profit-before-tax income for two consecutive years.
- Exceeded all goals and projections for growth, market share, and profitability; for example, doubled assigned market penetration each year for two consecutive years.
- Became recognized as a Five-Star Dealer and received the Dealer of the Year Award from Jeep for two consecutive years.

**GENERAL SALES MANAGER.** Stokes KIA, Winter Park, FL, (1996-98). Supervised eight sales professionals including the Used Car Manager, the New Car Manager, and the finance specialist. For this dealership with a $4.5 million inventory and gross sales of $19.5 million per year, increased market penetration by 49%. Was rated one of the top KIA dealerships.

**INTERIM OPERATOR & CONSULTANT.** Stokes Honda & Isuzu, Winter Park, FL, (1995-96). Was recruited to serve as Interim Operator and Consultant at Stokes Honda & Isuzu until a major buy/sell was negotiated and implemented. As a consultant in Sanford: In 60 days, turned around a franchise $75,000 a month and restored it to profitability.

**GENERAL MANAGER.** Summerton Chevrolet, Winter Park, FL, (1993-95). Supervised 54 individuals including one General Sales Manager, one Used Car Manager, one New Car Manager, and a New Truck Manager along with finance specialists, service and parts technicians, office personnel, the Finance Department, the body shop, and 20 sales professionals.
- Increased DTA to the Top 10 in a group of 45 dealers within 12 months.

**PERSONAL**  Can provide excellent personal and professional references. Dynamic and results-oriented.

Date

Exact Name of Person
Exact Title
Exact Name of Company
Address
City, State, Zip

**CONTROLLER** for a trucking company. His employer of more than 26 years has restructured and, to keep his job with the company, he must move to Richmond. He has decided to resign from the company and seek employment elsewhere.

Dear Exact Name of Person (or Dear Sir or Madam if answering a blind ad):

With the enclosed resume, I would like to make you aware of my considerable experience in the area of accounting, finance, budgeting, and controlling.

As you will see from my resume, I have a rather unusual work history, since I have worked for only one company. I began with Quality Truck Rental, Inc. in 1998 and was promoted through the ranks until I became a District Controller for one of Quality's 70 districts. For a district with a fleet of 800 vehicles, I received extensive recognition for exemplary performance in accounts receivable management as well as prudent accounting management in all areas.

Quality has been engaged in a process of eliminating administrative services performed at the district level and moving them to Richmond. I have played a key role in helping customers and staff adapt to the new concept. Although I have been strongly encouraged to be part of the restructured organization, I do not wish to move to Richmond. I can provide outstanding references at the appropriate time.

If you can use a professional with extensive experience in managing people while managing the bottom line for maximum profitability, I hope you will contact me to suggest a time when we might meet to discuss your needs. I am confident that I could become a valuable addition to your management team.

Yours sincerely,

Owens Kober

# OWENS KOBER

1110½ Hay Street, Fayetteville, NC 28305 • preppub@aol.com • (910) 483-6611

---

**OBJECTIVE**   To benefit an organization that can use an experienced manager who offers a background in accounting, finance, budgeting, and forecasting along with a proven ability to adapt to change while implementing new systems to enhance growth and profitability.

**COMPUTERS**   Highly proficient in utilizing computer software for financial analysis and word processing; extensive experience with software programs including Microsoft Excel, Microsoft Word, and Lotus 1-2-3.

**EDUCATION**   **Associate in Applied Science in Business Administration,** Sidona Technical Institute, Sidona, AZ 1998; named as class Honor Student.
- Excelled in professional training programs sponsored by Quality Truck Rental, Inc. related to cost accounting, financial analysis, forecasting, and budget preparation.

**EXPERIENCE**   **Excelled in handling a variety of special projects and multiple responsibilities while working for Quality Truck Rental, (Quality Transportation Services), locations in AZ, 2002-present: CONTROLLER.** Quality has restructured nationally, moving central support activities from its 70 districts to Richmond; I have played a key role in helping the company restructure and, although I have spent 26 enjoyable years with the company, I have decided not to relocate to Richmond.
- Can provide outstanding references from individuals at all company levels.

**REGIONAL CONTROLLER.** Tempe, AZ (2000-02). Assisted the General Manager with matters pertaining to financial analysis of the business while answering customer questions, resolving billing problems, and supporting the sales staff in obtaining answers and resolving problems related to the "migration" of administrative functions from the Tempe District to the Richmond Shared Services Center.

**DISTRICT CONTROLLER.** Tempe, AZ (1998-00). Excelled as District Controller of one of Quality's 70 districts, and managed up to seven Accounting Clerks in activities including accounts receivable and payable, repair expense accounting, vehicle cost records, vehicle licensing and permitting, and computer system administration.
- Ensured proper control of company assets in this $25 million district; oversaw $20 million in annual revenues while supporting the District Manager and General Managers with forecasting, budgeting, financial analyses of operations, general ledger maintenance, as well as monthly profit and loss statements.
- Prepared the district's annual financial plan, and am proud of our track record in nearly always exceeding profitability and revenue goals.
- Led the district to achieve outstanding results in internal audits conducted every 12-24 months by Quality officials.
- Received recognition for exemplary performance in accounts receivable management; was recognized for my initiative in implementing accounting controls.
- Provided the leadership in implementing PCs in the district, and served unofficially in the role of System Administrator.
- For a fleet of 800 vehicles, provided oversight of licensing for interstate operations.
- Analyzed financial statements including balance sheets and income statements.

*Other Quality experience:* **OFFICE MANAGER.** Milestown, AZ (1997-98).

**PERSONAL**   Excellent reputation and can provide outstanding personal and professional references.

Date

Exact Name of Person
Exact Title
Exact Name of Company
Address
City, State, Zip

**DIVISION GENERAL MANAGER**

Dear Exact Name of Person (or Dear Sir or Madam if answering a blind ad):

With the enclosed resume, I would like to make you aware of my in-depth experience related to the fleet maintenance industry. I would appreciate an opportunity to talk with you soon about how I could contribute to your organization through my versatile experience and the application of my analytical, financial, and organizational skills.

After completing my B.S. in Business Administration from Samford University, I was recruited by Montgomery Auto Distribution, Inc. (MADI). This is a major company within the fleet maintenance industry which provided me with great opportunities for growth and development. As a General Manager, I played a key role in starting up new locations in Alabama and Mississippi while acting as Contract Manager with government clients. My strong management skills played a role in making the company an attractive acquisition target; MADI sold its public transportation operation in 2003, but I continued working with them after being selected to take over management of three faltering operations in Mexico in 2003. I performed radical management restructuring which made the businesses profitable. Promoted in 2003 to Division General Manager, I have managed 31 locations in AL, LA, TX, and Mexico which produce more than $35 million annually. I have been extensively involved in contract negotiations and customer relations while restoring several of the region's 31 operations to profitability.

As Montgomery Auto Distribution continues to restructure, I am exploring opportunities with a select number of industry firms which require strong maintenance management expertise along with expert troubleshooting and problem-solving abilities. I did not sign a non-compete agreement as a condition of employment, and I am available for worldwide relocation and frequent travel as your needs require. In my position as General Manager, I have traveled 70% of the time as I visited the region's 31 operations. I am comfortable with extensive travel.

If you can use a strong leader with a proven ability to solve operational problems, negotiate effective contracts with customers, and start up new ventures, I hope you will contact me to suggest a time when we might discuss your needs. I can provide outstanding references.

Yours sincerely,

Kenneth P. Madden

# KENNETH P. MADDEN

1110½ Hay Street, Fayetteville, NC 28305 • preppub@aol.com • (910) 483-6611

**OBJECTIVE**  To contribute to the profitability of an organization that can use a resourceful problem solver who is experienced in managing multimillion-dollars operations while negotiating and managing contracts, training and motivating employees, and serving corporate, municipal, and government customers.

**EDUCATION**  **Master of Science in Business Administration,** Faulkner University, Montgomery, AL, 2002.
**Bachelor of Science in Business Administration,** Samford Univ., Birmingham, AL, 2000.

**EXPERIENCE**  **Have excelled in a track record of promotion with Auto Distribution Services, Inc. (ADSI) a major company in the fleet maintenance industry:**
DIVISION GENERAL MANAGER. Montgomery, AL (2003-present). Was promoted to General Manager of a region with operations in 31 locations in AL, LA, TX, and Mexico which produced more than $35 million annually; my job involved traveling 70% of the time.

- **Maintenance management:** Provided oversight for the maintenance of 12,500 vehicles used by municipalities, police departments, public utilities, emergency services organizations, and other organizations. Managed inventory in excess of $900,000. Reduced obsolete inventory by $100,000.
- **Personnel supervision:** Supervised 30 managers and 245 technicians and administrative personnel.
- **Financial management:** Provided oversight for annual payroll of $11.5 million; was responsible for profit and loss of operations in my region. Developed business plans and P&Ls.
- **Problem-solving:** Took over a region in which several of the 31 entities were losing money. I acted as a traveling management consultant and restored all troubled operations to profitability.
- **Contract negotiation and customer relations:** Was extensively involved in contract negotiations. Through my strong customer service skills, rescued several contracts which were in jeopardy with the result that all contracts have been renewed through 2005. Met with city managers and council members as needed during the annual contract negotiation process.
- **Leadership in safety and quality control:** Aggressively emphasized "safety as a lifestyle" with the result that 95% of locations experienced no lost time due to injuries.

AREA OPERATIONS MANAGER. Mexico (2003). Was handpicked to take over management of the company's three faltering operations in Mexico which had contract revenues of $4.9 million related to the maintenance of 1,300 pieces of equipment for various municipalities.

GENERAL MANAGER. Montgomery, AL (2000-2003). Acted as Contract Manager with government clients and oversaw operations at two corporate locations where more than 1,000 pieces of equipment and vehicles were maintained for municipal and government customers. Managed 17 employees.

GENERAL MANAGER. Hendrix's Nissan, Birmingham, AL (1995-2000). Managed one of the most successful Nissan automobile dealerships in Alabama. Supervised all aspects of automobile financing while also purchasing vehicles, negotiating contracts, and supervising 17 employees while working on my Bachelor's degree.

**PERSONAL**  Am a member of National Association of Fleet Administrators. Excellent references.

Date

Exact Name of Person
Title or Position
Name of Company
Address (no., street)
Address (city, state, zip)

**DRIVER & VEHICLE MAINTENANCE SUPERVISOR**

Dear Exact Name of Person (or Dear Sir or Madam if answering a blind ad):

I would appreciate an opportunity to talk with you soon about how I could benefit your organization through my experience and record of accident-free driving.

Currently serving as Driver/Vehicle Maintenance supervisor at Advanced Vehicle Technologies, Inc., Davidson, MD, I train and supervise 20 drivers maintaining a $760,000 inventory of vehicles. I have earned a reputation as a dependable and mature professional with outstanding motivational and communication skills. In addition to my many miles of safe driving, I also offer experience in supervising vehicle maintenance operations.

In previous positions, I have been a Testing Team Supervisor, Consultant, Service Representative, and Parts Manager. I offer a wide breadth of experience throughout the automotive field.

I hope you will call or write soon to suggest a time convenient for us to meet and discuss your current and future needs and how I might serve them. Thank you in advance for your time.

Sincerely yours,


Wendell G. Amberson

# WENDELL GEORGE AMBERSON

1110½ Hay Street, Fayetteville, NC 28305 • preppub@aol.com • (910) 483-6611

---

**OBJECTIVE**      To benefit an organization that can use an experienced driver who offers an accident-free record along with outstanding communication and organizational skills.

**VEHICLES**      **Am experienced in driving a variety of vehicles including the following:**

| | | |
|---|---|---|
| M915 tractor | M35A2 2 1/2-ton truck | M1009 3/4-ton truck |
| M1008 1 1/2-ton truck | M917 dump truck | M923 5-ton truck |
| M920 tractor | | |

**LICENSE**      Was issued a "Class A" Commercial Driver's License by the State of Maryland with endorsements for all categories except passenger vehicles.

**EXPERIENCE**      **DRIVER/VEHICLE MAINTENANCE SUPERVISOR.** Advanced Vehicle Technologies, Inc., Davidson, MD (2003-present). Train and supervise 20 drivers maintaining a $760,000 inventory of vehicles which include 10 tractors and 20 40-foot trailers.
- Accomplished more than 102,000 miles of accident-free driving.
- Was cited as an effective supervisor who "sets the example" for subordinates.
- Hold a record of perfect 100% accountability for all equipment.

**TESTING TEAM SUPERVISOR.** Bosal International North America, Ann Arbor, MI (2000-02). Awarded a commendation for "exceptionally meritorious achievements," managed a team of drivers testing engine components.
- Drove 50,000 miles with no accidents or incidents. Learned to remain calm and in control despite the hazards and extreme conditions. Was cited for "distinguished" performance.

**CONSULTANT.** Dow Automotive, Auburn Hills, MI (1997-99). Served as advisor on reliability and practicality of engineering designed automotive equipment. Test-drove vehicles as a final check. Logged more than 25,000 accident-free miles.

**SERVICE REPRESENTATIVE.** Allied Signal Automotive Aftermarket, Grand Rapids, MI (1994-96). Traveled extensively throughout the Midwestern states as a member of a team of specialists involved in major product line changeovers as well as providing merchandising support to large warehouses as requested.

**PARTS MANAGER.** J & S Auto Parts and Service, Grand Rapids, MI (1992-94). Supervised four people in a 10-bay service center with 20 employees; handled the purchase and resale of automotive and light truck parts to customers and company mechanics.
- Was praised for my "competence, technical expertise, and personal dedication."
- Gained in-depth knowledge of automotive and light truck troubleshooting and mechanical repairs along with the operating aspects of running the auto parts section.

**MECHANIC & SHOP FOREMAN.** Double Eagle Auto, Grand Rapids, MI (1990-91). Repaired foreign and domestic cars and light trucks; performed computer-controlled troubleshooting of engines, domestic and foreign.

**TRAINING**      Excelled in more than 750 hours of training courses including leadership, human relations, defensive driving, and summer and winter driving skills.

**PERSONAL**      Am very proud of my accomplishments in receiving promotion ahead of my peers. Work well under deadlines and pressure.

Date

Exact Name of Person
Title or Position
Name of Company
Address (no., street)
Address (city, state, zip)

**ENGINEERING EQUIPMENT REPAIRMAN & HEAVY TRUCK & EQUIPMENT REPAIRMAN**

Dear Exact Name of Person:   (if answering a blind ad, Dear Sir or Madam:)

I would enjoy an opportunity to talk with you soon, in person, about how my cost-effectiveness and expertise with heavy equipment and repair could substantially benefit your organization.

As you will see from my resume, my dedication and attention to detail has often resulted in significant savings. Most recently, I was responsible for reducing the cost of a bulldozer engine by repairing the engine instead of replacing it, saving approximately $37,500 at one time. My expertise in heavy mobile equipment has saved thousands of dollars in many other instances.

I have developed a reputation for doing the work right the first time, and am proud of my solid record. My experience in various service positions has permitted me to gain hands-on expertise with industrial equipment. This extensive training prepared me well for my supervisory experience. In addition, I have learned to work harmoniously with many different types of people and also enjoy taking the initiative in situations where repairs are warranted.

I am certain I could make valuable contributions to your organization, too. I am sure, realize cost-effective savings with repairs. I hope you will call or write me soon to suggest a time convenient for us to meet and discuss your current and future needs and how I might serve them. Thank you in advance for your time.

Yours sincerely,

Randall O. Dickerson

# RANDALL O. DICKERSON ("Randy")
1110½ Hay Street, Fayetteville, NC 28305 • preppub@aol.com • (910) 483-6611

---

**OBJECTIVE**  I want to benefit an organization that can profit from an experienced mechanic, repairman, trainer, and inspector whose troubleshooting skills and expert knowledge routinely result in valuable cost savings.

**EXPERIENCE**  **ENGINEERING EQUIPMENT REPAIRMAN AND HEAVY TRUCK AND EQUIPMENT REPAIRMAN.** Duraloy Division, Blaw Knox Corp, Scottsdale, PA (2003-present). Have successfully completed two contracts (one 16-month, one 6-month) inspecting and performing repairs on diesel trucks as well as a full range of construction equipment, including forklifts, cranes, and bulldozers.
- Determine nature and extent of repairs. Interpret instructions and specifications.
- Work closely with the Department of Transportation.
- Establish maintenance procedures and standards.
- Maintain these and other truck models: 953, AM2, AM5, AM8 Bischoff.
- Repair Stretford engines, power trains, and chassis components.
- Minimized downtime and save $37,500 by repairing instead of replacing a bulldozer engine. Saved $1,850 by repairing a Stretford engine exhaust system instead of replacing the turbocharger.
- Reduced by $6,250 the total cost of an Bewley automatic transmission through repairing the turbocharger instead of replacing the transmission.
- Train employees to be self-sufficient mechanics with engineering and truck equipment.

**MAINTENANCE ASSISTANT.** Continental Fabricators, Inc., St. Louis, MO (1999-03). Reduced the total cost of a textile machinery operation by 15% by properly maintaining machinery at correct specifications.

**HEAVY EQUIPMENT MECHANIC.** Bognar and CO., Inc., Harrisburg, PA (1997-99). Performed mechanical maintenance on numerous vehicles and industrial equipment.
- Received "Bognar Maintenance Achievement Award (BMAA)" for work on diesel engines and reducing overall manhours by making repairs.
- Gained skills and experience on diesel engines while advancing from helper to full mechanic in a very competitive system.

**Other experience:**
**MECHANIC.** CRANE Manufacturing, Harrisburg, PA (1996-97). Learned valuable skills in doing an excellent job under tight deadlines with limited resources while supporting the needs of this manufacturing company.

**TRAINING**  Completed training in vehicle air-conditioning and electrical systems, Harrisburg Area Community College, Harrisburg, PA.
Completed CRANE Manufacturing courses in repair and operation of heavy equipment engines and systems.
Acquired extensive "on-the-job" training with Duraloy Division, Blaw Knox Corp of Scottsdale, PA.

**PERSONAL**  Take great pride in my work and in training co-workers to attain efficient production. Am cost-conscious and hard-working. Enjoy international travel; am flexible about living and working conditions. Willing to relocate.

Date

Exact Name of Person
Title or Position
Name of Company
Address (number and street)
Address (city, state, and zip)

**FINANCE MANAGER**

Dear Exact Name of Person (or Sir or Madam if answering a blind ad):

I would appreciate an opportunity to talk with you soon about how I could contribute to your organization through my versatile experience, education, and the application of my analytical, problem-solving, and organizational skills.

As you will see from my enclosed resume, I successfully passed the CPA exam recently and received my B.S. in Business Administration degree with a concentration in Accounting from Franklin University at Columbus, OH. Currently the Finance Manager for a Ford dealership in Cincinnati, OH, I am involved in all aspects of financial activities including accounts payable and receivable, payroll processing, and sales tax processing as well as computer support and employee training activities.

Earlier experience has included Project Accountant for a multimillion-dollar construction company, Accounting Manager for a home furnishing store, and Administrative Assistant for an insurance company. I have been exposed to a wide range of work environments and also have gained experience in personal tax preparation while doing my own tax returns and those of several of my friends.

I am an enthusiastic, energetic, and outgoing individual who is known for my attention to detail and my ability to handle pressure and deadlines with professionalism and control.

I hope you will welcome my call soon to arrange a brief meeting to discuss your current and future needs and how I might serve them. Thank you in advance for your time.

Sincerely,

Thalia L. Samuels

Alternate last paragraph:
I hope you will call or write me soon to suggest a time convenient for us to meet and discuss your current and future needs and how I might serve them. Thank you in advance for your time.

# THALIA L. SAMUELS

1110½ Hay Street, Fayetteville, NC 28305 • preppub@aol.com • (910) 483-6611

---

**OBJECTIVE**  To offer analytical, problem-solving, and organizational skills as well as experience in accounting and financial planning to an organization that can benefit from my detail orientation, education, and ability to handle challenge, pressure, and deadlines.

**EDUCATION**  **Bachelor of Science Degree in Business Administration** with a concentration in **Accounting,** Franklin University, Columbus, OH, 1992.
**Associate of Arts Degree in Accounting,** Cedarville College, Cedarville, OH, 1990.

**EXPERIENCE**  **FINANCE MANAGER.** Allen-Moore Ford, Inc., Cincinnati, OH (2002-present). Contribute knowledge and problem-solving skills in ways which increased cash flow and the effectiveness of financial support operations in this dealership while handling the full range of financial activities including accounts payable and receivable and payroll accounting for 15 employees.

- Solve cash flow problems after investigating auto parts department procedures: design and implement inventory and accounts receivable activities.
- On my own initiative, master computer applications unique to this industry such as dealership warranties, sales reporting, and marketing programs.
- Handle bank reconciliations, sales tax processing for the dealership and a separate auto parts business, vehicle warranty repair administration, and employee insurance.
- Coordinate employee training programs using a satellite classroom set up.
- Maintain daily reports, ledgers, and computer records on dealership operations.

**CLIENT CONTACT SPECIALIST.** Landers & Dean Finance, San Antonio, TX (2000-02). Became recognized as a top-notch communicator and sales/customer service professional while calling on prospective and existing clients of this financial planning company which supports a clientele made up predominantly of military officers with a full range of financial planning and investment services.

- Received recognition from the highest levels of the company for my effectiveness as part of one of the company's most productive teams of Brokers, Administrative Assistants, and Client Contact Specialists.

**SALES AND MERCHANDISING REPRESENTATIVE.** Dell Publishing Company, Dayton, OH (1997-99). Built the company a reputation for quality services as first representative in this region; made regular visits to clients to ensure merchandise was displayed properly as well as obtaining new orders and ensuring proper disposal of obsolete and outdated items.

**ADMINISTRATIVE ASSISTANT.** American Airlines, Tokyo, Japan (1993-96). Gained knowledge of Japanese business ethics and culture while processing airline ticket billings and completing all required sales reports for a military sales office.

*Highlights of earlier experience:* Gained versatile skills and abilities in previous jobs:
As a **PROJECT ACCOUNTANT,** handled the costing of an average of $25 million worth of construction projects at any given time as well as the related percentage of completion payment requests to banks for a construction company.
As the **ACCOUNTING MANAGER,** supervised two employees while handling all phases of retail accounting for a home furnishings store: inventory, accounts receivable and payable, general ledger, financial statements, payroll for ten employees, and sales tax.

**PERSONAL**  Offer excellent analytical skills and the ability to develop workable strategies for problem-solving. Am effective in communicating with others through my caring, outgoing personality.

Date

Exact Name of Person
Title or Position
Name of Company
Address (no., street)
Address (city, state, zip)

**FLEET MAINTENANCE SUPERVISOR**

Dear Exact Name of Person (or Dear Sir or Madam if answering a blind ad):

I would appreciate an opportunity to talk with you soon about how I could contribute to your organization through my expertise in large fleet maintenance management along with my experience in managing assets and personnel.

In my present position as Fleet Maintenance Supervisor for the U.S. Postal Service, Sacramento, CA, I oversee a general support maintenance shop maintaining a fleet of more than 600 vehicles. I advise a senior official on potential problem areas and recommend solutions. Previously while serving in the U.S. Army, I oversaw activities including automotive, fuel, and electric component repair and rebuild operations.

My technical abilities, insistence on high-quality performance from my employees, and enthusiastic and energetic personality have enabled me to succeed while serving in every position held. As you will see from my resume, I have a B.S. degree in Interdisciplinary Studies from Darton College, Albany, GA.

I feel certain that you would find me to be an articulate and persuasive leader with a "track record" of success in building teams, increasing productivity and efficiency, and managing multimillion-dollar assets.

I hope you will welcome my call soon to arrange a brief meeting at your convenience to discuss your current and future needs and how I might serve them. Thank you in advance for your time.

Sincerely yours,


Jason L. Reaves


(Alternate last paragraph:
I hope you will call or write soon to suggest a time convenient for us to meet and discuss your current and future needs and how I might serve them. Thank you in advance for your time.)

## JASON LEE REAVES

1110½ Hay Street, Fayetteville, NC 28305 • preppub@aol.com • (910) 483-6611

---

**OBJECTIVE**  To benefit an organization that can use an astute manager who offers a proven ability to manage transportation services and vehicle maintenance for maximum safety and profitability.

**EDUCATION**  **B.S., Interdisciplinary Studies,** GPA 3.66, Darton College, Albany, GA, 1996.

**TRAINING**  Completed training programs which included logistics management and leadership schools as well as training as a military police officer.

**EXPERIENCE**  **FLEET MAINTENANCE SUPERVISOR.** U.S. Postal Service, Sacramento, CA (2003-present). Oversee maintenance support activities for a fleet of more than 600 vehicles. Collect data and prepare status reports on numbers of vehicles available for immediate use and on hold for repair parts.
- Distribute information on safety and equipment maintenance issues.
- Advise a senior official on potential problem areas and recommend solutions.
- Am known as an assertive manager who leads the way in producing quality results on a timely basis.

**Refined my skills while serving my counter in the U.S. Army:**
**MECHANIZED INFANTRY PLATOON LEADER.** U.S. Army, Germany (1997-02). In my first assignment as an officer, supervised and trained 30 people, controlled a $10 million equipment inventory, and oversaw equipment maintenance activities.
- Quickly earned a reputation as a young professional who could be counted on to react rapidly and use sound judgment when making decisions.
- Became effective in solving problems and operating under pressure and was selected to lead a support team to Bosnia which completed its mission with no incidents.
- Executed all missions without incident or loss to personnel or property.

**FULL-TIME STUDENT.** Darton College, Albany, GA (1994-96). Selected for a special program sponsored by the U.S. Army, attended college full time and upon graduation was commissioned into active duty service.
- Displayed a high level of leadership skills, personal drive, and dedication which resulted in my selection for this educational opportunity.

**MILITARY POLICE TEAM LEADER.** U.S. Army, Ft. Meade, MD (1992-94). Advanced quickly to the leadership role of my three-person team of military police officers providing law enforcement, traffic management, traffic investigation, and crime prevention support to a military community.
- Became highly effective as a leader and motivator; learned to welcome responsibility while ensuring that all tasks and duties were carried out successfully.
- Was singled out for my maturity and leadership qualities as a member of an advance task force providing relief following the devastation of a hurricane in Florida.
- Earned the honor of "Post Soldier of the Quarter" after winning at the company and battalion level against many more experienced candidates.

**COMPUTERS**  Proficient with numerous software programs including the Microsoft Office Suite.

**PERSONAL**  Married, 1 son. Enjoy the outdoors, cars, family, biking, sailing, and sports.

Date

Exact Name of Person
Title or Position
Name of Company
Address (No., street)
Address (city, state, zip)

## FREIGHT COORDINATOR

Fortune 500 Company
Although he is "held in high regard" by his current employer,
as he states in his cover letter, Mr. Palacios heard through the grapevine that his company was
going to downsize and he didn't want to be caught without options. Developing options is what his resume and cover letter are designed to do.

Dear Exact Name of Person: (or Dear Sir or Madam if answering a blind ad.)

I would appreciate an opportunity to talk with you soon about how I could contribute to your organization through my experience in all aspects of traffic and transportation management. I offer extensive knowledge of LTL, TL, Intermodal, rate negotiations, pool shipments, and cost analysis to determine the most economical method of shipping.

As you will see from my resume, I am currently site freight coordinator for a Fortune 500 company, and I have continuously found new ways to reduce costs and improve efficiency while managing all inbound and outbound shipping. On my own initiative, I have recovered $10,000 in claims annually while saving the company at least 40% of a $10 million LTL budget. In addition to continuous cost cutting, I have installed a new bar code system in the finished goods shipping area and have installed a new wrapping system.

In previous jobs supervising terminal operations, I opened up new terminals, closed down existing operations which were unprofitable, and gained hands-on experience in increasing efficiency in every terminal area.

With a reputation as a savvy negotiator, I can provide excellent personal and professional references. I am held in high regard by my current employer.

I hope you will call or write me soon to suggest a time convenient for us to meet and discuss your current and future needs and how I might serve them. Thank you in advance for you time.

Sincerely yours,


Pedro Palacios

(Alternate last paragraph:
I hope you will welcome my call soon to arrange a brief meeting at your convenience to discuss your current and future needs and how I might serve them. Thank you in advance for your time.)

# PEDRO PALACIOS

1110½ Hay Street, Fayetteville, NC 28305 • preppub@aol.com • (910) 483-6611

---

**OBJECTIVE**  To contribute to an organization that can use a skilled traffic management professional who offers a proven ability to reduce costs, install new systems, optimize scheduling, negotiate rates, anticipate difficulties, solve problems, and keep customers happy.

**EXPERIENCE**  **FREIGHT COORDINATOR.** DuPont Corporation, Wilmington, DE (2002-present). For this Fortune 500 company, have continuously found new ways to cut costs and improve service while managing all inbound transportation as well as outbound shipping totaling in excess of one million dollars in finished goods daily; supervise ten people.
- Saved the company at least 40% of a $10 million LTL budget by resourcefully combining my technical knowledge with my creative cost-cutting skills.
- Recovered $10,000 annually in claims; prepare all cargo claims documents for corporate office and oversee all procedures for proper claims documentation.
- Installed a bar code system in Finished Goods and also installed a new wrapping system.
- Reduced overtime by 90% while simultaneously cross-training some employees and improving overall morale.
- Became familiar with Total Quality Processes while analyzing transit times to ensure consistent and timely Just-In-Time delivery schedules.
- Am a member of the B & D corporate committee for North American rate negotiations; negotiate rates with various carriers on special moves.
- Justify capital appropriation requests for funding special projects; audit all freight bills and process them for payment.
- Prepare all documents for export shipments to Canada; also advise about the shipment of hazardous materials and maintain proper documentation placards and labels.
- Coordinate all site printing of product information and warranty cards.
- Have earned a reputation as a savvy negotiator with an ability to predict future variables that will affect traffic costs.

**SUPERVISOR.** International Freightways, Inc., Atlanta, GA (1998-02). Supervised up to 12 drivers while managing second-shift operations and controlling inbound and outbound freight at this terminal operation. Increased efficiency in every operational area; improved the load factor, reduced dock hours, and ensured more timely deliveries.

**INVENTORY SPECIALIST.** La-Z-Boy East, Inc., Florence, SC (1995-98). Learned the assembly process of this name-brand furniture manufacturer while managing replenishment of subassemblies for daily production.

*Highlights of other experience:*
- As Terminal Manager for Spartan Express, opened a new terminal in South Carolina; determined the pricing structure, handled sales, and then managed this new operation which enjoyed rapid growth.
- Gained experience in closing down a terminal determined to be in a poor location.
- As Operations Manager for a break bulk operation, supervised up to 12 people in a dock center while managing the sorting/segregating of shipments from origin to destination.

**EDUCATION**  Studied business management and liberal arts, Ohio State and LaSalle University. Completed extensive executive development courses in the field of transportation and traffic management sponsored by University of Toledo and Texas Technical University.

**PERSONAL**  Can provide outstanding personal and professional references. Will relocate.

Date

Exact Name of Person
Title or Position
Name of Company
Address (No., street)
Address (city, state, zip)

## FREIGHT TERMINAL MANAGER

*If you want to compare the resumes of two similar professionals, compare this resume with the resume of Pedro Palacios on the preceding pages. Mr. Velasquez emphasizes that he has worked for the same company for the past 14 years.*

Dear Exact Name of Person: (or Dear Sir or Madam if answering a blind ad.)

I would appreciate an opportunity to talk with you soon about how I could benefit Quality Shipping as a Freight Terminal Manager/Account Manager through my strong background in the transportation industry.

Known for my expertise in increasing sales and revenue while reducing costs, you will see by my enclosed resume that I have in-depth experience gained while working for the regional carrier McDonald Transportation. In my 14 years with this company I advanced to management roles after beginning in a ground-floor position as a Driver and Freight Handler. I am also a skilled accounts representative and enjoy the challenge of selling transportation services. I have become very adept at selling transportation services based mostly on quality and service rather than on price.

Throughout my career with McDonald Transportation, I consistently made changes which resulted in increased sales and revenue while reducing costs and eliminating unnecessary expenses. For instance, in my most recent position as Branch Terminal Manager at the Raleigh, NC, terminal I was credited with bringing about a 35% increase in sales and revenue, a 15% reduction in operating costs, and an increase in on-time rates from 89% to a near-perfect 98%.

Selected to attend corporate training courses in quality management, sales, and frontline supervisory techniques, I was appointed to Quality Improvement Teams beginning in 2000 and was elected as team chairman for 2001.

I am certain that you would find in me a talented manager who communicates effectively with others at all levels and is experienced in making sound decisions under pressure. With an excellent reputation within the transportation industry, I am a flexible and versatile individual who would consider serving your needs in a variety of capacities and functional areas. I can provide very strong references.

I hope you will welcome my call soon to arrange a brief meeting at your convenience to discuss your current and future needs and how I might serve them. Thank you in advance for your time.

Sincerely yours,

William Velasquez

# WILLIAM VELASQUEZ

1110½ Hay Street, Fayetteville, NC 28305  •  preppub@aol.com  •  (910) 483-6611

---

**OBJECTIVE**  To offer my reputation as a thoroughly knowledgeable professional with special abilities related to terminal operations, sales, quality management, and customer service gained while advancing to increasingly higher managerial levels within the trucking industry.

**QUALITY MANAGEMENT**  Appointed to Quality Improvement Teams in Georgia, North Carolina, and South Carolina (2000-03), was elected as chairman in 2001. Believe in total quality results, top to bottom.

**EXPERIENCE**  *Built a track record of promotion while becoming known for my expertise in increasing sales and reducing operational costs with McDonald Transportation, an interstate trucking company operating predominately in the southeastern U.S.:*
**FREIGHT TERMINAL MANAGER.** Raleigh, NC (2003-present). Continued to find ways to increase revenue and efficiency while managing all aspects of daily terminal operations ranging from staffing and training, to managing a sales territory, to supervising the terminal's account manager.
- Displayed a talent for introducing changes which increased annual sales/revenue 35%.
- Brought about a 15% reduction in operating costs while increasing on-time delivery rates to an almost-perfect 98% rate from the previous 89%.

**TERMINAL MANAGER.** Greensboro, NC (2000-03). Reduced operating costs 10% over a two-year period while directing total terminal operations including staffing and training employees in every section of the business; supervised two account managers.
- Increased annual sales and revenue 30% each year.

**ACCOUNT MANAGER** and **BRANCH TERMINAL MANAGER.** Baxley, GA (1998-00). Wore "two hats" as a combination Account Manager and Branch Terminal Manager; earned rapid promotion because of my success in sales and in hiring/supervising 15 people.
- Made improvements resulting in a 30% growth in sales and 18% decrease in costs.

**SALES REPRESENTATIVE.** Miami, FL (1995-98). Refined sales and customer service skills as the account manager for approximately 50% of the customer base for a company which provides sales and service within 80-100 miles of each local terminal.
- Maintained a strong repeat customer base while bringing about a 41% increase in sales,

**DISPATCHER/OPERATIONS MANAGER.** Orlando, FL (1993-95). Learned to remain in control under pressure and constant deadlines while scheduling deliveries and pick ups and dispatching trucks throughout the area.
- Applied my problem-solving skills by decreasing the number of missed pick ups 70%, thereby increasing customer satisfaction and boosting the bottom line.

**SHIPPING SUPERVISOR.** Orlando, FL (1990-93). Supervised ten dock workers; established truck routes; ensured shipments were on time with no errors or damage.
- Improved procedures so that the number of damage claims was greatly reduced.

**TRAINING**  Attended corporate professional development programs related to these and other areas:
Frontline supervisory practices          Sales and closing techniques
Breaking down work processes        Making quality improvements

**PERSONAL**  Offer an outstanding reputation within the transportation industry and can provide excellent references. Am skilled in competing based on quality and service, not just on price.

# CAREER CHANGE

Date

Exact Name of Person
Exact Title
Exact Name of Company
Address
City, State, Zip

**GAS STATION OWNER**

This individual is seeking a change from the industry where he has worked for most of his life. Notice that his cover letter is written so that it accentuates his skills and abilities which are transferable to other industries.

Dear Exact Name of Person (or Dear Sir or Madam if answering a blind ad):

With the enclosed resume, I would like to confidentially make you aware of my interest in exploring employment opportunities with your organization. I am in the process of negotiating the sale of a business, and I am enthusiastically looking forward to transferring my strong sales and management background into a quality organization.

**Background in Sales and Customer Service**

As you will see from my resume, I offer proven sales abilities. I have become skilled at the consultative style of selling as I have recommended products and services based on my analysis of customer needs. I feel confident that such a consultative style of selling would be effective in most business situations and in most companies. I have hired and managed numerous employees through the years, and I have always instilled in them an attitude of respect for the customer. My strong customer relations skills led to a very high word-of-mouth referral rate as well as an exceptionally loyal customer base. I am certain that I could make significant contributions to a company's bottom line through my aggressive emphasis on quality customer service as well as fair and honest dealings.

**Outstanding personal reputation**

In a small business, the owner and general manager defines the "personality" of the business, and I have always stood for integrity and fair dealings with customers. I have instilled in all employees the concept that they should never recommend any products or services to a customer which they would not purchase themselves if they were in the same situation. Over the years, my emphasis on fair dealings has contributed to an exceptionally stable work force as well as a loyal clientele. I have found that attitude is key in attracting and retaining quality employees as well as satisfied customers.

I am approaching your organization because I believe my background and skills would be a strong "fit" with your needs, and I am confident that I could quickly become a valuable asset to your company. I possess a talent for dealing effectively with people which I have refined through many years of sales and management experience. I hope you will give me the courtesy of an interview so that I can show you that I could become an appreciated member of your team.

Yours sincerely,

Karl N. Polansky, Jr.

# KARL N. POLANSKY, JR.

1110½ Hay Street, Fayetteville, NC 28305 • preppub@aol.com • (910) 483-6611

---

**OBJECTIVE**     To benefit an organization that can use an experienced professional with strong sales and management skills along with an ability to develop and maintain a loyal customer base.

**EDUCATION**     **Bachelor of Science degree in Recreation and Park Administration,** St. Joseph's College, Standish, ME, 1997.
**Associate of Arts degree in General College,** Standish Junior College, Standish, ME, 1995.
Completed extensive training sponsored by the Gulf Corporation related to management, total quality management, and hazardous materials management.

**EXPERIENCE**     **GAS STATION OWNER and GENERAL MANAGER.** Gadney's Gulf Service, Augusta, ME (2000-present). After college graduation, began working in an entry-level position with this full-service station and eventually became the station's owner and general manager. In 2002, negotiated the purchase of the station from Gulf, from whom we had previously leased.

- **Sales:** Have developed a highly effective style of consultative selling. Cross-sell the station's services through my ability to analyze customer problems and needs and then suggest products and services which meet those needs.
- **Reputation for integrity:** Have instilled in all employees an attitude of respect for customers. Customers know they receive fair service at a fair price, and employees are expected never to do anything to a customer's car that they wouldn't do to their own.
- **Personnel management:** Have hired and managed multiple individuals who have remained in my employment for many years. Am experienced in hiring, training, and motivating employees. Have been highly successful in building team spirit and motivating employees to produce their best work. Believe in leadership by example.
- **Financial management:** Continuously oversee inventory and maintain inventory carrying costs at the lowest possible level. Work with accountants and bookkeepers.
- **Mechanical operations management:** Oversee the mechanics who operate the station's three bays. I provide oversight as the mechanics provide services ranging from minor oil changes and repairs to electronic diagnostics on both U.S. and imported cars.
- **Vendor relations:** Maintain strong working relationships with vendors who include Advance Auto Parts, NAPA, CarQuest, and major dealerships such as Quality Chevrolet-Geo, Buckingham's Buick, and many others.
- **Community service:** Believe strongly that businesses should be good corporate citizens, and we have sponsored a basketball youth team for several years as a way of supporting local activities and local youth.

**Other experience:**
**ASSISTANT RANGER.** Farmington State Park, ME. Excelled in an internship and worked closely with the park supervisor, two park rangers, and other rangers.

**AFFILIATIONS**     First Methodist Church, Past Moderator and Vice Moderator, Board of Deacons.
- Also served on the Property, Stewardship & Finance, and Christian Education Committees.

**HOBBIES**     Hunting, fishing, softball, yard work.

**PERSONAL**     Outgoing individual with exceptional interpersonal skills. Known for my ability to gain the trust of others and establish warm working relationships with others. Experienced in multi-tasking and handling simultaneous responsibilities. Outstanding personal and professional reputation.

Date

Exact Name of Person
Title or Position
Name of Company
Address (number and street)
Address (city, state, and zip)

**GENERAL AUTO SALES MANAGER**

Dear Exact Name of Person (or Sir or Madam if answering a blind ad):

With the enclosed resume, I would like to express my interest in exploring employment opportunities with your organization.

With 20 years in the automotive industry, I am a management professional experienced in all phases of the industry, including used car sales and financing as well as general sales management. Originally recruited by my present employer for a newly created position, I have advanced with Hank Wallace of Flagstaff, AZ, and am highly valued as a resourceful and effective General Sales Manager. Although I am held in high regard by the executives of this large dual dealership, I have made the decision to selectively explore other opportunities and would ask that my interest in your organization be kept in confidence at this time.

Recruited as the dealership's first Outside Buyer, I was promoted to Used Car General Sales Manager. Soon after, I enjoyed a further promotion to General Sales Manager. In the first job I took the store from a losing operation to a multimillion-dollar producer and then advanced to oversee a sales staff which increased from 28 to 36 and led them in building a 30% increase in sales—the highest rate of growth of any dealership in the region. My accomplishments include earning a prestigious recognition award from Toyota and being one of only three people in the region to earn the "Toyota Professional Used Car Manager Recognition Award" in consecutive years. Because of my reputation and expertise, I was the only General Sales Manager once invited to be a member of an automotive team comprised of only General Managers except for myself.

If you can use an astute manager who excels in finding solutions for the tough problems while leading the way to increased sales, profitability, and customer satisfaction, I hope you will contact me to suggest a time when we might meet to discuss your needs. I can provide outstanding references at the appropriate time.

Sincerely,

Molly Sue Bickford

# MOLLY SUE BICKFORD

1110½ Hay Street, Fayetteville, NC 28305 • preppub@aol.com • (910) 483-6611

**OBJECTIVE** To benefit an organization that can use a high-powered management professional with exceptional problem-solving, communication, and motivational skills along with a strong background as a sales trainer, general sales manager, and used car manager.

**EDUCATION & TRAINING** Completed the Southwest Toyota Training Program for General Sales Managers.
Completed Dale Carnegie courses, Saturn Culture Manager Training, and numerous seminars focusing on management, marketing, and customer service.
Graduated from Jefferson High School, Tucson, AZ.

**EXPERIENCE** **With Hank Wallace Toyota and Chrysler Jeep Eagle, Flagstaff, AZ, have advanced in a track record of accomplishments while establishing records in numerous areas:**
**GENERAL AUTO SALES MANAGER.** (2001-present). Described as a top-notch manager who consistently establishes new sales records in a competitive region, was recruited by this dealership to a position created for me and am enjoying rapid advancement in the management of this large multi-line dealership.
- Guided the used car department to a number one ranking in the group.
- Was recognized as Sales Manager of the Year 2002.
- Following a 2001 division into Hank Wallace Toyota and Hank Wallace Chrysler Plymouth Jeep, became Sales Manager of used car operations for Chrysler Plymouth Jeep store.
- Became the only General Sales Manager on a top-level automotive team focusing on reliability which was comprised mainly of General Managers.
- Lead the two stores to top sales satisfaction and customer service satisfaction ratings.
- Consistently earn formal evaluations which describe me in part as "the best used car manager I have ever worked with" and as a manager whose performance "could not be improved on."
- Earned the "Toyota Professional Used Car Manager Recognition Award" (2001): this honor is given to the country's top 20% of used car managers and recognizes expertise in total retail sales, department gross profits, return on investments, and inventory management; was one of only three people to win this award in consecutive years.

**GENERAL SALES MANAGER & USED CAR MANAGER.** (2000). Increased a 28-person staff of sales professionals to 36 and was soon promoted to General Sales Manager.
- Led a motivated and highly successful team to a 30% increase in sales which was recognized as the largest increase in the district.

**OUTSIDE BUYER.** (1998-00). Originally recruited as the dealership's first Outside Buyer, built a reputation as a results-oriented professional.
- Put $100,000 on the statement monthly by skillfully managing the wholesale buying for Toyota and Jeep Eagle; took the store from a losing store to a multimillion-dollar store.

**Highlights of earlier experience:** Fresno, CA:
**Business Manager and General Sales Manager.** Star Leasing – advanced from supervising sales, parts, and service while selecting the right mix of cars and trucks, to working with banks to arrange individual contracts; trained eight Finance/Insurance Managers.
**Sales Manager.** Max Turner Chevrolet – sold new and used cars while controlling the details of wholesale and retail used car purchases.

**PERSONAL** Excellent personal and professional references on request. Outstanding problem solver.

Date

Exact Name of Person
Title or Position
Name of Company
Address (number and street)
Address (city, state, and zip)

**GENERAL MANAGER**

Auto Auction Business Senior managers often want to "test the waters," even when they enjoy their current position and responsibilities. That's what has motivated this senior manager to approach a select number of employers in industries which interest him. Notice that he has only one job on his resume, and his numerous functional responsibilities are highlighted within his chronological resume.

Dear Exact Name of Person: (or Sir or Madam if answering a blind ad.)

With the enclosed resume, I would like to make you aware of my interest in discussing the possibility of employment with your organization.

As you will see from my enclosed resume, I have been excelling in a track record of accomplishment with a 50-year-old company that produces gross revenue of more than $100 million annually. While earning a reputation as a dedicated businessman known for honesty and intelligence, I provided the leadership in helping this company strengthen its market share and improve its ability to serve its customers in a timely fashion. On my own initiative I took on the task of building a trucking division within the organization so that the company could be more responsive to customer needs and be able to rapidly take advantage of business opportunities. The company now has a 12-truck fleet and gross sales have increased by nearly 40% during the past six years.

I have earned a reputation as an outstanding communicator, and I have found that my communication skills have enabled me to tactfully resolve difficult customer problem, find remedies to employee issues, as well as aggressively develop new business and new accounts.

You would find me in person to be a congenial, straightforward individual who is skilled in every aspect of public relations and customer service. I can provide outstanding personal and professional references within the auto auction industry, banking community, and from numerous other sources.

If you can use a go-getter with exceptionally strong sales and marketing abilities along with a strong make-it-happen attitude and aggressive bottom-line orientation, I hope you will contact me to suggest a time when we might meet to discuss your goals and how I might help you achieve them.

Yours sincerely,

Neil Harriss

# NEIL HARRISS

1110½ Hay Street, Fayetteville, NC 28305 • preppub@aol.com • (910) 483-6611

---

**OBJECTIVE** To contribute to an organization that can use a dynamic and hard-working manager who offers strong communication skills and management experience along with a proven track record of success in applying my entrepreneurial abilities, sales skills, and marketing know-how to boost bottom-line profitability, improve customer satisfaction, and gain market share.

**EDUCATION** Received **B.S. degree in Political Science,** University of North Carolina at Chapel Hill, Chapel Hill, NC, 2000.
- Member of Alpha Pi Fraternity; served as Social Chairman for two years.

Completed numerous professional development courses related to sales, management, and motivational techniques sponsored by organizations including Partners in Success.

Graduated from high school at Beaver Creek High School, Beaver Creek, GA 1997.
- Was Captain of the football team; played varsity baseball and basketball.
- Was named to Who's Who Among High School Students

**EXPERIENCE** **GENERAL MANAGER.** Harriss Auto Auction, Maysfield, GA (2002-present). Played a key role in the growth of this business with $100 million in annual sales; this is the oldest company of its type in the world; it was founded in 1928, and is still privately held. The company holds weekly used car auctions strictly for dealers. From 2000-present, the business has enjoyed explosive growth, with the number of employees increasing by 25% while gross sales increased by 40%.

- Have been involved in every aspect of organizing and managing auctions which involve Chrysler Credit, GMAC, NationsBank, and First Union as well as the trade-ins of local dealers.
- *Initiative and entrepreneurial abilities:* On my own initiative, provided the leadership which enabled this 50-year-old company to strengthen its ability to provide excellent customer service in a highly competitive industry. I took on the task of building a trucking fleet for the company so that it could better compete in the areas of customer satisfaction, timeliness, and the quality of service provided. The company has grown from a one-truck operation into a 12-truck fleet.
- *Problem solving and troubleshooting:* Became well known for my energetic approach to solving customer complaints or problems; always took prompt action and negotiated a fair resolution of dissatisfactions.
- *Employee supervision:* Managed up to 150 individuals and earned their respect for my willingness to listen and desire to resolve personnel problems tactfully and quickly; hired, fired, and trained employees and maintained a low personnel turnover rate.
- *Regulations compliance:* Became very knowledgeable of Department of Transportation regulations and other regulations governing trucking and transportation.
- *Computer operations:* Assisted in integrating the AS400 into the company's operation, and have become knowledgeable of the capabilities of the AS400, which the company recently upgraded and enhanced.
- *Total Quality Management:* Became known for my dedication to customer service and customer satisfaction through my hands-on management style, and continuously monitored the company's quality performance and dedication to customer satisfaction.

**AFFILIATIONS** Masonic Lodge member. Member, Maysfield United Methodist Church
Through Harriss Auto Auction, affiliated with the National Auto Auction Association (NAAA) and Georgia Independent Auto Dealers Association (GADA)

**PERSONAL** Feel that the key to my success in business has been my skill as a communicator. Am known for my tact and diplomacy in resolving problems. Can provide outstanding references.

Date

Exact Name of Person
Exact Title
Exact Name of Company
Address
City, State, Zip

**GENERAL MANAGER & FOUNDER**

Dear Exact Name of Person (or Dear Sir or Madam if answering a blind ad):

With the enclosed resume, I would like to formally express my interest in exploring employment with your organization. I believe my background is tailor-made to your needs, and I would welcome the opportunity to talk with you.

As you will see from my resume, I have embarked upon a career as an entrepreneur, and I have founded and managed three successful businesses. One of those businesses was a club/casino business in Nevada, and I provided oversight for all aspects of food and beverage operations including purchasing, sanitation, employee hiring and training, and quality control. In Delaware, I built "from scratch" an automobile dealership which became one of the most successful dealerships on the East Coast, and I eventually sold that company to an industry firm. Most recently, I assumed ownership of Premium Cars of Norwalk, CT, and manage all aspects of this business, including supervising four personnel, negotiating financing, providing quality service, and maintaining prudent cost controls.

Early on, I served my country with distinction in the U.S. Army, and I rose rapidly from the enlisted ranks to Warrant Officer while serving as a Club Night Manager, Branch Chief, and Airdrop Technician. I was praised for my attention to detail, emphasis on quality assurance, and superior problem-solving skills. Later, after I rose to the rank of Warrant Officer, I excelled in management positions, and I routinely managed budgets ranging between $700,000 to $1.5 million while overseeing property management, supply operations, and logistics.

Through my experience as a military officer and as a successful entrepreneur, I have become a skilled problem solver, and I have acquired extensive overseas experience as well as strong management skills. I would be available to travel and relocate anywhere in the world as your needs require. I hope you will contact me to arrange for an interview.

Sincerely,

Albert A. Li

# ALBERT ALLEN LI ("Al")

1110½ Hay Street, Fayetteville, NC 28305 • preppub@aol.com • (910) 483-6611

---

**OBJECTIVE**  I want to contribute to an organization that can use a resourceful manager who offers a proven ability to organize and manage automobile dealerships along with experience in directing food and beverage service in club environments.

**EDUCATION**  Earned an **Associate of Arts degree in History**, Delaware State University, Dover, DE, 1990.
Extensive formal and hands-on training in club operations, food and beverage service management, supply and inventory control, logistics, contract negotiation and contract management, and personnel supervision.

**EXPERIENCE**  **GENERAL MANAGER & (FOUNDER).** Premium Cars of Norwalk, Norwalk, CT (2003-present). Manage all aspects of this pre-owned car business which includes supervising four personnel, negotiating financing, providing quality service, and maintaining prudent cost controls in order to remain within budgetary guidelines.

**OWNER (FOUNDER).** Black Jack Casino, Reno, NV (2001-2002). Established "from scratch" a company which became known for its outstanding food and beverage as well as its quality service. Refined my skills in club management and became an expert in food and beverage control until I closed the business.
- Hired, trained, and supervised 72 employees; provided oversight for all financial management including accounts receivable and accounts payable.
- Ordered food and beverages; managed a sophisticated club operation which catered to a wide range of tastes and preferences in food and beverage.
- Acquired expert knowledge of food handling laws; maintained top sanitation rating.

**OWNER (FOUNDER).** Car Company Extraordinaire, Dover, DE (1997-01). Established this company "from scratch" and built it into one of the most successful automobile dealerships on the East Coast. Supervised all aspects of automobile financing while also purchasing vehicles, negotiating contracts, and supervising 27 employees.
- Hired, trained, and supervised a sales staff which gained a reputation as a sales force committed to quality results both in customer satisfaction and in bottom-line profitability.
- Sold more than 7,000 vehicles in six years.

**Highlights of U.S. military experience: Served with distinction in the U.S. Army:**
**AIRDROP TECHNICIAN.** Locations worldwide. For four consecutive years, led my section to be selected out of hundreds of competitors as "the #1 airdrop section in the world." This was a distinction which recognized my leadership and dedication to quality results.
**BRANCH CHIEF.** Ft. Ord, CA. After beginning my career as an enlisted soldier, was promoted to Chief Warrant Officer. Was handpicked for various management positions with the Special Forces. In one position, managed $13 million in property and equipment while managing budgets of $700,000 to $1.5 million.

**HONORS**  Served as **President**, Norwalk Independent Automobile Dealers Association, 2003.
Served as **President**, Connecticut Independent Automobile Association, 2003.
Selected as "**Quality Dealer**" in DE, 1998; selected local "Quality Dealer," 2000.
Received more than 20 medals, awards, and ribbons while serving in the U.S. Army.

**PERSONAL**  Lived and worked in numerous countries while serving in the U.S. Army. Held a Secret security clearance. Would welcome the opportunity to work overseas for extended periods.

Date

Exact Name of Person
Title or Position
Name of Company
Address (no., street)
Address (city, state, zip)

**GENERAL MANAGER & OWNER**

Dear Exact Name of Person (or Dear Sir or Madam if answering a blind ad):

I would appreciate an opportunity to talk with you soon about how I could contribute to your organization through my "track record" of success in sales and management.

You will see from my resume that I have been highly effective in increasing sales, reducing operating costs, and building a growing and successful business during my years with Astor Auto Supply Co. in Clarkston, GA. My efforts in improving and expanding services resulted in competitive prices through streamlining and consolidating facilities and assets.

A well-rounded professional, my main strengths lie in my success in the areas of sales and retail management. As General Manager, Owner, Vice President, and Operations Manager for the same company, I also gained experience in administrative, bookkeeping, advertising, and warehousing operations.

I hope you will call or write me soon to suggest a time convenient for us to meet and discuss your current and future needs and how I might serve them. Thank you in advance for your time.

Sincerely yours,

Neville D. Levitz

# NEVILLE DAVID LEVITZ

1110½ Hay Street, Fayetteville, NC 28305 • preppub@aol.com • (910) 483-6611

---

**OBJECTIVE**  To benefit an organization that can use a mature professional who offers a solid background of experience related to sales and retail management with special knowledge and expertise in the area of automotive parts supply and distribution procedures.

**EXPERIENCE**  *Expanded and built on a strong base of customer satisfaction while developing a successful automotive supply business, Astor Auto Supply Co., Clarkston, GA*:

**GENERAL MANAGER and OWNER.** (2002-present). Continually find ways to improve efficiency and services while overseeing day-to-day operations and supervising five employees. Increased the business's "competitive edge" by merging the warehouse functions into the main business location.
- Streamlined operations and cut costs by eliminating a system of outside sales and through the warehouse merger. Handle administrative activities including preparing weekly payrolls and monthly sales tax reports.
- Maintain control over inventory actions including ordering replacement stock weekly.
- Prepare monthly statements using data gained by posting accounts daily.
- Set up the schedules and ensure that payments are made to vendors.
- Arrange bank loans and make daily deposits.
- Deal with delinquent accounts and collect amounts due from them.
- Developed effective advertising by working with newspaper and radio specialists.

**VICE PRESIDENT and GENERAL MANAGER.** (1997-01). Continued to control the day-to-day operation and expand the customer base while completing a functional reorganization and the purchase of a major share of the business.
- Established and oversaw the operation of a branch warehouse.
- Developed new accounts with other area parts store locations.
- Purchased vehicles and expanded the outside sales routes.
- Prepared weekly payrolls and monthly reports and statements.

**OPERATIONS MANAGER.** (1990-96). Was responsible for major increases in sales revenues while building a successful and continually growing business.
- Increased average monthly sales from $17,000 to approximately $60,000.
- Made daily contacts with major customers in order to develop a strong customer base and held the customers through a competitive pricing system. Implemented the company's first outside sales route and then expanded it from only two days a week to four.

*Highlights of other experience*: Advanced within the U.S. Civil Service System as a Budget Analyst and Accounting Technician at Ft. Bragg, NC, the nation's largest Army base.
- Received, analyzed, classified, and controlled accounting documents.

**CIVIC ACTIVITIES**  Enjoy contributing to community activities and have been active in organizations such as:
- Served two terms (2001-02 and 2000-01) as the president of the Mid-Georgia Private Industry Council (PIC) and also contributed to the Planning and Oversight Committees.
- Was a key player in establishing and coaching a soccer program at Clarkston High School when no regular school funds were allocated for the program.
- As a Boy Scout leader took 30 troop members to Virginia for the National Jamboree.
- Served a term as President of the Clarkston Jaycees.

**PERSONAL**  Attended several workshops on employment and job training as a member of the PIC. Offer a thorough knowledge of the auto parts industry and strong sales and communication skills.

Date

Exact Name of Person
Title or Position
Name of Company
Address (no., street)
Address (city, state, zip)

**GENERATOR MECHANIC**

Dear Exact Name of Person (or Dear Sir or Madam if answering a blind ad):

I would appreciate an opportunity to talk with you soon about how I could benefit your organization through my technical power generation skills, my knowledge of electrical and diesel equipment, as well as my experience in testing and inspection. I can confidently assure you that I can maintain any system in the field of power generation.

As you will see from my resume, I worked most recently for United Construction Company, an American-owned company, in Bosnia as a Generator Mechanic performing organizational, preventive, and field maintenance on diesel engine generators for the United Nations. We provided 24-hour service under often hostile and dangerous conditions. In my previous job I worked as an Electrical Generation Power Technician and assisted with depot-level 10,000-hour as well as 1,000- and 4,000-hour inspections. Through combining my creative problem-solving ability with my technical expertise, I have saved thousands of dollars through early detection of equipment defects, rapid on-site problem solving, and troubleshooting stubborn malfunctions. In prior jobs in the Air Force, I earned a reputation as a skilled troubleshooter, plant operator, and technician.

You will see from my resume that I am knowledgeable of a wide variety of equipment by manufacturers including Wilson Gen Sets, Lister, Yamaha, Fairbanks, Schoemaker, DAF, Onan, Caterpillar, Hydrodiesel, Perkins, Nuremburg, White Superior, MAN, Allis-Chalmers, Emerson UPS System, Volvo, Duetz, and Detroit. I am skilled in working in-house as well as on mobile power generation systems.

I would like to thank you in advance for your prompt response to this letter and look forward to discussing your current and future needs and how I might serve them.

Sincerely yours,


Vernon R. Blanding

# VERNON R. BLANDING ("Vern")

1110½ Hay Street, Fayetteville, NC 28305 • preppub@aol.com • (910) 483-6611

| | |
|---|---|
| **OBJECTIVE** | To contribute my outstanding technical power generation skills, knowledge of electrical and diesel equipment, and experience in testing and inspection to an organization that can use a professional who can maintain and operate any system in the field of power production. |
| **AREAS of EXPERTISE & CLEARANCE** | • Troubleshoot solid state devices including electromechanical devices.<br>• Experienced in diesel mechanics; read/interpret diagrams and schematics.<br>• Use equipment including phase rotation meters, energy analyzers, clamp-on amp meters, voltage continuity testers, portable load banks, maintenance tools, ohmmeters, voltmeters, analog and digital circuit testers, multimeters, and voltage probes.<br>• Entrusted with a **Secret** security clearance with SBI.<br>• Familiar with equipment, generator sets, and switchgear from manufacturers such as: |

| | | | |
|---|---|---|---|
| Wilson Gen Sets | Yamaha | Fairbanks | Nuremburg |
| Schoemaker | White Superior | DAF | MAN |
| Onan | Allis-Chalmers | Caterpillar | Emerson UPS System |
| Hydrodiesel | Volvo | Perkins Duetz | Detroit Lister |

**EDUCATION & TRAINING**

USAF trained, 13 years of experience in Electrical Power Production - Generator Technician:
    intrusion alarm detection                generator troubleshooting
    depot-level diesel generator maintenance    aircraft barrier systems
    effective training techniques               (ICS) diesel maintenance

**EXPERIENCE**

**GENERATOR MECHANIC.** United Construction Company, Mostar-Sarajevo/Bosnia-Herzegovina (2002-present). As a mechanic on a mobile generator team, perform organizational, preventive, and field maintenance on diesel engine generators for all military and civilian support provided by the United Nations; provide 24-hour service and respond to emergency calls related to generator and distribution panel malfunctions.
- Provide technical generator operating training to tenant organizations pertaining to generators ranging from 3.9 to 400 KVA - manual and autosync.
- Conduct preventative maintenance inspections for 134 operating generator sets.
- Performed 200- through 10,000-hour inspections, engine and generator.
- Install auxiliary systems; maintain and adjust switch gear and distribution components.

**POWER TECHNICIAN.** Sprint Federal Services International Company, Athens, Greece (2001-02). Performed preventive maintenance inspections in addition to operating and maintaining all prime, standby, and associated power plant equipment including four 300-KW White-Superior diesel generators supplying power to a remote radio station.
- Assisted with three depot-level 10,000-hour as well as 1,000- and 4,000-hour inspections.
- Traced a problem that had caused four power outages within a month to its source, resolving the problem within 36 hours with no additional outages.

**SPECIAL EQUIPMENT TECHNICIAN.** Sprint Federal Services International Company, Berlin, Germany (1996-00). Inspected and maintained 16 intrusion detection systems providing security for sophisticated missile computer systems at a NATO facility.

**POWER PRODUCTION SPECIALIST.** U.S. Air Force, locations worldwide (1990-95). Maintained mobile diesel and gasoline-driven generator sets, conducted training, and was accountable for more than $400,000 worth of equipment.

**PERSONAL**      Highly skilled troubleshooter. Will relocate worldwide. Work well with others.

Date

Exact Name of Person
Exact Title
Exact Name of Company
Address
City, State, Zip

**INSPECTOR**   Dear Exact Name of Person (or Dear Sir or Madam if answering a blind ad):

With the enclosed resume, I would like to express my interest in exploring employment opportunities with your organization.

As you will see from my resume, I offer extensive technical knowledge related to automobile repair, maintenance, and troubleshooting. I am currently an Inspector at UPS, Syracuse, NY, where I inspect a fleet of wheeled vehicles. Previously, I was Shop Foreman at Hopkins Trucking Lines in Batavia, NY, and managed up to 10 personnel maintaining 28 types of vehicles and generators. Before that, I served as Senior Mechanic at Greyhound Bus Lines in Oakdale, NY where I ensured all buses and subsidiary automobiles for official use were in good repair.

In addition to my technical training in the Army, I completed two years of college course work in Automotive Technology. With a reputation as a resourceful problem solver, I have repaired equipment ranging from engines to transmissions. I am proficient at troubleshooting electrical problems, and I am adept in utilizing computer technology for problem solving.

While serving with distinction in the U.S. Army, I earned widespread respect for my ability to fix equipment which others could not. During a special assignment in Haiti in 1996, I worked persistently on a generator which has not worked in two years. I was successful in restoring the generator to operational condition and that permitted the residents of the town of Les Cayes, Haiti, to have electricity and running water for the first time in two years. I also trained personnel in Haiti to operate and repair vehicles.

I am confident that you would find me in person to be a congenial individual who could enhance the effectiveness of your organization. I am skilled at all aspects of customer service in addition to my technical expertise, and I thoroughly enjoy working with others to deliver a quality product in an efficient and quality manner. I can provide outstanding references, and I hope you will contact me to suggest a time when we might meet to discuss your needs.

Sincerely,

Frank M. Hai

# FRANK M. HAI

1110½ Hay Street, Fayetteville, NC 28305 • preppub@aol.com • (910) 483-6611

---

**OBJECTIVE**  I want to contribute to an organization that can use a versatile professional with extensive skills related to vehicle repair, maintenance, and troubleshooting.

**EDUCATION**  Completed two years of college course work related to Automotive Technology, Liberal Arts, and other areas, Manhattan College, Riverdale, NY.

**CERTIFICATION & SKILLS**  A+ Certified, CompTIA, March 2001.
Offer strong troubleshooting and problem-solving skills related to both computers and autos:
*Computers:* Built computers from scratch; repaired/upgraded equipment including computers, printers, and monitors, and loaded software. Proficient with computers and software including Word, Excel, and PowerPoint.
*Automobiles and generators:* Repaired equipment ranging from engines to transmissions; proficient at troubleshooting electrical problems.
*Languages:* Fluently speak, read, and write Spanish.
*Clearance:* Held a Top Secret security clearance while in military service.

**EXPERIENCE**  **INSPECTOR.** UPS, Syracuse, NY (2002-present). Inspect a fleet of wheeled vehicles and special purpose equipment. Conduct safety inspections to ensure vehicles are maintained in accordance with organizational and government regulations.
- Reviewed//prepared operations reports and made determinations on vehicle needs.

**SHOP FOREMAN.** Hopkins Trucking Lines, Batavia, NY (2000-02). Managed up to 10 personnel maintaining 28 types of vehicles and generators; was Advisor to four transportation organizations; acted as Inspector. Displayed my versatility overseeing activities ranging from dispatching, to training, to using computers for report preparation and record keeping.

**SENIOR MECHANIC.** Greyhound Bus Lines, Oakdale, NY (1997-00). Supervised 11 individuals maintaining a fleet of 60 vehicles.
- Ensured all buses and subsidiary automobiles for official use were in good repair.

**Excelled in a "track record" of promotion with the U.S. Army, locations worldwide:**
**2000-01: ASSISTANT OPERATIONS MANAGER.** Supervised three people involved in preparing training schedules for a 600-person organization.
**1999-00: OPERATIONS MANAGER.** Prepared written portions of important documents published for use by the Special Operations.
**1998-99: OPERATIONS ADVISOR.** Was Consultant and trusted advisor to an executive on matters related to Special Forces operations in the Caribbean; planned and managed multiple special projects and was commended in writing for developing "superb training plans."
**1997-98: INTELLIGENCE ANALYST.** Analyzed data and utilized it in preparing area studies and operations reports for use by the Special Forces; accounted for $400,000 in assets. Served as a Team Leader on several projects. Restructured the Program of Instruction for the 1997 Commando Course in Antigua.
**1996: OPERATIONS MANAGER.** Directed operations of the Dominican Republic National Directorate for Drug Control; trained personnel on computer intelligence-related software.
**1995-96: ADVISOR, CARIBBEAN HEADQUARTERS.** During the United Nations mission in Haiti, was personally commended by the U.N. Force Commander; trained personnel in vehicle repair in remote areas of Haiti.

**PERSONAL**  Resourceful problem solver. Excellent references upon request.

Date

Exact Name of Person
Exact Title
Exact Name of Company
Address
City, State, Zip

**LONG-HAUL TRUCK DRIVER**

Dear Exact Name of Person (or Dear Sir or Madam if answering a blind ad):

With the enclosed resume, I would like to make you aware of my interest in exploring employment opportunities with your organization. I can provide outstanding references and would cheerfully accept worldwide relocation according to your needs.

As you will see from my resume, I offer versatile skills in two technical fields along with strong management and leadership skills which were refined during the process of serving my country in the U.S. Army.

**Technical expertise:** The recipient of numerous medals and awards for superior performance as a U.S. Army supervisor and manager, I gained valuable experience as a POL Specialist. I began my military career as a Petroleum Supply Supervisor supervising 12 employees involving in aircraft refueling operations throughout the army base at Fort Rucker. In a subsequent position in Kentucky, I supervised 28 employees in aircraft refueling and defueling operations. Because of my technical expertise and quality control knowledge, I was handpicked for positions as a Petroleum Products Supervisor, Distribution Manager, Petroleum Station Manager, and Pump Station Manager. While serving in Japan, I was praised widely for the positive influence I had on others. In my most recent experience as a Long-Haul Truck Driver, I have received special recognition every year and recently I was honored with a Truck Driving Safety Award from the National Association for Truck Drivers for "no accidents (or incidents) in four years." I hold a Class A CDL with Endorsement X (HAZMAT/tanker certification).

**Management skills:** My management skills were refined in military service, as I constantly operated in an environment in which there was "no room for error." With a reputation as a manager who emphasized safety and quality control at all times, I maintained accountability for multimillion-dollar equipment while dispensing hundreds of thousands of aviation fuel without mishap. On numerous occasions I transformed substandard operations into models of efficiency. For example, as a Petroleum Station Manager, I inherited a failing section and, through strong leadership, I transformed its operational readiness status from 54% to 96%.

If you can use a dynamic communicator with a talent for establishing effective relationships and managing profitable business activities, I hope you will call or write me to suggest a time when we might meet in person to discuss your needs. I can provide outstanding references at the appropriate time.

Yours sincerely,

Xavier A. Washington

# XAVIER A. WASHINGTON
1110½ Hay Street, Fayetteville, NC 28305 • preppub@aol.com • (910) 483-6611

---

**OBJECTIVE**      I want to contribute to an organization that can use a versatile professional with experience in managing the distribution, storage, and maintenance of petroleum and aviation fuel along with specialized expertise related to the handling and transportation of hazardous materials.

**LICENSES & CERTIFICATIONS**      Class A CDL with Endorsement X (HAZMAT certification); completed Roadway Express Truck Driving School Proficient in operating forklifts ranging from 3K to 10K. Certified as a professional POL Fuel Handler and Petroleum Supply Specialist, U.S. Army.

**EDUCATION**      Completed more than two years of college-level course work sponsored by the U.S. Army which included Quartermaster School; completed courses including the Senior Leadership Development Course, Instructor Development Course, Counseling Techniques Course, and training related to fuel handling, petroleum supply management, and drug and alcohol abuse.

**CLEARANCE, LANGUAGE**      Held secret security clearance
Working knowledge of Spanish

**EXPERIENCE**      **LONG-HAUL TRUCK DRIVER.** Central Transport International, Richmond, VA (2001-present). Have received a safety award annually every year since I have been employed by Central Transport International; travel throughout the southeast while obeying all federal laws and government regulations. Received a prestigious Truck Driving Safety Award from the National Association for Truck Drivers for "no accidents (or incidents) in four years."

**TERMINAL PUMP STATION MANAGER.** Hess, Inc., Richmond, VA (1999-01). Supervised 18 personnel in pipeline and terminal operations while also serving as a Master Driver in special projects which required a skilled HAZMAT manager.

**Other U.S. Army experience:**
**PETROLEUM STATION MANAGER.** U.S. Army, Fort Huachuca, AZ (1996-99). Managed 13 people involved in the receipt, storage, issuing, distribution, and use of petroleum and water. Inherited a failing section and, through strong leadership, transformed its operational readiness status from 54% to 96%. The section subsequently received a commendable rating.
- **Communication skills:** On my own initiative, wrote the organization's POL standards operating procedures and organized its basic load requirements pertaining to packages.
- **Inventory control skills:** Maintained accountability for equipment valued at over $1.3 million. Dispensed more than 193,000 gallons of fuel without mishap.
- **Safety and environmental control:** Implemented a model ecological control program; trained personnel in emergency procedures to use in the event of spills or fires.

**DISTRIBUTION MANAGER.** US Army, Camp Casey, Korea (1995-96). Was praised for "exceptional technical expertise and initiative" while supervising and managing 15 workers at six different locations; provided oversight for petroleum and water operations.
- During a special project in Okinawa, Japan, established and managed petroleum at remote sites. Was described as providing "outstanding petroleum support."

**AIRCRAFT REFUELING SUPERVISOR.** US Army, Fort Campbell, KY (1992-95). Supervised 28 employees in aircraft refueling/defueling operations; tested for particulate contamination and free water in fuels.

**PERSONAL**      Excellent personal and professional references. Recipient of more than a dozen awards.

Date

Exact Name of Person
Title or Position
Name of Company
Address (no., street)
Address (city, state, zip)

**MAINTENANCE & OPERATIONS SUPERVISOR**

Dear Exact Name of Person (or Dear Sir or Madam if answering a blind ad):

Can you use a hard-working young professional who has the proven ability to learn quickly, an eye for details, well-developed leadership skills, and experience in the transportation field and office administration?

I offer a background which includes maintenance and management of an automobile rental agency in Geneva, OH, as well as office administration, clerical experience, and handling customer service/sales/inventory control.

I feel that through my enthusiasm, ability to absorb new information quickly, and broad range of skills, I am capable of stepping into new environments and rapidly being able to contribute to my employer's efficiency and profitability.

I hope you will welcome my call soon to arrange a brief meeting at your convenience to discuss your current and future needs and how I might serve them. Thank you in advance for your time.

Sincerely yours,


Ricky G. Kennison III


(Alternate last paragraph:
I hope you will call or write soon to suggest a time convenient for us to meet and discuss your current and future needs and how I might serve them. Thank you in advance for your time.)

# RICKY G. KENNISON III

1110½ Hay Street, Fayetteville, NC 28305 • preppub@aol.com • (910) 483-6611

---

**OBJECTIVE**    To benefit an organization that can use a versatile and adaptable young professional who offers an eye for detail along with specialized experience related to transportation, clerical administration, and providing leadership.

**SPECIAL SKILLS & ABILITIES**
- Offer experience in using computers for word processing and record keeping.
- Am familiar with a variety of software including the following:
    Word        Excel        PowerPoint        Access
- Was entrusted by the U.S. Army with a **Secret** security clearance.
- Am skilled in troubleshooting and repairing track vehicles.

**EXPERIENCE**    **MAINTENANCE & OPERATIONS SUPERVISOR.** Renault Rentals, Geneva, OH (2002-present). Oversee eight subordinates while leading a team of specialists operating and maintaining a rental agency.
- Earned a reputation as a skilled troubleshooter who could be counted on to "set the example" for other team members by the quality of my performance.
- Make contributions to the success of the company by ensuring vehicles are clean and well maintained.
- Raised the prestige of the company by participating in parades and public appearances.
- Received an award for providing excellent customer service.

**ADMINISTRATIVE SPECIALIST.** Advanced Technology Corp., Geneva, OH (2000-01). Polished my clerical skills and office management knowledge collecting information from subordinate company managers, then using the information to prepare and type training schedules for a 3,000-person organization.
- Produced detailed materials including memorandums, graphics, charts, operations plans, and reports.
- Initiated an accelerated system of report collection which in turn allowed information to be processed and perfected before it was sent on to a higher headquarters level.
- Excelled in a job which required outstanding coordination and time management abilities.

**ENTERTAINMENT PROMOTER.** Roller Skate U.S.A., Dayton, OH (1998-00). Used my creativity to develop promotion campaigns and entertainment which customers enjoyed and which contributed to satisfaction and repeat business.

**SALES ASSOCIATE.** Wal-Mart, Ft. Richardson, AK (1995-97). Displayed my versatility by handling several functional areas including:

    providing customer service          operating a cash register
    stocking merchandise                taking inventory
    facilities maintenance and upkeep   conducting store security

- Became known for my dependability and willingness to learn new things.
- Earned a reputation as a customer-oriented young professional.

**TRAINING**    Received more than 340 hours of specialized instruction in leadership techniques, how to conduct training, computer operations, and first aid.

**EDUCATION**    Studied Communications, Cedarville College, Cedarville, OH.

**PERSONAL**    Earned six U.S. Army Achievement Medals for professionalism which placed me "ahead of my peers" in positions above my actual military rank.

Date

Exact Name of Person
Title or Position
Name of Company
Address (no., street)
Address (city, state, zip)

**MAINTENANCE DIRECTOR**

Dear Exact Name of Person (or Dear Sir or Madam if answering a blind ad):

I would appreciate an opportunity to talk with you soon about how I could benefit your organization through my extensive experience in heavy equipment and vehicle maintenance management.

While serving as Maintenance Director for Commercial Equipment Leasing, Buffalo, NY, I have built a "track record" of excellent performance while consistently being evaluated as an expert in the area of construction equipment and wheeled vehicle maintenance. I am proud of my accomplishments in finding innovative ways to increase productivity while reducing costs and developing training to enhance performance.

My special area of expertise, and the field where my experience has been concentrated, is heavy equipment/vehicle maintenance. I have managed two auto repair shops at dealerships, served as Maintenance Operations Supervisor at the Buffalo Airport and as Maintenance Technician at the Jamestown Airport at facilities maintaining construction equipment and vehicles for airfield expansions.

I offer a combination of management expertise, technical abilities, and creative problem-solving skills which make me a versatile and adaptable professional who is known for "setting the standards" for others to follow.

I hope you will welcome my call soon to arrange a brief meeting at your convenience to discuss your current and future needs and how I might serve them. Thank you in advance for your time.

Sincerely yours,

Clark D. Chang

# CLARK DAVID CHANG

1110½ Hay Street, Fayetteville, NC 28305 • preppub@aol.com • (910) 483-6611

---

**OBJECTIVE**  To contribute to an organization through my extensive experience in heavy equipment and vehicle maintenance as well as through my management abilities.

**SPECIAL SKILLS & AREAS OF EXPERTISE**

- Offer experience in the repair and maintenance of heavy equipment by manufacturers including Caterpillar, Case, John Deere, AM General, Barber-Green, Hyster, Allison, and Cedar Rapids.
- Have expertise related to forklifts, asphalt plants, pavers, rollers, scrapers, bucket loaders, rock-crushing equipment, and trucks including tractor trailers.
- Use computer software including Word, Excel, Access, and PowerPoint.
- Can read and interpret electrical diagrams and schematics as well as hydraulic diagrams.
- Offer expertise related to power generation, gas turbine engines, and diesel engines.
- Skilled in welding, fabrication, and as a machinist.

**EDUCATION & TRAINING**

B.A. in **Business Administration,** Clarkson University, Potsdam, NY, 1989.
Excelled in management and leadership training as well as in extensive technical programs related to specialized equipment including:

| | |
|---|---|
| Caterpillar 130G grader | MW24C Case bucket loader |
| power generation | hydraulics |
| gas turbine engines | engineering equipment repair |

**EXPERIENCE**

**MAINTENANCE DIRECTOR.** Commercial Equipment Leasing, Buffalo, NY (2003-present). Develop maintenance plans for an organization with 730 items of construction equipment and wheeled vehicles; train employees in proper maintenance procedures; establish and enforce safety/environmental programs.

- Set up innovative new training for mechanics and supervisors which contributed to the 12% increase in operational readiness rates. Was recognized as the resident "expert" and advisor on issues related to equipment availability and maintenance procedures.
- Analyzed maintenance operations and forecasted future requirements.

**MAINTENANCE SHOP MANAGER.** Davis Ford-Lincoln, Buffalo, NY (2000-02). Supervised 40 employees performing direct support repairs on vehicles. Initiated changes which reduced repair time and costs. Implemented a highly effective quality control program.

**VEHICLE MAINTENANCE MANAGER.** Martin New & Used Autos, Newark, NJ (1997-99). Supervised the maintenance and repair shop of this large car dealer employing 30 mechanics. Advised clients on what repairs were needed on their vehicles and coordinated the arrangements for scheduling and making the repairs.

- Used test measuring and diagnostic equipment to troubleshoot malfunctions.

**MAINTENANCE OPERATIONS SUPERVISOR.** Buffalo Airport, Buffalo, NY (1995-97). Supervised 30 mechanics at a maintenance facility supporting 200 items of construction equipment and vehicles. Handled all aspects of a $3 million-dollar airfield rebuilding project; made budget estimates.

**MAINTENANCE TECHNICIAN.** Jamestown Airport, Jamestown, NY (1990-94). Became familiar with OSHA and EPA oil analysis standards while supervising employees maintaining over 800 pieces of construction equipment and vehicles.

**PERSONAL**  Am very skilled in training others and leading them to put forth their personal best efforts.

Date

Exact Name of Person
Title or Position
Name of Company
Address (no., street)
Address (city, state, zip)

**MAINTENANCE MANAGER**

Dear Exact Name of Person (or Dear Sir or Madam if answering a blind ad):

I would appreciate an opportunity to talk with you soon about how I could contribute to your organization through my excellent performance record which includes both technical and mechanical skills as well as the ability to provide training, supervision, and managerial abilities.

As you will see from my resume, I offer more than ten years of experience as a light and heavy wheeled vehicle mechanic and power generation equipment technician. In my current position as Shop Supervisor at Allied Auto Electric, Annapolis, MD, I have been credited with turning around a failing maintenance operation. I direct two clerks and five mechanics in all aspects of maintenance support. In a previous job with the U.S. Postal Service, Baltimore, MD, I supervised five persons and was awarded three awards in recognition of my efforts. Throughout my employment, I have earned a reputation as a creative leader who could be counted on to see that the details were taken care of which ensured that operations ran smoothly. I have consistently been singled out for advancement and described as a professional who meets challenges head on and achieves outstanding results through leadership by example.

My versatile background has included providing direct supervision for up to 27 employees, overseeing all aspects of running maintenance operations, developing and conducting effective training programs, and managing logistics support activities. I have received numerous commendation and achievement awards for my exceptional duty performance, leadership and concern for my employees, and contributions which directly resulted in success for my department and for the organization as a whole.

I believe you would find me to be an enthusiastic and ambitious individual who works well under stress and time constraints.

I hope you will welcome my call soon to arrange a brief meeting at your convenience to discuss your current and future needs and how I might serve them. Thank you in advance for your time.

Sincerely yours,

Jerry C. O'Reilly

# JERRY CHAD O'REILLY

1110½ Hay Street, Fayetteville, NC 28305 • preppub@aol.com • (910) 483-6611

| | |
|---|---|
| **OBJECTIVE** | To offer a combination of excellent electrical and mechanical skills along with outstanding managerial and supervisory abilities to an organization that can use a mature, detail-oriented professional who is also recognized as a hard-charging and creative trainer and motivator. |
| **TECHNICAL KNOWLEDGE** | Experienced in reading schematics and wiring diagrams, am highly skilled in the repair, service, and inspection of a wide range of equipment including, but not limited to: |

      generators up to 100KW     trucks up to 10 tons     trailers up to 40 feet
      air compressors up to 250CFM     floodlights     gas and diesel heaters
      4,000 and 6,000-lb. forklifts     4,000-lb. cranes   hoists
      water and fuel pumps up to 350GPM

**gas engines:** up to 20HP Hercules engines
**diesel engines:** Cummins, Detroit, and White V-6, V-8, and V-10 straight 6, 4, and 2-cylinders
Use diagnostic equipment including calibrators, potentiometers, and multimeters.

**EXPERIENCE**

**MAINTENANCE MANAGER.** Allied Auto Electric, Annapolis, MD (2002-present). Credited with turning around a failing maintenance operation, directed two clerks and five mechanics in all aspects of support for a $1 million inventory of 80 generators.
- Displayed my knowledge and versatility overseeing activities ranging from dispatching, to training, to using computers for report preparation and record keeping.
- Molded employees into a team which went from failing to "no faults found" ratings.

**MAINTENANCE SUPERVISOR.** U.S. Postal Service, Baltimore, MD (1998-01). Developed a maintenance program which led to commendable 95% availability rates as the manager of a five-person department with 33 line items of equipment valued in excess of $2 million.
- Was singled out to conduct the organization's maintenance training program.
- Exceeded standards by averaging 6% zero balance for a 180-line-item inventory.
- Was awarded *three* awards in recognition of my efforts and long hours which directly resulted in the shop's superior rating in a major inspection which found no faults in the areas of automated records and inventory.
- Supervised five employees and ensured error-free operation of the automated logistics system including all aspects of ordering parts and maintaining records.

**POWER GENERATION SHOP FOREMAN.** Hood Construction Company, Baltimore, MD (1994-97). Earned advancement to a supervisory role and several awards for my performance in supervising up to 27 people maintaining and operating as many as 50 vehicles, 17 power units, and 234 items of material-handling equipment.
- Was consistently evaluated as displaying technical competence, sound judgment, and a true concern for ensuring high standards of training for and performance by employees.
- Motivated and led employees to outstanding accomplishments under tight deadlines.

**POWER GENERATION EQUIPMENT INSPECTOR.** U.S. Army, Germany (1991-93). After contributing skills and knowledge which led to a low maintenance backlog, was chosen to oversee quality control and provide technical guidance for eight separate companies.

**TRAINING**    Excelled in training including power generation mechanics, wheeled vehicle mechanics, fuel handling, leadership development, and maintenance management.

**PERSONAL**    Have a Secret security clearance. Excel in motivating others through my strong work ethic, insistence on results, and positive approach. Am available for relocation worldwide.

Date

Exact Name of Person
Title or Position
Name of Company
Address (number and street)
Address (city, state, and zip)

**MANAGER TRAINEE**

Dear Exact Name of Person (or Dear Sir or Madam if answering a blind ad):

I would appreciate an opportunity to talk with you soon about how I could contribute to your organization through my fleet management experience with an emphasis on providing strong customer service support.

As you see on my enclosed resume, I am currently Manager Trainee at Atlantic Rent-A-Car in Bismarck, ND. I was groomed to manage this branch of this international rental car agency including fleet management, personnel administration, customer service, and direct sales.

Previously, I have shown my keen sales ability in a variety of positions including Licensed Insurance Agent, Administrative Assistant, and Assistant Manager. My interest now is in fleet management as I have found this interesting and enjoyable, albeit challenging, employment.

You would find me to be a results-oriented professional who believes that one of the keys to success in business is treating customers graciously and building relationships that last. I pride myself on loyalty to my employer, and I think that building and cementing the employer's customer base for future repeat business is probably the most important contribution an employee can make to her employer.

I hope you will welcome my call soon to arrange a brief meeting at your convenience to discuss your current and future needs and how I might serve them. Thank you in advance for your time.

Sincerely yours,

Sasha L. Polanski

(Alternate last paragraph:
I hope you will call or write me soon to suggest a time convenient for us to meet and discuss your current and future needs and how I might serve them. Thank you in advance for your time.)

## SASHA L. POLANSKI
1110½ Hay Street, Fayetteville, NC 28305   •   preppub@aol.com   •   (910) 483-6611

| | |
|---|---|
| **OBJECTIVE** | To offer my reputation as a detail-oriented young professional who can handle deadlines and stress while contributing my time management, administrative, and office operations abilities to an organization that can benefit from my people skills and concern for others. |
| **EXPERIENCE** | **MANAGER TRAINEE.** Atlantic Rent-A-Car, Bismarck, ND (2002-present). Was groomed to manage a branch of this international rental car agency including handling fleet management, personnel administration, customer service, and direct sales. |
| | **LICENSED INSURANCE AGENT.** Prudential Insurance, Bismarck, ND (2001-02). Refined communication skills while developing a network of clients selling medical insurance. |
| | **ADMINISTRATIVE ASSISTANT.** U.S. Coast Guard, Bismarck, ND (1998-00). Maintained the personnel, medical, and training records for 33 employees while providing a senior executive and the senior manager with clerical and administrative support. |

- Provided the personnel manager with freedom from the day-to-day details of records management which allowed him more time for counseling and supervising.
- Contributed to the unit's recognition with an Outstanding Achievement Award.
- Became very skilled at managing my time effectively, handling an average of 400-500 cases a year as compared to 200 to 300 for most stations of its size.
- As a Certified Radio Watch Stander, received calls from disabled vessels and dispatched emergency help.

**ASSISTANT MANAGER.** Cicero Community Store, Cicero, IL (1993-97). Refined my time management and public relations skills while handling areas ranging from ordering and stocking merchandise, to making bank deposits and picking up cash for use in the store, to opening and closing the store.

**LAW ENFORCEMENT VOLUNTEER.** Police Explorers, Cicero, IL (1991-93). In this program (PAL) which is sponsored by the Boy Scouts of America, gained exposure to numerous areas of police department operations including:

| | |
|---|---|
| dispatching officers in response to 911 calls | questioning witnesses |
| investigating accidents and crime scenes | fingerprinting suspects |

- Was cited by the Chief of Police for my assistance at the city's fourth annual alcohol and drug awareness exposition and singled out for my enthusiasm and professional image.

**ATHLETIC & COMMUNITY INVOLVEMENT**

Won numerous awards for my participation in varsity sports including field hockey and basketball while attending high school.

Received a Certificate of Appreciation for my assistance during a Halloween toy drive to benefit a county foster children's program.

**TRAINING**

Completed extensive military training programs emphasizing such diverse areas as:

| | |
|---|---|
| CPR and first aid | risk assessment |
| environmental protection | family advocacy |
| drug and alcohol screening | health and nutrition |
| emergency medical technology | hazardous material handling |

**PERSONAL**

Am proud of my reputation as an independent thinker of strong character and personal values. Have been described as a compassionate and giving individual who is very concerned with the feelings of others.

Date

Exact Name of Person
Exact Title
Exact Name of Company
Address
City, State, Zip

## MECHANIC & SHOP FOREMAN

Dear Exact Name of Person (or Dear Sir or Madam if answering a blind ad):

With the enclosed resume, I would like to make you aware of my interest in exploring employment opportunities with your organization and introduce you to my experience and certifications related to your business.

As you will see from my resume, I hold a Diploma in Auto Mechanics and am completing an Associate of Science in Auto Mechanics. An ICS Certified Mechanic, I am also ASE Certified in engine repair. Currently in France, I work at a U.S. car dealership repairing foreign and domestic cars and light trucks. As you will note from my resume, I previously served as General Manager at Kramer Cadillac in Decatur, IL. I also performed computer-assisted troubleshooting of engines, domestic and foreign. I became a valuable member of the management team and acted as Shop Foreman.

My experience in the military helped me refine my technical skills and management ability. As an Operations Manager in two different organizations, I trained and managed up to 12 employees while accounting for $4.5 million in equipment which included a fleet of vehicles. In another assignment, I managed a mechanized platoon and controlled a $5 million inventory which included vehicles, communications equipment, and other items. In a job as a Vehicle Operations Supervisor, I trained and supervised 31 employees while controlling equipment and a fleet of vehicles. I completed training as a Heavy Tracked Driver, and I became a skilled driver with an outstanding safety record. Early in my military career I was selected to serve as a Commander's Personal Driver. As my career progressed, I was promoted rapidly ahead of my peers and was selected for numerous executive development programs.

Throughout my experience I have developed strong customer service and management skills as well as superior technical abilities and an aggressive bottom-line orientation. If my background and skills interest you, I hope you will contact me to suggest a time when we could meet in person to discuss your needs. I can provide outstanding references. Thank you in advance for your time.

Yours sincerely,

Manuel F. Lopez

# MANUEL F. LOPEZ

1110½ Hay Street, Fayetteville, NC 28305  •  preppub@aol.com  •  (910) 483-6611

---

**OBJECTIVE**   I want to contribute to an organization that can use a certified auto mechanic with an outstanding safety record along with extensive experience in training and supervising others.

**CERTIFICATIONS**   ICS Certified Mechanic; ASE Certified Mechanic and certified in engine repair.
**& SKILLS**   Licensed to drive all vehicles in the Army, 26 tons and below, tracked; and 5 tons and below.

**EDUCATION**   **Associate of Science in Auto Mechanics,** Richland Community College, Decatur, IL (completing degree).
Received a Diploma in Auto Mechanics, ICS.
Graduated from a two-month executive development program, 2002.
Graduated from leadership development, communication, security management, other courses.
**Computers:** Received Certificates from formal training in Microsoft, UNIX, and software.

**EXPERIENCE**   **MECHANIC & SHOP FOREMAN.** American Parts and Cars, France (2002-present). With a U.S. dealership, became part of management; repaired foreign and domestic cars and light trucks; performed computer-controlled troubleshooting of engines, domestic and foreign.
- Supervised 12 mechanics and maintained adequate parts availability.

**GENERAL MANAGER.** Kramer Cadillac, Decatur, IL (1997-01). Supervise shop and sales managers as well verify accuracy of loan contracts for this busy dealership.
- Led the store to receive official recognition as "one of the best dealerships in the state."
- Ensure customer service satisfaction.
- Have been credited with having the best and most successful used car department.

**OPERATIONS MANAGER.** Advance Auto Parts, Joliet, IL (1995-97). Was commended for exhibiting "great proficiency" while managing the operation of a highly complex computerized system with a state-of-the-art SUN computer for inventory control.
- Trained staff on the UNIX-based SUN analysis system to ensure availability of parts.
- Provided leadership in managing the transition to a new computerized inventory system.

**Refined my mechanical skills while serving in the U.S. Army:**
**OPERATIONS MANAGER.** U.S. Army, Germany (1993-95). Trained and managed up to 12 employees in two different organizations while accounting for up to $4.5 million in equipment which included a fleet of vehicles; accounted for and serviced wheeled vehicles including M2A2 Bradleys, M577A2s, M998 HMMWVs, and M113A3s.
- Was commended for managing a maintenance program that became the standard.

**MECHANIZED PLATOON MANAGER.** U.S. Army, Germany (1990-92). In charge of a 30-person organization, was personally accountable for a $5 million inventory which included M2A2 Bradley Infantry Fighting vehicles, and weapons and communications equipment.
- Was evaluated as "the best platoon sergeant in the company" and selected for a prestigious promotion in competition with 28 other skilled professionals.
- During a six-month assignment in Bosnia, maintained vehicles at a 96% readiness rate.

**VEHICLE OPERATIONS SUPERVISOR.** U.S. Army, Ft. Polk, LA (1986-89). Was selected for this position over seven other outstanding managers; trained and supervised 31 employees while controlling equipment and a fleet of M2A2 Bradley vehicles worth over $6 million.

**PERSONAL**   Received numerous honors including 3 badges and 12 medals. Excellent references on request.

# CAREER CHANGE

Date

Exact Name of Person
Title or Position
Name of Company
Address (no., street)
Address (city, state, zip)

**OWNER/FOUNDER of an Auto Audio Store**

Dear Exact Name of Person (or Dear Sir or Madam if answering a blind ad):

I would appreciate an opportunity to talk with you soon about how I could contribute to your organization through my superior communication and sales abilities along with my reputation as a dependable professional and creative thinker.

You will see from my resume that I have a talent for sales with a history of success at all levels. I have been an area sales representative for national companies and have been exposed to the methods of pricing and operating at manufacturer's, retail, and distributor's levels. I am accustomed to the demands of traveling and dealing with others through my years of experience with automotive products.

More recently I have been successful in setting up a unique business which has undergone more than one functional reorganization due to public demands and need for my products. Starting as a rep for a three-state area, my automotive parts and accessories business grew into a successful retail location.

I am certain that through my talent for relating to people, my persuasive and professional manner, and experience I could make valuable contributions to your organization.

I hope you will welcome my call soon to arrange a brief meeting at your convenience to discuss your current and future needs and how I might serve them. Thank you in advance for your time.

Sincerely yours,

Oliver L. Li

(Alternate last paragraph:
I hope you will call or write me soon to suggest a time convenient for us to meet and discuss your current and future needs and how I might serve them. Thank you in advance for your time.)

# OLIVER LARRY LI ("Olly")

1110½ Hay Street, Fayetteville, NC 28305 • preppub@aol.com • (910) 483-6611

---

**OBJECTIVE**  I want to offer my versatile background in sales and business management to an organization that can benefit from the experience of a mature hard-charger with a reputation for unquestioned honesty and integrity and the ability to relate to people at all levels.

**EXPERIENCE**  *Built a successful service business from scratch while developing a strong repeat customer base in a very competitive market*:
**OWNER/FOUNDER.** Auto Audio, Fullerton CA (2001-present). Reorganized and expanded an existing business in order to take advantage of the public's wish to buy quality automobile sound systems at competitive prices, as well as installed equipment.
- Handle day-to-day operational activities ranging from hiring to training/supervising employees.
- Refined my knowledge of customer loan processing and purchasing procedures.
- Apply my extensive sales background and depth of product knowledge to ensure the business continually operates at a profit.

**OWNER/FOUNDER.** Lou's Automotive Sales d.b.a. Paradise Wheels and Accessories, Fullerton, CA (1994-2000). Established the unique concept of the area's first retail sales outlet strictly for automotive accessories and served retail customers and wholesale dealers.
- As a full-time manufacturer's representative until 1992, called on auto parts dealers and wholesale distributors in three states for Edelbrock, Octane 104, Bandit Wheel Accessories, Doug Thorley, Sail Tech, and Wail Industries, earned the money to start my own retail operation.
- Took one manufacturer's (Bandit Wheel Accessories) regional volume of sales from $20,000 to $1.2 million annually.
- Sold three major manufacturers attending a Las Vegas trade show on my abilities and gained the right to represent their products in a three-state area.
- Learned to deal with the general public by representing the distributors at trade shows and auto races throughout the area. Became very effective in dealing with people at all levels while making frequent visits to small, independently owned garages and installers.

*Highlights of other experience*:
- Called on department stores and chains, including discount chains, drug store chains, and wholesale distribution on all lines.
- Gained insight into the most productive techniques for building and organizing a sales territory for the highest volume as an area sales representative of automotive supplies.
- Developed my supervisory, sales, and merchandising skills as a representative for Remington Rand electric shavers, Helene Curtis beauty products, and Purex products, originally fragrance soap division consisting of fragrant colognes and fragrant soaps.

**EDUCATION**  Completed business-related courses while attending Fullerton College, Fullerton, CA.

**SPECIAL SKILLS & KNOWLEDGE**  Offer a versatile background in areas and activities including the following:
- Selling and managing sales personnel
- Working with beauty and health aids and automotive accessories
- Dealing with suppliers; negotiating with manufacturers and handling purchasing

**PERSONAL**  Am known for my ability to find solutions to problems and maximize available resources. Offer a broad base of knowledge at every level of sales including retail, distributorships, and as a regional sales rep for national companies. Traveled in Nevada, California, and Arizona.

Date

Exact Name of Person
Title or Position
Name of Company
Address (number and street)
Address (city, state, and zip)

## PARTS DEPARTMENT MANAGER

Great minds think alike, as they say, and Mr. Oliver Li from the preceding page and Jeremiah Horenkamp have similar objectives: Both want to work for a large international company which will send them to an exotic location, probably in the Middle East, where they can apply their hands-on skills in automotive repair and maintenance.

Dear Exact Name of Person: (or Dear Sir or Madam if answering a blind ad.)

With the enclosed resume, I would like to indicate my interest in your organization and my desire to explore employment opportunities.

As you will see from my enclosed resume, I am experienced in all aspects of parts management and maintenance shop supervision. Prior to my current job with AutoMax, I reduced costs and improved customer satisfaction in jobs managing up to seven mechanics maintaining a fleet of vehicles. Although I am excelling in my current position and am held in high regard by my employer, I am interested in exploring opportunities with international companies that can use a maintenance expert available for worldwide relocation.

I hope you will welcome my call soon to arrange a brief meeting at your convenience to discuss your current and future needs and how I might serve them. Thank you in advance for your time.

Sincerely yours,


Jeremiah Horenkamp

(Alternate last paragraph:
I hope you will call or write me soon to suggest a time convenient for us to meet and discuss your current and future needs and how I might serve them. Thank you in advance for your time.)

# JEREMIAH HORENKAMP

1110½ Hay Street, Fayetteville, NC 28305 • preppub@aol.com • (910) 483-6611

---

**OBJECTIVE**  To benefit an organization that can use a motivated young professional with strong problem-solving and organizational skills who offers a background as an automotive maintenance supervisor, parts manager, mechanic, and retail merchandiser.

**EXPERIENCE**  **PARTS DEPARTMENT MANAGER.** AutoMax, El Paso, TX (2002-present). Manage all operational aspects of the parts department of this busy automotive supply wholesaler. Supervise seven employees; daily utilize a computer with customized software.
- Reset displays throughout the store, merchandising all areas according to the plan-o-gram as well as district and regional guidelines.
- Oversee and direct the stocking, merchandising, and recovery of the sales floor.
- Open and close the store, balancing the safe and completing all daily operational paperwork, shortage/overage reports, etc.
- Control inventory shrinkage; implement and train staff in the implementation of loss prevention procedures and guidelines.
- Increase average sales per customer by reminding staff of our target average and encouraging "plus selling" of related items.

**MAINTENANCE SHOP SUPERVISOR.** U.S. Army, Fort Buffalo, TX (1998-02). Ensured that the shop workers under my supervision followed proper maintenance, safety, and hazardous material handling and disposal procedures.
- Supervised a staff of 7-10 mechanics.
- Scheduled work assignments and training cycles for staff.
- Ensured security and maintenance of more than $150,000 worth of equipment.
- Developed streamlined procedures for common repairs, reducing labor time by 50%.

**VEHICLE MAINTENANCE TECHNICIAN.** U.S. Army, Fort Buffalo, TX (1994-1998). Performed major and minor repairs as well as preventive maintenance on wheeled vehicles.
- Operated welding equipment, brake lathes, battery testers, impact wrenches, winches, and overhead cranes.
- Utilized computer diagnostic equipment to troubleshoot vehicle malfunctions.
- Completely rebuilt engines and transmissions.

**SHOP SUPERVISOR.** MotorWorld, Tempe, AZ (1994). Opened and closed the shop, balancing the safe, and preparing the cash register tills for the next day's business. Supervised and trained four employees. Assisted mechanics with repairs and prepared bills for customers.

**TRAINING**  Excelled in a number of military and civilian training courses, including the following:
- Oral Communication and Emergency Lifesaver courses, Buffalo Technical Community College, Buffalo, TX, 1996-1997.
- Junior Leadership Course, Distinguished Honor Graduate (Top student in class), 1995.
- Wheeled Vehicle Repair, Distinguished Honor Graduate (Top student in class), 1995.
- Driver Training Course; trained in the operation of medium and heavy duty trucks, as well as the transportation of hazardous materials, 1995.
- Wrecker Operator Course; trained to operate rollback, winch, and block-and-tackle wreckers to recover stalled vehicles, 1995.
- Licensed to operate 6,000- and 10,000-lb. forklifts and other heavy power equipment.

**PERSONAL**  Excellent personal and professional references are available upon request.

Date

Exact Name of Person
Title or Position
Name of Company
Address (number and street)
Address (city, state, and zip)

## PRESIDENT & GENERAL MANAGER

This successful automobile industry entrepreneur is seeking a new challenge after a career which has included starting up dealerships, troubleshooting problems in existing dealerships as a consultant, and managing large-scale operations.

To whom it may concern:

With the enclosed resume, I would like to make you aware of my interest in contributing to your organization through my considerable management experience as well as my proven motivational, sales, and organizational skills.

Although most of my business savvy has come from "real-world" experience, I do hold an M.S. degree in Business Administration, a Master's degree in Guidance and Counseling, and a B.S. degree. After earning my college degree, I worked for several years as a High School Teacher until economics forced me to seek a simultaneous part-time job as a Salesman for used and new cars with a prominent dealership. That part-time job opened my eyes to my talent for selling cars and motivating others, and thus began an impressive career in the automotive industry.

After attending Ford Motor Company's two-year Dealer Trainee Program, I became General Manager of a Ford dealership. I was successful in turning around that dealership which had experienced multimillion-dollar losses in three previous years, and I led it to show a profit of $500,000—its first profit in four years. Subsequently, I served as a Consultant to start-up dealerships and to mature dealerships in need of a strong manager to resolve sales and profitability problems.

As General Sales Manager of another dealership, I played a key role in increasing market penetration by 60%. I was then recruited to serve as President and General Manager of a dealership. I led the company to achieve gross sales of $32 million a year along with a $1 million profit-before-tax income for three consecutive years. We received the Outstanding Dealer's Award for three consecutive years, and were recognized as a five-star dealer—the ultimate achievement in customer service—for two years.

Most recently, I have managed a successful start-up of a used car dealership which became a major force in the market in less than two years.

I can provide excellent personal and professional references at the appropriate time, and I can assure you that I am a dynamic individual with an outstanding reputation within the industry along with an aggressive bottom-line orientation.

Sincerely,

Carson Oleksiw

# CARSON OLEKSIW

1110½ Hay Street, Fayetteville, NC 28305  •  preppub@aol.com  •  (910) 483-6611

---

**OBJECTIVE**  To benefit an organization that can use a dynamic leader who has excelled in recruiting and training personnel, developing and implementing human resources policies, as well as troubleshooting problems with creative solutions.

**EDUCATION**  **Master of Science in Business Administration,** University of Tampa, Tampa, FL, 1999.
**Masters of Science in Guidance and Counseling,** Tampa State College, Tampa, FL.
**Bachelor of Science Degree,** Macklin University, Macklinburg, GA, 1988.
Completed two-year Dealer Trainee Program, Ford Motor Company, Detroit.

**EXPERIENCE**  **PRESIDENT & GENERAL MANAGER.** Carson's Used Cars, Tampa, FL (1999-02). Supervised 15 individuals including six sales professionals, two finance specialists, one manager, one assistant sales manager, office personnel, and the Recon Department.
- Founded a company which rapidly became a major competitor.

**PRESIDENT & GENERAL MANAGER.** Beverly Hills BMW, Beverly Hills, FL (1995-99). Supervised 60 individuals who included 18 sales professionals, two finance specialists, the Used Car Manager, the New Car Manager, the Service and Parts Manager, the Service Department, the Recon Department, and the office personnel.
- Led the company to achieve gross sales of $32 million a year, and achieved a $1 million profit-before-tax income for three consecutive years.
- Became recognized as a Five Star Dealer.
- Exceeded all goals and projections for growth, market share, and profitability; for example, doubled assigned market penetration each year for three consecutive years.
- Received "Just the Best" award and the Outstanding Dealer's Award for three consecutive years.

**GENERAL SALES MANAGER.** Bradenton Subaru, Brandenton, FL (1991-95). Supervised 10 sales professionals including the Used Car Manager, the New Car Manager, and the finance specialist.
- For this dealership with a $6 million inventory and gross sales of $25 million per year, increased market penetration by 60%.
- Was rated one of the top dealerships in FL.

**INTERIM OPERATOR & CONSULTANT.** Ford Motor Company (1983-91). Was recruited to serve as Interim Operator and Consultant by Ford Motor Company and placed in charge of a large dealership until a major buy/sell was negotiated and implemented; also acted as roving consultant and problem solver for new dealerships and for dealerships in trouble.
- As a consultant for one dealership in Wisconsin: In 90 days, turned around a franchise which had been losing $100,000 a month and restored it to profitability.
- As a consultant for an Indiana dealership: Led a new dealership to achieve phenomenal results in profitability and sales through effective advertising, merchandising, and expense control.
- Experience prior to 1983: Excelled in sales management roles with automobile dealerships in FL and WI.

**PERSONAL**  Excellent personal and professional references. Dynamic and results-oriented.

Date

Exact Name of Person
Title or Position
Name of Company
Address (no., street)
Address (city, state, zip)

**POWER PLANT MECHANIC**

Dear Exact Name of Person (or Dear Sir or Madam if answering a blind ad):

I would appreciate an opportunity to talk with you soon about how I could contribute to your organization through my technical knowledge and experience in power plant operations and electrical power production.

Recently serving as Power Plant Assistant Manager, I have become known as a skilled operator, technician, and supervisor. I have additionally been selected to oversee training programs and have found ways to upgrade training for greatly improved operational efficiency. Before my promotion to my current job, I had operated a 3.9 megawatt prime power plant for 10,000 hours of uninterrupted, error-free production.

As you will see from my resume, I have recently received my associate's degree in Electrical and Mechanical Technology and am continuing my education in a program leading to a degree in Business Management.

I am a person who believes that my dedication and eagerness to learn have allowed me to earn a reputation as a productive high-quality worker who can be counted on and can handle pressure calmly.

I hope you will welcome my call soon to arrange a brief meeting at your convenience to discuss your current and future needs and how I might serve them. Thank you in advance for your time.

Sincerely yours,


Paul T. Goshen

(Alternate last paragraph:
I hope you will call or write soon to suggest a time convenient for us to meet and discuss your current and future needs and how I might serve them. Thank you in advance for your time.)

# PAUL THOMAS GOSHEN

1110½ Hay Street, Fayetteville, NC 28305 • preppub@aol.com • (910) 483-6611

---

**OBJECTIVE**   To apply my outstanding technical knowledge of power production and power plant operations to an organization that can use a well-trained professional.

**TECHNICAL EXPERTISE**   Possess outstanding electrical and mechanical knowledge related to equipment and power generation systems including:

| | |
|---|---|
| Diesel generators — 15- to 1,250-kilowatt | General Electric switchgear |
| Circulating oil and water pumps | Crankshaft deflection gauges |
| Inside/outside Micrometers | Air compressors |
| Centrifuges | Multimeters |
| Dial indicators | Feeler gauges |

**EDUCATION & TRAINING**   **Associate of Science Degree in Electrical and Mechanical Technology**, Holyoke Community College, Holyoke, MA, 1992.
Am studying Business Management, the University of Massachusetts, Boston.
Excelled in specialized training in the following areas:

| | |
|---|---|
| Electrical power plant production | Diesel engine troubleshooting |
| Advanced electronic troubleshooting | Records management |
| Repair/maintenance of aircraft arresting systems | |

**EXPERIENCE**   **POWER PLANT MECHANIC.** Regional Power Plant of Boston, Boston, MA (2002-present). Was hired on the basis of error-free performance and proven leadership skill to handle a variety of operational areas in a 3.9-megawatt prime power plant with six 650-kilowatt Nordberg diesel generator sets, power plant subsystems, and auxiliary equipment.
- Establish maintenance and repair priorities and schedule plant operations.
- Maintain detailed equipment performance records and analyze data to ensure compliance with government operational guidelines. Inspect, troubleshoot, and maintain main station battery-charging systems, electrical distribution switchgear, and diesel generator sets.

**POWER PLANT OPERATOR** and **SHIFT SUPERVISOR.** City of Springfield, MA (1998-01). Supervised eight employees and conducted on-the-job training while ensuring efficiency and safety in a 3.9-megawatt prime power plant.
- Operated error-free for more than 10,000 hours over this period with no interruptions to service. Performed corrosion control services which saved the government $50,000.
- Maintained detailed records of instrument reading observations on six 650-kilowatt Nordberg diesel electric generator sets.

**POWER PRODUCTION SPECIALIST.** U.S. Air, Miami, FL (1995-97). Handled installation, operation, maintenance, and inspection of 15-100KW 60-hertz diesel generator sets.
- Greatly increased efficiency by totally reorganizing generator training.

**ELECTRIC POWER PRODUCTION TECHNICIAN.** Con Edison, Boston, MA (1992-94). Operated from two to four 1,250-kilowatt dual-fuel generator sets; inspected switchgear, engine, and generator components; observed and maintained records of pressure, temperature, levels, and operating conditions on all equipment.
- Played a key role in a project which resulted in a 20% increase in the plant's thermal efficiency by rebuilding two three-story cooling towers.

**PERSONAL**   Received two Air Force Achievement Medals for "exceptional job knowledge and outstanding leadership." Will relocate worldwide. Secret security clearance.

Date

Exact Name of Person
Title or Position
Name of Company
Address (street, no.)
Address (city, state, zip)

**PUBLIC RELATIONS SPECIALIST & SALES MANAGER**

Dear Exact Name of Person (or Dear Sir or Madam if answering a blind ad):

I would appreciate an opportunity to talk with you in person about my desire to serve the needs of Yamaha Motor Corporation as a Y.E.S. sales representative.

As you will see from my resume, I offer expert knowledge of and great enthusiasm for the Yamaha Extended Service (Y.E.S.) program. After initiating and implementing the Y.E.S. program for our dealership, I led the dealer to be named #1 in the country in sales of Y.E.S. contracts — we were 30 contracts ahead of the nearest competitor. In a 2002 contest, I won a CD player for selling the highest volume of Y.E.S. contracts in our district. I have played a key role in guiding the business to $2.9 million in sales from $1.6 million over a three-year period, and I have earned a reputation as a dependable hard worker with exceptional public relations, decision making, and promotional skills.

I also offer expert knowledge of the product made by Yamaha. The first new motorcycle I owned was a Yamaha — bought 18 years ago. I have owned eight Yamahas and have worked extensively on Yamaha motorcycles. I am very familiar with the mechanical aspects of such cycles, especially dirt bikes.

My sales skills are considered top-notch, and I attribute my sales expertise to the outstanding training I have received as well as the gifted sales professionals I have had the honor of working for. I feel I earned the equivalent of "a master's degree in sales" through the training I received from my boss of the last four years, Matt Donovan, who has more than 10 years of experience selling and administering extended service contracts including Y.E.S. contracts.

In addition to my expert product knowledge and sales skills, I also offer a thorough understanding of the Yamaha organization. I have had the honor of meeting both Japanese and U.S. presidents of Yamaha Motor Corporation at the national Yamaha dealer show in Tampa in 2003, and I am a personal friend of a professional racer for Team Yamaha. I have worked closely with several dealerships and know owners of many dealerships in GA.

I feel certain that you would find me to be a talented communicator who could become a valuable resource to the Yamaha organization as a Y.E.S. sales representative. I hope you will call or write me soon to suggest a time when we might meet to discuss the position in person.

Yours sincerely,

Daniel M. Thibbs

# DANIEL MICHAEL THIBBS

1110½ Hay Street, Fayetteville, NC 28305 • preppub@aol.com • (910) 483-6611

**OBJECTIVE**  To apply my knowledge and experience related to motorcycle sales and track design along with my skills in public relations to an organization in need of an enthusiastic and adaptable young professional.

**TRAINING and EDUCATION**  
**Excelled in specialized training including the following:**
- **Yamaha Extended Service (Y.E.S.)** — how to increase profits by selling Y.E.S. contracts- Valdosta, GA, 2001
- **Kawasaki Customer Service** — how to offer the best and most complete customer service – Columbia, SC, 2001
- **Finance and Insurance** — techniques for offering the best services to suit the customer's needs — the Clemson, SC, motorcycle trade show, 2002
- **HRSI Financing** — using the newest methods of providing insurance and financing — Winston-Salem, NC, 2002
- **Yamaha Water Vehicles** — seminars conducted by Charles Regent of the District Water Vehicle Division — Gainesville, GA, 2001-03
- **Yamaha Motorcycles** — "A New Day" — Tampa, FL, 2003

Completed two years of college course work.

**SPECIAL SKILLS and EXPERIENCE**
- Am currently involved in designing and building a super-cross track in Valdosta, GA, for the Jaycees.
- Offer seven years of professional motorcycle racing experience; have been riding Yamaha, Kawasaki, Honda, and Suzuki cycles for over 15 years.
- Am experienced in moto-cross track promotion and in scheduling events.
- Designed and built the Riders Up MX Raceway in Macon, GA.
- Have owned and operated personal watercrafts since 2000.

**EXPERIENCE**  **PUBLIC RELATIONS SPECIALIST** and **SALES MANAGER.** Donovan Enterprises, Inc., dba Donovan's Cycle World, Tampa, FL (2001-present). Increase sales and dealer visibility in the community while overseeing sales, customer service, marketing, and public relations.
- Initiated and put into place the Yamaha Extended Service contract program which led to increased dealer profits.
- Led the dealership to be named #1 in the country in sales of Y.E.S. contracts — we were 30 contracts ahead of the nearest competitor. In a 2002 national contest, won a CD player for selling the highest volume of Y.E.S. contracts in our district.
- Earned recognition among the "Top 50" Yamaha dealerships, out of more than 1,400 in the country, based on units sold and customer satisfaction.
- Introduced successful public relations ideas including giveaways and a demonstration ride program. Played a major role in the dealership's ability to operate and survive loss of revenue due to the economic setback.
- Guided the business to $2.9 million in sales from $1.6 in three years.
- Provide "behind-the-scenes" service by running credit checks, approving or disapproving loans, and handling paperwork to complete sales. Make decisions on displays.

**Other experience:** Earned a reputation as a dependable hard worker.
- Partially financed my education working in a Yamaha dealership, Gainesville, GA: assembled bikes and prepared them for sale.

**PERSONAL**  Am proud of my strong family background — belong to a large, close-knit Christian family.

Date

Exact Name of Person
Title or Position
Name of Company
Address (number and street)
Address (city, state, and zip)

**PURCHASING MANAGER,**
Industrial Materials
This junior professional is approaching a wide range of companies, including some companies in her industry. Although it is not likely that a company she approaches will contact her current employer before talking with her, she explicitly requests in the second paragraph of her letter that the reader hold her initial expression of interest in confidence.

Dear Exact Name of Person: (or Dear Sir or Madam if answering a blind ad.)

I would appreciate an opportunity to talk with you soon about how I could contribute to your organization through my extensive background in purchasing parts and services for a manufacturing firm.

You will see from my enclosed resume that I have been with Goodyear Consumer Products, Inc., in St. Louis, MO, for several years. Although I enjoy this position and have advanced with the company from a Materials Buyer position to Purchasing Manager, I am interested in confidentially exploring opportunities within your company.

Because of my ability to reduce costs and negotiate product contracts with a wide variety of vendors, I have received numerous awards and honors recognizing my purchasing expertise and management ability. I believe that you would find me to be an enthusiastic and outgoing professional who offers strong organizational abilities and attention to detail.

I hope you will welcome my call soon to arrange a brief meeting at your convenience to discuss your current and future needs and how I might serve them. Thank you in advance for your time.

Sincerely yours,


Dean Hardwick

(Alternate last paragraph:
I hope you will call or write me soon to suggest a time convenient for us to meet and discuss your current and future needs and how I might serve them. Thank you in advance for your time.)

# DEAN HARDWICK

1110½ Hay Street, Fayetteville, NC 28305 • preppub@aol.com • (910) 483-6611

---

**OBJECTIVE**  To offer my extensive background in purchasing and my aggressive bottom-line orientation to an organization that can use a positive and enthusiastic professional known for attention to detail as well as expertise in all aspects of purchasing both parts and services.

**EXPERIENCE**  **PURCHASING MANAGER & MATERIALS BUYER.** Goodyear Consumer Products, Inc., St. Louis, MO (2002-present). Began as a Materials Buyer and was promoted to Purchasing Manager in charge of a five-person department; provide oversight of the purchasing of a wide range of products valued at six million annually.
- Received a letter of appreciation from the company president in recognition of my accomplishments and contributions including my ability to continually reduce costs, June 2003.
- Wrote the standard operating procedures (SOPs) used by all purchasing department personnel, not only at the St. Louis central office but also at the 12 field offices.
- Oversee MRO (Maintenance, Repair, and Operating) purchasing contracts for plant services at 16 plants; negotiate contracts valued at $25 million annually.
- In 2003, negotiated a contract for additional commodities including labels and instruction books.
- Have acquired expertise in commodity buying including the purchasing of all electrical and electronic parts, fasteners, screw machine, and imported parts including finished goods.
- In 2002, chaired a task force which developed a new line of ceiling fans: the project was successfully completed ahead of schedule and within corporate budget guidelines and restrictions.
- On my own initiative, established a new buyer training program which has led to numerous efficiencies; set up a complete how-to system and oversaw the implementation of a new automated system used for tracking inventory and purchasing.

*Highlights of previous experience:* Refined skills as a Clerk/Typist and Secretary for a Human Relations/Equal Opportunity Office and the Director of Personnel and Community Affairs for an Army post in Germany.
- Earned several letters and certificates of commendation and a Sustained Performance Award in recognition of my professionalism and accomplishments as a government employee.

Became familiar with the functions of a purchasing office as a Departmental Secretary, Goodyear Industries, Inc., St. Louis, MO.

Gained experience in jobs as a Office Clerk/Claims Handler/Dispatcher for a trucking company and Real Estate Salesperson.

**EDUCATION**  **Associate of Science degree in Industrial Management Technology,** St. Louis Technical Community College, MO, 1999.
Completed 60 credit hours in **Personnel Management** through a correspondence course.
Attended Bohecker's Business College, Ravenna, OH: received training in the field of executive secretarial duties.

**PERSONAL**  Active in church activities, have served as vice president and secretary of the women's organization; served on the finance committee. Am a friendly and enthusiastic individual.

Date

Exact Name of Person
Title or Position
Name of Company
Address (number and street)
Address (city, state, and zip)

**QUALITY CONTROL INSPECTOR**

Dear Exact Name of Person (or Sir or Madam if answering a blind ad):

I would appreciate an opportunity to talk with you soon about how I could contribute to your organization through the application of my knowledge and skills in the field of transportation.

In my current position, I provide technical advice and guidance as well as training support for all levels of vehicle maintenance and operations. My responsibilities include providing quality control inspections and monitoring maintenance programs. I also conduct safety inspections to ensure vehicles are maintained in accordance with organizational and government regulations. In all positions I have filled, I have earned numerous awards and accolades for my expertise in planning and supervising transportation operations throughout the world in locations which have included Germany and Japan.

You will see from my enclosed resume that I am accustomed to overseeing multimillion-dollar inventories of vehicles and associated equipment and have provided direct supervision for a work forces as large as 300 civilian employees. I have specialized in providing transportation on a large scale for both personnel and cargo by rail, air, highway, and water for international and domestic shipment.

If you can use a well-trained and knowledgeable logistics and transportation specialist who can provide leadership, supervision, and control for shipment of cargo and/or personnel, I hope you will call or write me soon to suggest a time convenient for us to meet and discuss your current and future needs and how I might serve them. Thank you in advance for your time.

Sincerely,

Gary N. Sheckles

# GARY N. SHECKLES

1110½ Hay Street, Fayetteville, NC 28305 • preppub@aol.com • (910) 483-6611

---

**OBJECTIVE**     To offer my strong background in transportation and logistics support activities to an organization that can benefit from my knowledge of domestic and international shipping of both personnel and cargo by train, truck, plane, or ship.

**EXPERIENCE**     **QUALITY CONTROL INSPECTOR.** Airborne Express, Ann Arbor, MI (2003-present). Provide technical assistance and guidance as well as training support for all levels of maintenance and driver support for a fleet of more than 250 vehicles.

- Inspect maintenance programs of subordinate units for violations of maintenance and safety procedures and requirements. Conduct safety inspections to ensure vehicles are maintained in accordance with organizational and government regulations; prepare special and regular reports.
- Contributed to the successful integration of a new type of vehicle into operations.

**HIGHWAY OPERATIONS SUPERVISOR.** All America Auto Transport, Detroit, MI (2000-02). Received several awards for my accomplishments while supervising a transportation and maintenance section with equipment valued at $4.5 million; supervised 33 people.

- Negotiated transportation costs and contracts with carriers and scheduled routes for motor transport equipment; managed a $1.5 million annual operating budget.
- Inputted data and used a PC-generated spreadsheet for preparing monthly usage reports.
- Trained and then certified at least 20 tractor-trailer truck drivers.

**VEHICLE MAINTENANCE AND OPERATIONS SUPERVISOR.** Samson Construction Company, Flint, MI (1997-99). Trained and supervised 30 employees while providing technical guidance on maintenance and operations.

- Controlled a $2.5 million inventory of 11 five-ton trucks, seven 2-1/2-ton trucks, and 12 40-foot tractor trailers along with associated tools and equipment.
- Prepared regular reports to management on department expenses, safety record, and vehicle availability. Contributed my knowledge during the testing phase for new vehicles which were being integrated into the company's inventory.

**TRUCKING COMPANY SUPERVISOR.** Universal Truck & Auto, Inc., Berlin, Germany (1994-96). Received several awards and the praise of the U.S. Ambassador to Germany for my leadership which ensured the availability and efficient utilization of a fleet of more than 60 commercial vehicles, sedans, trucks, and buses and a transportation budget of $3.5 million.

**OPERATIONS SUPERVISOR.** Allied Van Lines, Tokyo, Japan (1991-93). Supervised six subordinates and maintained records for a fleet of 60 five-ton tractors, 150 2-1/2-ton trailers, and 20 five-ton cargo trucks.

- Led the company to accumulate more than 200,000 accident-free miles in four months.

**OPERATIONS MANAGER.** Old Dominion Freight Line Co., Richmond, VA (1987-90). Supervised 21 employees maintaining and operating a fleet of 10-ton trucks and a light van: trained personnel in vehicle maintenance, loading, safe driving, and record keeping.

**EDUCATION & TRAINING**     Pursing **Associate in Applied Science Transportation,** University of Michigan, Ann Arbor, MI. Completed advanced coursework in transportation operations, management, and leadership as well as in MS Office and spreadsheets, hazardous material handling, and safety.

**PERSONAL**     Member, American Society of Transportation and the National Transportation Association.

Date

Exact Name of Person
Title or Position
Name of Company
Address (no., street)
Address (city, state, zip)

**REGIONAL MARKETING REPRESENTATIVE**

Dear Exact Name of Person (or Dear Sir or Madam if answering a blind ad):

Can you use an adaptable young professional who calmly handles pressure, is highly self-motivated and excels in motivating others, and offers a "track record" of rapid progression?

As you will see from my resume, I have worked for three employers and in each case earned promotions and advancement to increasing levels of responsibility on the basis of my performance. I offer a reputation as a very fast learner who can provide expertise in numerous areas ranging from sales, to office and computer operations, to credit analysis and marketing.

In my most recent position with Paramount Automotive Acceptance Corp. in Fort Worth, TX, I earned promotion from Administrative Assistant to Credit Analyst to Regional Marketing Representative over a four-year period. I helped develop programs which increased the company's volume and scope of business while displaying a talent for organization and attention to detail.

I feel that as a self-starter and fast learner known for my adaptability, I offer valuable skills which could make me an asset to your organization.

I hope you will welcome my call soon to arrange a brief meeting at your convenience to discuss your current and future needs and how I might serve them. Thank you in advance for your time.

Sincerely yours,


Rachel Ann Jamieson


(Alternate last paragraph:
I hope you will call or write soon to suggest a time convenient for us to meet and discuss your current and future needs and how I might serve them. Thank you in advance for your time.)

# RACHEL ANN JAMIESON

1110½ Hay Street, Fayetteville, NC 28305 • preppub@aol.com • (910) 483-6611

**OBJECTIVE**  To contribute to an organization that can use a mature young professional who offers a proven ability to learn quickly and adapt easily through the application of outstanding planning, organizational, and communication skills as well as a talent for motivating others.

**EXPERIENCE**  *Built a "track record" with Paramount Automotive Acceptance Corp., Fort Worth, TX:*
**REGIONAL MARKETING REPRESENTATIVE.** (2003-present). Was successful in maintaining and expanding the company's base of automobile dealers as well as in marketing the advantages of the company's services to prospective new dealerships.
- Produced a "well-designed" Corporate Dealership Training Manual and the layout for a hand-held calculator programmed specifically to meet company needs.
- Played a major role in establishing the guidelines for this newly created position and personally trained and serviced 70% of the dealer base.
- Apply my outstanding communication and listening skills while working closely with personnel from the Better Business Bureau, Chamber of Commerce, Dunn and Bradstreet, and Army Community Services to investigate and gather information.
- Use my outstanding organizational skills while setting up and scheduling meetings and training sessions in addition to ensuring dealer files are always up to date.

**CREDIT ANALYST.** (2001-03). Reviewed credit applications, making sure information was complete and met corporate guidelines and policies; analyzed this data to make informed credit decisions in order to maximize credit purchases and minimize losses.
- Was a major force in the development of a program which purchased civilian contracts for a company which had previously dealt almost entirely with military customers.
- Purchased approximately $300,000 in contracts each month.
- Earned a reputation for objectivity, creativity, and flexibility under pressure.

**ADMINISTRATIVE ASSISTANT.** (1999-01). Learned and refined computer operating skills and responded with "tact and diplomacy" to customer and dealer inquiries and complaints while maintaining files, handling clerical duties, processing payments, and investigating and gathering information from credit bureau and customer files.
- Earned promotion to Credit Analyst on the basis of my professionalism.
- Processed in excess of $400,000 in loans in my first month with the company.

*Refined my sales and clerical skills in this progression with Moore's Jewelers:*
**SALES ASSOCIATE.** Augusta, GA (1998). Gained experience in selling fine jewelry.

**SALES ASSOCIATE.** Columbus, GA (1995-97). Handled a variety of daily functions ranging from processing items brought in for repairs, tagging items for sale, conducting daily inventories, and ringing up sales. Discovered and refined my "natural" sales abilities.

**ADMINISTRATIVE ASSISTANT. Columbus**, GA (1994). Applied my attention to detail while assisting in processing mail and walk-in payments, entering payment data in the computers, ringing up sales, preparing daily bank deposits, and conducting inventories.

**SPECIAL SKILLS**
- Operate 10-key calculators, typewriters, and multi-line phones.
- Troubleshoot computer problems and am experienced in Word and Excel

**PERSONAL**  Am recognized as a highly self-motivated professional who excels in leading and motivating others. Offer a reputation for flexibility and adaptability. Will travel.

Date

Exact Name of Person
Title or Position
Name of Company
Address (number and street)
Address (city, state, and zip)

**RENTAL AGENT SUPERVISOR**

Dear Exact Name of Person (or Sir or Madam if answering a blind ad):

With the enclosed resume, I would like to express my interest in exploring employment opportunities with your organization.

As you can see from my enclosed resume, I am a management professional experienced in all phases of the car rental industry, including general sales management. Currently I am the Rental Agent Supervisor at AAA Car Rental in Chicago. Although I am held in high regard by the executives of this busy agency, I have made the decision to selectively explore other opportunities and would ask that my interest in your organization be kept in confidence at this time.

If you can use an astute manager who excels in finding solutions for the tough problems while leading the way to increased sales, profitability, and customer satisfaction, I hope you will contact me to suggest a time when we might meet to discuss your needs. I can provide outstanding references at the appropriate time.

Sincerely,

Serena M. Alvarez

# SERENA MARIA ALVAREZ

1110½ Hay Street, Fayetteville, NC 28305 • preppub@aol.com • (910) 483-6611

---

**OBJECTIVE**  I want to contribute to an organization that can use a hard-working professional with a background of accomplishments in the car rental industry, along with outstanding communication skills, public relations know-how, hands-on computer experience, as well as my experience in training and supervising employees.

**EXPERIENCE**  **RENTAL AGENT SUPERVISOR.** AAA Car Rental, Chicago, IL (2003-present). Use the SABRA computer system to make automobile reservations for clients needing local and national transportation.
- Train and supervise new rental agents.
- Reconcile internal agency problems.
- Record and deposit daily transactions.
- Through my strong customer service and sales skills, have made significant contributions to record profitability in 2003 despite sour economic conditions.

**RESERVATIONIST.** Travelers' Club, Inc., Chicago, IL (2001-2003). Through the use of the PARS computer system was able to process car rental and hotel reservations.
- Made reservations for up to 100 members via telephone.
- Provided club members with current company information.
- Coordinated hotel timeshare accommodations for multinational customers.
- Rented limousines and arranged for long-distance taxi rides and rental cars.

**CAR RENTAL AGENT.** Enterprise Rent-A-Car, Tucson, AZ (1998-2001). Through the use of my excellent people skills was able to successfully accommodate the transportation needs of a primarily Spanish-speaking clientele.
- Rapidly obtained a working knowledge of the Spanish language.
- Provided insurance rates and service replacement rates for clients involved in automobile accidents.

**CUSTOMER SERVICE SUPERVISOR.** Yokum Family Restaurant, Costa Mesa, CA (1996-1998). While supervising and training employees, effectively resolved customer complaints to maintain a high standard of customer satisfaction.
- Trained and supervised three cashiers and a wait staff of 12.
- Coordinated restaurant operations with management and corporate offices.

**TELEMARKETING MANAGER.** Diamond Specialty Construction, Orange, CA (1993-1996). Controlled the daily operations of a busy telemarketing office while supervising and training employees.
- Established an extensive potential clientele sales database.
- Trained four employees to be effective telemarketers.

**CUSTOMER SERVICE SUPERVISOR.** Johnny's Big Boy Restaurant, Glendale, CA (1992-1993). Used my public relations skills to ensure customer satisfaction, handling customer complaints and requests.
- Trained new employees.
- Supervised cashiers and bus boys.

**PERSONAL**  Have ability to motivate others to perform at maximum potential. Enjoy dealing with the public. Outstanding references on request.

Date

Exact Name of Person
Exact Title of Position
Exact Name of Company
Address (no., street)
Address (city, state, zip)

**SALES CONSULTANT**

Dear Exact Name of Person (or Dear Sir or Madam if answering a blind ad):

With the enclosed resume, I am writing to express my strong interest in joining your organization in some capacity which can utilize a dynamic communicator and "make-it-happen" young professional with a strong bottom-line orientation along with excellent customer service skills.

As you will see from my resume, I have been excelling since 2000 in a field where women are often not successful. As a Sales Consultant with a well regarded car dealership, I have been recognized as "Sales Consultant of the Month" numerous times while earning a reputation as a congenial colleague. In my prior position with a company in the transportation industry, I earned rapid advancement because of my resourcefulness, problem-solving skills, and customer relations abilities.

Although I can provide outstanding personal and professional references at the appropriate time, I do ask that you not contact my current employer until we have a chance to meet and talk in person.

I can assure you that I could become a valuable asset to your organization, as I have to every employer for whom I have worked. I am a current resident of Conway and graduated from R.U. Mitchell High School in 1999, so I can assure you that my roots in the community are permanent. I am seeking an organization I can contribute to and grow with over the long-term.

If you can use a proven performer with versatile sales experience and office skills, I hope you will contact me to suggest a time at your convenience when we might meet to discuss your needs. Thank you in advance for your time.

Sincerely,

Julia E. Samuels

# JULIA E. SAMUELS

1110½ Hay Street, Fayetteville, NC 28305  •  preppub@aol.com  •  (910) 483-6611

---

**OBJECTIVE**  To benefit an organization that can use a dynamic communicator, quick learner, and proven sales professional who offers skills related to customer service and word processing along with a reputation as a loyal and reliable hard worker and creative problem solver.

**EDUCATION**  Graduated from R.U. Mitchell High School, Conway, AR, 1999.
Obtained annual certification as a Certified Sales Professional, and always scored between 89% and 95% on all portions of sales certification exams.
Completed extensive training sponsored by Subaru Auto in these and other areas:
Understanding Your Customers      Selling in the New Millennium
Effective Sales Prospecting       Professional Telephone Skills

**EXPERIENCE**  **SALES CONSULTANT.** Guillard Mazda Dealers, Conway, AR (2003-present). Have been recognized as "Sales Consultant of the Month" ten times, and have contributed to the growth and profitability of the company in numerous other ways while becoming known as a dependable hard worker and congenial colleague.
- Act as a model/spokesperson for the dealership in television commercials.
- Represent the company at training seminars related to finance and leasing.
- Train new employees in all aspects of selling automobiles including completing the extensive paperwork required to close the sale.
- Established a loyal base of repeat customers and obtain a strong word-of-mouth business while building a base of referrals, prospecting for new customers, and converting new prospects into clients.
- Have thoroughly enjoyed representing a line of outstanding automotive products, and became known for my enthusiastic sales style as well as my honest presentation.
- Utilize computer programs to locate products and to research products.

**CUSTOMER SERVICE COORDINATOR.** Thompson's Transportation & Distribution Center, Little Rock, AR (2000-03). After securing employment with Tempo Temporary Services, excelled in a long-term assignment with a company in the transportation industry; became known as a gracious and articulate communicator while working with rental car customers and rental agents as well as with customers seeking outbound shipment of private automobiles.
- Utilized Microsoft Access and Excel while preparing, searching, and transmitting information needed for outbound shipments and rental car services; input delivery dates.
- Made myself very valuable to my supervisor, who increasingly turned to me for assistance in solving difficult customer problems with resourcefulness and tact.
- Was being groomed for rapid promotion, but my husband was transferred.

*Highlights of other experience:*
**RENTAL ASSISTANT.** Century 21 Realtors, Conway, AR (1999-00). For a major realty company, assisted rental agents in all aspects of rental management; received rental applications, determined suitability of applicants, prepared and explained rental agreements, collected rent and security deposit monies, received repair and maintenance requests, completed tenant termination forms, and reviewed computer reports.

**CLERK/SECRETARIAL ASSISTANT.** Town Hall of Conway and City Council's Office, Conway, AR (1998-99). Worked during the summers and after school while in high school.

**PERSONAL**  Am known for my ingenuity, resourcefulness, and creativity.

Date

Exact Name of Person
Title or Position
Name of Company
Address (number and street)
Address (city, state, and zip)

**SALES REPRESENTATIVE**

Dear Exact Name of Person (or Sir or Madam if answering a blind ad):

I would appreciate an opportunity to talk with you soon about how I could contribute to your organization through my versatile experience, education, and the application of my analytical, problem-solving, and organizational skills.

As you will see from my enclosed resume, I serve as Sales Representative for Valley Ford-Lincoln-Mercury in Santa Clara, CA. At Valley Ford, I have consistently averaged 15 unit sales per month as well as doubling the per unit back-end and developing relationships with alternative finance organizations. I am known for my ability to find a way to "get a deal bought." I have received my B.S. degree in Political Science from Rollins College in Winter Park, FL.

Earlier experience includes Front Office Supervisor at Days Inn, San Diego, CA, where I juggled multiple responsibilities. I developed excellent communication, organization, and customer relations skills while making reservations and scheduling group conventions, forecasting, and reconciling rate discrepancies.

I am an enthusiastic, energetic, and outgoing individual who is known for my attention to detail and my ability to handle pressure and deadlines with professionalism and control.

I hope you will welcome my call soon to arrange a brief meeting to discuss your current and future needs and how I might serve them. Thank you in advance for your time.

Sincerely,

Josh N. Charles

(Alternate last paragraph:
I hope you will call or write me soon to suggest a time convenient for us to meet and discuss your current and future needs and how I might serve them. Thank you in advance for your time.)

# JOSH NATHAN CHARLES

1110½ Hay Street, Fayetteville, NC 28305  •  preppub@aol.com  •  (910) 483-6611

---

**OBJECTIVE**  To continue to contribute to the success and prosperity of a major automobile dealership through my talents as an articulate manager, skilled motivator, and creative problem solver as well as through my reputation as an outstanding sales professional with a flair for finding alternative finance avenues.

**EDUCATION**  **Bachelor of Science Degree in Political Science,** Rollins College, Winter Park, FL, 1992.

**EXPERIENCE**  **SALES REPRESENTATIVE.** Valley Ford-Lincoln-Mercury, Santa Clara, CA (2002-present). Have consistently averaged 15-unit sales per month as well as doubling the per unit back-end while also developing relationships with alternative finance organizations and becoming known for my ability to find a way to "get a deal bought."
- Became known as the "resident computer expert" as the Systems Manager while handling upgrades and technical troubleshooting, as well as serving as software support technician while mastering CrediNet, CompuServe, ADP, Dashboard For Windows, and Concepts software programs.
- On my own initiative, successfully completed Consumer Finance Management training through the Apex Group, 12/02.

**FRONT OFFICE SUPERVISOR.** Days Inn, San Diego, CA (1999-02). Juggled multiple responsibilities within this busy front office serving corporate-level customers from around the world.
- Computed and monitored average daily rate (ADR).
- Refined computer knowledge while working on a variety of systems including Holidex 2000, MSI, Tesa Lock System, and WordPerfect. Earned a track record of success using Signature Marketing Program after three months of extensive implementation.
- Developed excellent communication, organization, and customer relations skills while making reservations and scheduling group conventions, forecasting, and reconciling rate discrepancies.
- Honed general accounting skills while performing accounts payable/receivable functions.

**FRONT OFFICE MANAGER.** King Motel, El Cajon, CA (1996-99). Supervised 15 desk clerks and the housekeeping staff while ensuring that the administrative operations of the organization were precisely followed.
- Performed payroll functions, managed time cards, and handled promotions and raises.
- Ensured that employees were scheduled according to booking ratios.

**FRONT DESK SUPERVISOR.** Palace Hotel, Fort Lauderdale, FL (1992-94). Refined management and organizational skills while administratively supervising this 425-room hotel with 10 three-bedroom suites, catering to foreign dignitaries and VIPs.
- Used my bilingual skills to help register international guests and dignitaries.
- Ensured standard front office procedures were followed and improved the ADR.
- Earned quick advancement from restaurant supervisor to desk clerk and then to Front Desk Supervisor when Park Plaza was bought by Omni.
- Applied my marketing and communication skills to increase and build loyal clientele.

**PERSONAL**  Am an extremely articulate and highly motivated team player with a "do-whatever-it-takes" attitude; always willing to go the extra mile for the satisfaction in a job well done. Am extremely computer-literate with knowledge of multiple operating systems as well as experience using most software packages.

Date

Exact Name of Person
Title or Position
Name of Company
Address (no., street)
Address (city, state, zip)

**SALES REPRESENTATIVE & EUROPEAN DELIVERY MANAGER**

Dear Exact Name of Person:

I believe I am exactly the person you are looking for in your recent employment ad for an aggressive, hard-driving district sales manager for Volvo sales in the Jackson, MS area.

These 3 highlights in particular from my resume will, I hope, illustrate why I am the dynamic, experienced, proven sales professional you seek:

- I already have demonstrated my ability and desire to contribute to the continued success of imported automobiles through numerous sales honors awarded on the basis of superior product knowledge as well as excellent "people" skills.

- In my current job as a Sales Representative and Import Delivery Manager, I have developed an outstanding track record as an excellent trainer, manager, and sales "pro" in a highly competitive market. Frankly, however, sales success has been easier for me to achieve because I am so truly proud to represent exciting, unique product line and I have developed an intimate understanding of ideal customer.

- I am dedicated to a career in auto sales and would thoroughly enjoy the travel of a district manager's life. I am fortunate to have the natural energy, industry, and enthusiasm required to put in the long hours necessary for effective sales performance and management.

I am certain I could be enormously valuable to Volvo at the district level through my excellent experience with and technical training regarding its products, its customers, and its employees. And I am equally sure you would find me in person to be a warm, energetic young professional who is thoroughly "sold" on Volvo.

I hope you will call or write me soon to suggest a time convenient for us to meet and discuss your current and future needs and how I might serve them. Thank you in advance for your time.

Yours sincerely,

Thomas D. Hammonds

# THOMAS D. HAMMONDS

1110½ Hay Street, Fayetteville, NC 28305  •  preppub@aol.com  •  (910) 483-6611

---

**OBJECTIVE**  I want to contribute to the success of an organization that can use a dynamic sales professional who has distinguished himself through numerous sales accomplishments on the basis of superior product knowledge as well as excellent "people" skills.

**EXPERIENCE**  **SALES REPRESENTATIVE AND EUROPEAN DELIVERY MANAGER.** Bob Maddox Auto Imports, Jackson, MS (2003-present). Train, motivate, and manage a 4-person sales force selling 6 lines of imported automobiles in a highly-competitive market serving a diverse regional clientele, including Naval and Marine professionals.
- Use historical data and business judgment to project monthly sales quotas.
- Keep sales force informed on changes in "Import Development Program."
- Maintain a sales force that is thoroughly "product knowledgeable" of the European lines.
- Have developed the "art" and expertise of selling to and servicing "high-line" automobile customers.

**SALES REPRESENTATIVE.** Coastal BMW Sales, Jackson, MS (1999-03). Developed quickly into a top performing salesperson by mastering proven techniques related to high-volume automobile sales.
- Learned valuable time management skills in organizing my own daily work schedule for maximum productivity.
- Earned a reputation as a "whiz" at turning a prospect into a sale.

**OPERATIONS MANAGER.** Sears, Jackson, MS (1996-99). Handled wide-ranging responsibilities related to merchandising management, wholesale buying, and inventory control. Supervised 3 people.
- Improved the efficiency of a profitable department.
- Developed "attention to detail" philosophy in performing the discipline of daily reconciliation of department activities.

**STORE MANAGER.** Dillard's, Jackson, MS (1995-96). For a busy, top-of-the-line clothing store, supervised 4 sales associates while developing excellent skills in store management and customer relations.

**TRAINING**  Excelled in numerous sales and management training programs, including:
BMW "Product Knowledge and Technical Training" and Volvo: "Drive and Buy Program", Saab: "Intro-line", and the Mazda: "Drive and Buy Program."

**SALES AWARDS**  Have won numerous sales honors awarded to "Salesperson of the Quarter" and based on precise test scores and seminar performance, 2003-04.

**PERSONAL**  Have capability for learning new things quickly. Enjoy motivating others to excel. Have an ability to make an excellent first impression on customers. Am flexible and adaptable.

Date

Exact Name of Person
Title or Position
Name of Company
Address (number and street)
Address (city, state, and zip)

**SALES MANAGER**
for an automobile dealership
A desire to move up to a General Manager position is the motivation behind this resume and cover letter.

Dear Exact Name of Person: (or Sir or Madam if answering a blind ad.)

With the enclosed resume, I would like to make you aware of my desire to become General Manager of a BMW Automobile Dealership.

As you will see from my enclosed resume, I have excelled in a track record of accomplishment with BMW of Columbia, MD. I am proud of the results I achieved as Sales Manager, Finance & Insurance Manager, Used Car Manager, and General Sales Manager. My exceptionally strong leadership skills have been refined in the highly competitive environment of the automobile sales business, and I offer a reputation as a powerful leader and motivator with the ability to inspire people to perform to their highest levels of competence. You will notice on my resume that I have used my outstanding personal reputation and ability to influence others to take action in high-visibility community leadership roles when a trusted leader was needed to take on a tough job and mobilize people to accomplish difficult tasks.

I am willing to relocate according to company needs in order to accomplish my goal of becoming General Manager of a dealership. I can assure you in advance that I am confident in my ability to take a good dealership and make it great or to transform a troubled operation into a well-oiled machine. My skills as a motivator and team builder are highly respected, and I can provide outstanding references throughout the industry.

Please favorably consider my desire to take the next logical step in my career of becoming a General Manager and suggest a time when we might meet to discuss your goals and how I might help you achieve them. I will look forward to your response.

Yours sincerely,

William Cislak

# WILLIAM CISLAK

1110½ Hay Street, Fayetteville, NC 28305 • preppub@aol.com • (910) 483-6611

---

**OBJECTIVE**  To benefit an organization that can use a General Manager with exceptional motivational and communication skills who offers a strong background as a sales trainer and a track record of excellence as a general sales manager, used car manager, and finance manager.

**EDUCATION**  **Bachelor of Arts degree in Philosophy,** University of Florida, Gainesville, FL, 1994.
**Associate of Arts in General Education,** Florida Community College, Jacksonville, FL, 1992.

**COMMUNITY LEADERSHIP**  **Offer a reputation as a highly respected local leader who believes in helping my community:**
**2001-03:** Appointed President, Columbia Middle School Athletic Booster Club; organized the club from scratch, served as its first president, and created revenue-generating plans.
**1998-00:** President, Columbia Sports Association. Took control of a small athletic association comprised of 8 teams totaling 120 people and, in three years, transformed it into a 43-team organization with more than 700 people affiliated. Established new programs for children including flag football and persuaded city government to better equip fields.

**EXPERIENCE**  *With BMW of Columbia, MD, have advanced in the following "track record":*
*2002-present:* **SALES MANAGER.** Advanced to this position after excelling as Used Car Manager and Sales Manager, was tasked with the additional responsibility of overseeing the operation of the entire sales department; continued to serve as Used Car Manager.
- Supervise up to 14 employees, including Automotive Sales Representatives, Finance Managers, and Sales Managers.
- Serve as director of employee training for all departments; track completion of training courses required by BMW and ensure that all employees receive proper instruction.
- Achieved and consistently maintain a Customer Service Index of #1 among all Automotive Group dealerships.
- New car sales consistently exceed National, South Area, and Territory averages.

*1999-02:* **USED CAR MANAGER.** Promoted from a Sales Man position; responsible for managing all operational aspects of the Used Car department.
- Monitor used car inventory, ensuring that the dealership doesn't become overstocked, controlling the number of overaged units, and ordering program vehicles to meet the dealership's needs.
- Perform appraisals of vehicles being traded in based on condition, black book value, and existing unsold inventory of the same or similar used vehicles.
- Due to my initiative, net profit for the used car department increased by 47%, and is currently returning a net-to-gross profit ratio greater than 29%; the used car department is consistently ranked in the top four among all BMW dealerships.

*1996-99:* **SALES MANAGER and FINANCE & INSURANCE MANAGER.** Hired by BMW of Columbia to serve as Sales Manager of the existing sales team; also acted as a backup Finance and Insurance Manager.
- Supervised a staff of Automotive Sales Representatives; set daily, weekly, and monthly sales goals and motivated them to achieve or exceed those goals.
- As Finance Manager, maximized the dealership's profit by selling and promoting the sale of aftermarket products such as extended warranties and credit life insurance.

**Other experience: DIRECTOR OF TRAINING and INSURANCE SALES REPRESENTATIVE.** Nationwide Insurance, Columbia, MD (1995-96). Supervised training of all new and existing Nationwide agents for all of Maryland, teaching sales techniques, products, and services.

**PERSONAL**  Excellent personal and professional references on request. Outstanding reputation.

# CAREER CHANGE: from military to civilian

Date

Exact Name of Person
Exact Title
Exact Name of Company
Address
City, State, Zip

**SENIOR ADVISOR & LOGISTICIAN**

Dear Exact Name of Person (or Dear Sir or Madam if answering a blind ad):

With the enclosed resume, I would like to make you aware of my experience and accomplishments as well as the multiple abilities I offer in diverse areas including logistics and inventory control management, law enforcement, and human resource management.

As you will see from my resume, I have advanced to the highest enlisted rank of Command Sergeant Major in the U.S. Army. I was handpicked for my current position as Senior Advisor and Logistician because of my outstanding reputation and diverse background. While supervising 37% of Army training at 20 different geographical locations in 8 states, I have transformed a stagnant mid-level management training program into a vital, relevant, executive-level training experience. I have also improved retention of quality employees through better communication and creative job re-engineering.

In my previous assignment as a Senior Advisor and Consultant for a 6,250-person organization in Fort Carson, CO, I was cited as a "dynamic leader with impeccable judgment." In a senior leadership role with this logistics organization which provided support services for personnel located at sites throughout the Southwest, I was described as a "visionary leader" who truly cared about the personal and professional problems and circumstances of personnel within the organization. As a mentor and counselor, I developed improvements to all areas of training, living and working conditions, and issues which impacted on morale.

Throughout a distinguished career I have excelled in high-visibility roles where my expertise in logistics management and my skills with people have combined to result in better working conditions, improved productivity, and strong results in every measurable area of operations. Widely recognized as an innovative thinker and creative problem solver, I have been recognized with honors which include a Humanitarian Service Medal, two U.S. Army Commendation Medals, and three Meritorious Service Medals.

If you can use a mature and self-confident management professional with a reputation for high moral and ethical standards along with a concerned and fair manner of dealing with others, I hope you will call me soon to suggest a time when we might meet and discuss your organization's needs and how I could help meet them.

Sincerely,

Jason Griffin

# JASON GRIFFIN
1110½ Hay Street, Fayetteville, NC 28305  •  preppub@aol.com  •  (910) 483-6611

---

**OBJECTIVE**   To offer a distinguished track record of accomplishments and reputation as an assertive, dedicated, and visionary management professional with a background in such diverse areas as logistics and inventory control management, training/counseling, and law enforcement.

**EDUCATION**   **Associate of Science Degree in Liberal Arts, concentration in Law Enforcement,** University of California-Army Branch, Fort Irwin, CA.

**EXPERIENCE**   *Advanced to the highest enlisted rank of Command Sergeant Major while excelling in multiple roles requiring planning, motivational, and resource management expertise, U.S. Army:*

**SENIOR ADVISOR & LOGISTICIAN.** U.S. Army, Fort Irwin, CA (2003-present). Was handpicked for this position which involves supervising 37% of Army training which is conducted at 20 different geographical locations in 8 states.
- Am the trusted "right arm" and advisor to a CEO; provide counsel on matters affecting the quality of life for over 45,000 officers, enlisted soldiers, and their families.
- Took over a stagnant mid-level management training program (the noncommissioned officer training program) and transformed it into a vital executive training experience which is thoroughly relevant to modern needs.
- Manage the human resources function related to the professional retention of a workforce of 2,500 people. Have significantly improved the retention of quality individuals through better communication and resourceful job re-engineering.

**SENIOR ADVISOR AND CONSULTANT.** U.S. Army, Ft. Carson, CO (2001-03). Cited as a "dynamic leader with impeccable judgment," advised the senior executive of a logistics organization with more than 6,250 people on personnel and quality-of-life issues as the leader of 20 subordinate human resources/personnel administration managers throughout Southwest.
- Was recognized as a "hands-on" counselor and mentor who cared deeply about the issues and problems faced by military personnel and 8,250 family members.

**LOGISTICS COMMAND SENIOR ADVISOR.** Panama City, Panama (1998-01). Consistently evaluated as a "principled leader" and "aggressive and innovative problem solver," managed operational logistics support and an annual budget of $255 million for an organization with 7,950 people dispersed throughout 75 separate installations.

**SUPPORT SERVICES MANAGER.** US Army, Ft. Drum, NY (1995-98). Recognized for my sound recommendations and high standards, managed a support group for 12 installations and 12 communications sites in an organization with a $48 million annual operating budget and more than 12,850 combined personnel and family members.
- Managed a diverse organization with an airfield, training center, and large supply center while revitalizing all levels of training as well as living quarters maintenance programs.

**MANAGER OF HUMAN RESOURCES AND PERSONNEL ADMINISTRATION.** US Army, Fort Hood, TX (1988-94). Was recognized as a "tireless and totally selfless" leader while holding this position in three consecutive assignments overseeing a wide range of administrative, training, team building, and health issues and advising senior management on related issues and concerns for organizations with as many as 175 personnel.

**PERSONAL**   Consistently recognized for high standards, integrity, morals, and work ethic.

Date

Exact Name of Person
Exact Title
Exact Name of Company
Address
City, State, Zip

**SENIOR CLAIMS REPRESENTATIVE**

Dear Exact Name of Person (or Dear Sir or Madam if answering a blind ad):

With the attached resume, I would like to make you aware of my interest in the position as Claims Manager for your West Phoenix, AZ office. I feel as though my expertise and skills would be assets for Chrysler Dodge in the Material Damage Claims Manager position.

**Extensive claims expertise**

Shortly after receiving my college degree from University of Arizona, I embarked upon a career as a Claims Representative and I have been promoted to Senior Claims Representative and Office Team Leader within Chrysler Dodge. While excelling in all aspects of my job, I have contributed significantly to numerous task forces designed to improve the efficiency of claims processing and customer satisfaction. I have trained and mentored numerous junior adjusters, and I have set an example for them to follow in my positive attitude, work ethic, and aggressive pursuit of advanced training and professional development courses. In Chrysler Dodge's 10-adjuster office, I function as the Litigation Adjuster and have acquired much experience in settling disputes through mediation.

**Proven management and communication skills**

In addition to the numerous management courses I took while earning my college degree, I have refined my management and communication skills in jobs as an assistant manager for a shoe store, small business manager, and district sales representative. I offer a proven ability to establish effective working relationships, and I enjoy the responsibility of training, coaching, and developing junior employees.

**Outstanding track record**

I recently completed my annual performance appraisal and received exemplary scores on all performance areas. Chrysler Dodge has recognized my management abilities: the company offered me a management position in California.

I am well acquainted with Chrysler Dodge's reputation for excellence, and I would appreciate an opportunity to discuss the MD – Claims Manager position in Phoenix with you. Although I can provide outstanding references from Chrysler Dodge at the appropriate time, I would appreciate your holding my expression of interest in your company in confidence until we discuss the position. Thank you in advance for your time and professional courtesies.

Yours sincerely,

Victor H. Westbrook

# VICTOR H. WESTBROOK

1110½ Hay Street, Fayetteville, NC 28305 • preppub@aol.com • (910) 483-6611

---

**OBJECTIVE**  To benefit in an organization that can use a resourceful problem solver with strong analytical, communication, and management skills who has excelled as a claims adjuster in all aspects of automobile and homeowners property/claims settlement including material damage (MD).

**EDUCATION**  **Bachelor of Science in Leisure Science,** University of Arizona, Tucson, AZ, 2001.
- Played varsity football, 1998-00; was active in intramural sport including softball, basketball, co-ed football, and football.
- Placed on Honor Roll in 2001, Dean's List in 2000, and Athletic Dean's List in 1999.
- Completed numerous courses in management and excelled in internships which tested my ability to plan, program, manage, and evaluate recreational programs and activities.

**LICENSE**  Arizona Property & Casualty (AP&C) license
Licensed as a Notary Public through 2005
Completed BCD 25 designation; planning to pursue further BCD 25 courses.

**SCHOLARSHIP FOUNDER**  Founded and, with three partners, funded an ongoing scholarship which presents $2,500.00 yearly to a deserving person to further his/her education; the scholarship is called the Hope Scholarship and has existed for six years.

**EXPERIENCE**  **SENIOR CLAIMS REPRESENTATIVE & OFFICE TEAM LEADER.** Chrysler Dodge Corporation, Insurance Division, Tucson, AZ (2003-present). Have become respected for my material damage (MD) expertise in an office with 10 adjusters; function as the Litigation Adjuster and have acquired vast experience in settling disputes through mediation.
- Handle daily office claims management responsibilities including the disbursement of claims load to adjusters in the following cities: Tempe, Phoenix, Yuma, Scottsdale, Sierra Vista, and Flagstaff.
- As the Office Team Leader, I examine files, provide direction toward claim settlement, and handle external and internal complaints.
- Assume responsibilities as office supervisor in the office manager's absence.
- Approve authority requests and all extended hours scheduling.
- Have trained many adjusters, and continuously set an example for other adjusters through my positive attitude, work ethic, and aggressive pursuit of advanced training and certifications.
- Have played a key role on numerous company task forces designed to streamline claims performance, improve cross claims coordination, and increase the contact percentage as well as customer satisfaction of loss participants.
- Coordinated the company's local Litigation, Adjustment and Recovery Team (LAR), and was a quarterly award winner within Chrysler Dodge for my contributions to the LAR Team.
- Demonstrated my ability to adapt to changing environments during the transition period following 2004 when Denmarck, Inc. was bought by Chrysler Dodge; we implemented numerous modifications internally as I was promoted to Senior Claims Representative.

**TRAINING**  Received Chrysler Dodge Certificates of Completion from numerous industry and company training programs.

**PERSONAL**  Can provide outstanding references from all employers. Pride myself on my dedication to physical fitness. Six years of experience in all aspects of automobile and homeowners property/ claims settlement including extensive experience in material damage (MD) specialty.

Date

Exact Name of Person
Exact Title
Exact Name of Company
Address
City, State, Zip

**SENIOR MECHANIC**

Dear Exact Name of Person (or Dear Sir or Madam if answering a blind ad):

With the enclosed resume, I would like to make you aware of my interest in exploring employment opportunities with your organization and introduce you to my background.

As you will see from my resume, I am currently Senior Mechanic with John Deere Tractors, Atlanta, GA. I supervise up to seven individuals who are generator mechanics, wheeled mechanics, and air conditioning specialists. I also personally function as a Quality Inspector and conduct scheduled and unscheduled inspections of wheeled and track vehicles. Previously, I held the position of Shop Foreman & Quality Control Manager with the U.S. Army. My major accomplishment was providing the smooth transitioning of 57 units from diesel generation to quiet generators without problem or delay. As I served my country with distinction in the U.S. Army, I became an expert in the areas of generator maintenance. Because of my strong management ability, I was selected to hold positions as Shop Foreman and Supply Manager.

In my spare time, I have completed college coursework designed to enhance my technical knowledge and skills. I graduated with highest honors with an A.A. degree in Telecommunications, and I am certified as a Registered Telecommunications Cable Installer. My background in the power generation field has helped me to quickly master and apply telecommunications principles.

If my background and skills interest you, I hope you will contact me to suggest a time when we could meet in person to discuss your needs. Thank you in advance for your time.

Yours sincerely,

Morris O. Parnisis

# MORRIS O. PARNISIS

1110½ Hay Street, Fayetteville, NC 28305 • preppub@aol.com • (910) 483-6611

**OBJECTIVE** To benefit an organization that can use a highly trained and versatile professional who offers experience in automotive and property maintenance management.

**EDUCATION** Completed training conducted by the U.S. Army related to leadership and management, power generation repair, and professional driving skills.

**Generator maintenance:** Extensively trained in generator operations and maintenance, 1990-99.

**Vehicle maintenance:** Extensively trained in automotive operation, maintenance, and troubleshooting for the U.S. Army's medium tactical vehicles, 1997.

**Management:** Excelled in the U.S. Marine Corps Leadership Training Program, 1995.

**Technical training:** In my spare time, completed multiple technical courses, including these:

| | |
|---|---|
| Refrigeration and air conditioning | Principles of gasoline and fuel systems |
| Accident prevention management | Electrical system component repair |
| Station installation and repair | Electricity mathematics; electronics |
| Chemical detection and reporting | Transistors and semiconductors |
| Hazardous materials and waste handling | Automotive engines |
| Cable splicing | Fiber Optics OSP and LAN |

**A.A., Telecommunications**; graduated with highest honors (4.0 GPA) from Victoria College, Victoria, TX, 2002.

Completed courses in DC/AC circuitry, semiconductor devices, mathematics, and other areas, El Paso Community College, TX, 2000.

**CERTIFICATION** Certified as BICSI Registered Telecommunications Cable Installer by the BICSI telecommunications association.

Hold the Mechanic Badge; certified in automotive repair and maintenance, Department of the Army.

**EXPERIENCE** **SENIOR MECHANIC.** John Deere Tractors, Atlanta, GA (2003-present). Train and supervise up to seven individuals who are generator mechanics, wheeled mechanics, and mechanics.

- Perform scheduled and unscheduled maintenance; personally function as a Quality Inspector and conduct scheduled and unscheduled inspections of various facilities and equipment.
- Received a prestigious award recognizing my "devotion to duty and attention to detail."

**SHOP FOREMAN & QUALITY CONTROL MANAGER.** U.S. Army, Victoria, TX (2000-02). Planned and implemented maintenance support activities for 57 college units while training and supervising eight maintenance technicians. Maintained 100% readiness on power generation assets.

- Provided expert guidance related to the overhaul of power generation equipment, internal combustion engines, and associated equipment.
- Received a prestigious award recognizing multiple achievements: was praised for the technical leadership I provided as 57 units transitioned from diesel generation to quiet generators without problems or delays.
- During a massive flood, volunteered to work many additional hours repairing and setting up pumps. During several special projects, was praised in writing for "initiative, sound judgment, and outstanding professional ability."

**PERSONAL** Can provide outstanding personal and professional references. Held Secret security clearance.

Date

Exact Name of Person
Title or Position
Name of Company
Address (no., street)
Address (city, state, zip)

**SENIOR POWER PRODUCTION SPECIALIST**

Dear Exact Name of Person (or Dear Sir or Madam if answering a blind ad):

I would appreciate an opportunity to talk with you soon about how I could benefit your organization through my personnel management skills and my proven power generation equipment expertise.

While serving as Senior Power Production Specialist at Amtec Precision Products, Inc., Elgin, IL, I schedule and conduct training for 20 employees in the maintenance section. I ensure compliance with quality control guidelines for 90 items of power generation equipment. My experience and knowledge extends from gasoline and diesel engines to 60 kilowatt generators.

You would find me a reliable individual with a talent for motivating others and a desire to give "110 percent" in the performance of any task.

I hope you will welcome my call soon to arrange a brief meeting at your convenience to discuss your current and future needs and how I might serve them. Thank you in advance for your time.

Sincerely yours,


Roger Lee Marley


(Alternate last paragraph:
I hope you will call or write me soon to suggest a time convenient for us to meet and discuss your current and future needs and how I might serve them. Thank you in advance for your time.)

# ROGER LEE MARLEY

1110½ Hay Street, Fayetteville, NC 28305 • preppub@aol.com • (910) 483-6611

**OBJECTIVE**  To contribute through my outstanding technical skills in maintaining power generation equipment to an organization that can use my experience in budget management, personnel supervision, and training.

**AREAS of EXPERTISE**
- Troubleshoot and repair gasoline and diesel engines.
- Read and interpret schematics and wiring diagrams.
- Maintain and operate vehicles up to five-ton size.
- Use computers for record keeping and inventory control.
- Maintain and operate heavy construction equipment including bulldozers, graders, and bucket loaders.
- Am licensed by the U.S. government to operate generators up to 60 KW.

**EXPERIENCE**  **SENIOR POWER PRODUCTION SPECIALIST.** Amtec Precision Products, Inc., Elgin, IL (2002-present). Learned to use automated systems for record keeping while scheduling and conducting training for 20 employees in a maintenance section.
- Ensure compliance with quality control guidelines for 90 items of power generation equipment.
- Maintain up-to-date records of material availability.

**SUPERVISORY POWER GENERATION TECHNICIAN.** Northwood University, Midand, MI (1999-01). Handled areas including: troubleshooting and repairing up to 60 KW generators, repairing and operating heavy construction equipment, receiving work requests, and processing an average of 46 work orders daily.
- Polished my communication skills conducting daily briefings for superiors.

**SUPERVISORY MOTOR VEHICLE MECHANIC.** U-Haul Rentals, New Orleans, LA (1997-1998). Managed the training and performance of 25 employees maintaining a $10 million-dollar inventory of wheeled vehicles. Trained personnel to use new automated equipment used for keeping maintenance logs and records.
- Guided the section to high scores during maintenance inspections.
- Was often sought out to provide professional and personal guidance.

**MAINTENANCE/INVENTORY CONTROL MANAGER.** White-Harris Buick, Albuquerque, NM (1995-96). Supervised 30 mechanics and controlled a 350-line parts inventory
- Emphasized safety in all phases of work performance.
- Initiated a flex-time schedule for mechanics which resulted in increased employee morale and customer satisfaction.
- Utilized diagnostic equipment to troubleshoot malfunctions.

**INVENTORY CONTROL MANAGER.** AutoZone, Moline, IL (1992-94). Managed 14 employees maintaining thousands of items in stock to be sold to vehicle owners.
- Became expert in locating parts for walk-in retail customers.

**TRAINING**  Completed programs in auto body repair, front end alignment, and welding, Jackson Community College, Jackson, MI.
Received nine months of military leadership and technical training.

**PERSONAL**  Have received praise for my technical and supervisory skills. Am known as a go-getter who will get the job done right.

Date

Exact Name of Person
Title or Position
Name of Company
Address (no., street)
Address (city, state, zip)

Dear Exact Name of Person (or Dear Sir or Madam if answering a blind ad):

With the enclosed resume, I would like to introduce myself and make you aware of the considerable experience in purchasing, contracting, property management, finance, and operations management which I could put to work for you. I am currently in the process of relocating to the Florida area where my extended family lives, and I would appreciate an opportunity to talk personally with you about how I could contribute to your organization.

With my current employer, I have been promoted to Senior Purchasing Manager. I am responsible for the property management of more than 5,000 vehicles and a fleet of 72 service vans. I also prepare and resourcefully utilize a budget of more than $1.6 million annually for repair parts, outside services, support equipment, and materials. On my own initiative, I have totally streamlined the bidding process. In consultation with the System Manager, I implemented a new computer program to track bids, thereby transforming a previously disorganized manual process into an efficient computerized system. Additionally, I streamlined purchasing procedures while taking over a job which had previously been done by two people. Using available software, I have also established accounting and budgeting programs for a small business.

In all my previous jobs, I have been recognized—sometimes with cash bonuses—for developing new systems which improved efficiency and customer service. For example, while working for the U.S. Embassy in Miami, I created a computerized method of financial reporting which greatly enhanced the budgeting and fiscal accountability functions. In another job as a Purchasing Agent, I exceeded expected standards while handling critical functions including making decisions on the most advantageous sources, assisting in bidding solicitations, and evaluating quotations for price discounts and reference materials.

I have never been in a job where I did not find creative and resourceful ways to cut costs, improve bottom-line results, and strengthen relationships with customers.

I hope you will call or write me soon to suggest a time convenient for us to meet and discuss your needs and how I might serve them. Thank you for your time.

Sincerely,

Robert Rountree

---

**SENIOR PURCHASING MANAGER, Government Contracting.** Notice the bold fourth paragraph, where he simply states that he has never been in a job where he didn't find ways to improve profitability and strengthen customer relationships. This ought to interest prospective employers in Florida!

# ROBERT ROUNTREE

1110½ Hay Street, Fayetteville, NC 28305 • preppub@aol.com • (910) 483-6611

---

| | |
|---|---|
| **OBJECTIVE** | To contribute to an organization that can use a resourceful purchasing manager who is skilled in contract negotiation, operations management, and personnel administration. |
| **EDUCATION** | Completed one year of **Master of Science Degree** work in **Urban Management,** Texas State University, Mercerville, TX, 1995-96.<br>Earned **B.S. in Health Education,** University of Washington, Washington, DC, 1991.<br>Received **A.A. in General Education,** Miami Dale Community College, Miami, FL, 1986.<br>Completed executive development and non-degree-granting training programs in:<br>    Cost Accounting    Managerial Accounting    Procurement<br>    Computer Operations    Inventory Control    Budget Administration |
| **COMPUTERS** | Lotus 1-2-3, dBase IV, WordPerfect, Managing Your Money, Windows 95, others |
| **EXPERIENCE** | **SENIOR PURCHASING MANAGER.** Briley & Co., Ft. Hood, TX (2002-present). Have acquired a broad understanding of government contracting procedures while achieving an excellent track record of promotion in the finance and purchasing field.<br>• Was originally employed as a Purchasing Agent in 2003 to replace two buyers; have been promoted to Senior Purchasing Manager in charge of five associates.<br>• Am responsible for an annual budget of approximately $2.1 million of which $1.6 million is used by me to purchase repair parts, outside services, support equipment, and materials.<br>• Responsible for property management: within a $150,000 monthly budget oversee maintenance and repairs performed on 5,000 vehicles and a fleet of 72 vans.<br>• In a formal letter of appreciation, was commended for saving at least $400,000 annually by combining my extensive purchasing knowledge with my creative problem-solving skills.<br>• On my own initiative, streamlined the bidding process; developed a new system for obtaining price quotes from potential vendors and worked with the System Manager in developing a computer program to track quotes: this transformed the manual quotation to an efficient new process which reduced the time necessary to prepare quotes.<br>• Established excellent working relationships with vendors all over the country, and am known for my ability to quickly find difficult-to-obtain parts for critical needs.<br>• Knowledgeable of government contracting and new product testing.<br><br>**CONSULTANT & VICE PRESIDENT OF FINANCE.** Branson Enterprises, Miami, FL (1999-02). Played a key role in helping the owner build a new business; established budgeting and accounting systems. Negotiated the details of the company's largest contract.<br><br>**PURCHASING MANAGER.** Contracting Division of the U.S. Air Force, Washington, DC (1997-99). Handled critical functions including making decisions on the most advantageous sources, assisting in bidding solicitations and acceptance, and evaluating quotations for price discounts as well as delivery/transportation costs. Developed outstanding relationships and received a Laudatory Best Operation performance appraisal with cash bonus.<br><br>**PROCUREMENT OFFICER.** The American Embassy in Miami (1994-97). Began working for the Embassy as a Warehouse Manager and, holding a Top Secret security clearance, excelled in managing warehouse operations and in relocating warehouse contents to new facilities.<br>• Because of my problem-solving ability, was promoted to Procurement Officer; took over a disorganized operation and created a computerized method of reporting Local Operational Funds (LOF) which enhanced efficiency of the budgeting and fiscal functions. |
| **PERSONAL** | Outstanding personal and professional references. Will cheerfully travel/relocate. |

Date

Exact Name of Person
Title or Position
Name of Company
Address (no., street)
Address (city, state, zip)

Dear Exact Name of Person (or Dear Sir or Madam if answering a blind ad):

At the encouragement of Jim West, I am sending you the enclosed resume. I am very interested in becoming a member of the Cableton district management team through my versatile background in service, parts, and sales management.

As you will see from my resume, I am presently employed as a Service Manager with Thurston Chrysler Plymouth Suzuki, Inc., in Canby, OR. Although I am well respected for my expertise and professionalism by this company, I would very much like to move into a corporate position in which I can apply my strong consulting and communication skills.

I am confident that my extensive experience in all areas of service, parts, and warranty operations, along with my ability to consistently maintain high customer satisfaction scores in service and sales, would allow me to become a valuable part of your team. In addition, I am certain that you would find me to be a hard-working and reliable professional who prides myself on doing every job to the best of my ability.

I welcome the opportunity for additional training and am willing to travel according to your needs.

I hope you will contact me soon to arrange a time convenient for us to meet and discuss your current and future needs and how I can help serve them. Thank you in advance for your time and consideration.

Sincerely,

Lee Southerland

## SERVICE MANAGER

There's an old saying, "A change is as good as a rest." In some instances in our careers, that's true, too. Here you see the resume and cover letter of an automobile industry professional seeking to transfer his industry knowledge from a management position inside a dealership to a consulting and training role inside a specialized training organization. Notice in the first paragraph of his letter that he "drops a name" of an industry colleague and provides a reference. The position he seeks requires extensive travel, so he clarifies that he would welcome extensive travel.

# LEE B. SOUTHERLAND

1110½ Hay Street, Fayetteville, NC 28305 • preppub@aol.com • (910) 483-6611

| | |
|---|---|
| **OBJECTIVE** | To benefit a progressive automotive organization through my experience in service, parts, and sales as well as through my proven ability to train and motivate others to achieve the highest levels of job knowledge and productivity. |
| **EXPERIENCE** | *Excelled in a track record of promotions with Thurston Chrysler Plymouth, Suzuki, Inc., Canby, OR (2001-present):*<br>**SERVICE MANAGER** (Suzuki) and **ASSISTANT SERVICE MANAGER** (Chrysler/Plymouth). Oversee service operations including performing service write ups, dispatching, effectively explaining recommended repairs, conducting sales, as well as handling special orders and inventory control.<br>• Process warranty claims; help launch new vehicles through creative advertising and marketing of accessories.<br>• Refined management and administrative skills while managing employees, handling weekly and monthly financial and inventory reports, and performing daily computer operations.<br>• Demonstrate effective public relations and communication skills while maintaining excellent customer and dealer relations.<br>• Earned several performance awards while handling service write ups, dispatching, explaining recommended repairs, as well as conducting sales, warranty counseling, and customer relations.<br>• Sold new and used vehicles as a Sales Representative (2002-03) while becoming skilled at the minute details of contracting and inventory control; became a 2003 Chrysler Certified Sales Representative.<br>• Was recognized as "Employee of the Month" on several occasions and "Employee of the Year," 2002. |
| **SPECIAL SKILLS** | Offer detailed knowledge of computers along with industry-specific software programs including the ADP and SCAT systems. Offer strong communication, time management, and customer relations skills. |
| **EDUCATION and TRAINING** | Excelled at various corporate-sponsored training programs and seminars including these:<br>• American Suzuki Electronic Fuel Injection 95-97 EFI, June 2003<br>• American Suzuki warranty seminar, 2002<br>• Product Introduction Technical Training — an overview of Suzuki automobiles, service, and repairs, 2002<br>• SME-SMO1, SM The Essential Service Management System, 2001<br>• SME-SMO2, SM Work Distribution, Work Performance, 2001<br>• Studied Business at Maryland University and Gaithersburg Technical Community College. |
| **PERSONAL** | Know the importance of being willing to be flexible and versatile when working in service industries. Effective decision maker with strong administrative and public relations skills. |

Date

Exact Name of Person
Title or Position
Name of Company
Address (number and street)
Address (city, state, and zip)

**SERVICE STATION MANAGER**

A service station manager does not frequently need a resume, but this particular manager decided he wanted out of daily management activities and back into full-time technical activities. He is seeking a highly paid position as a mechanic in a foreign location.

Dear Exact Name of Person: (or Dear Sir or Madam if answering a blind ad.)

With the enclosed resume, I would like to indicate my interest in your organization and my desire to explore employment opportunities.

As you will see from my enclosed resume, I am experienced in all aspects of managing an automotive business, and I offer strong knowledge of accounting, finance, and purchasing as well as automotive repair. I am selling my ownership in the service station which my partner and I started "from scratch" in order to make myself available for worldwide relocation with a company that can utilize my expert mechanical and maintenance knowledge. An experienced industrial mechanic, welder, and automotive mechanic, I have received numerous awards and honors for technical expertise.

I hope you will welcome my call soon to arrange a brief meeting at your convenience to discuss your current and future needs and how I might serve them. Thank you in advance for your time.

Sincerely yours,

Conrad Kael

(Alternate last paragraph:
I hope you will call or write me soon to suggest a time convenient for us to meet and discuss your current and future needs and how I might serve them. Thank you in advance for your time.)

# CONRAD KAEL

1110½ Hay Street, Fayetteville, NC 28305 • preppub@aol.com • (910) 483-6611

---

**OBJECTIVE**      To contribute to an organization that can use a skilled operations manager with a proven ability to establish and manage successful new ventures along with extensive expertise in every aspect of the automotive business.

**COMPUTERS**      Highly proficient in utilizing a variety of software programs to enhance bottom-line efficiency and profitability; experienced with Windows 95 and with various types of software used for accounting and inventory control including ShopPro.

**EXPERIENCE**      **SERVICE STATION MANAGER.** ALL AMERICAN BP, Lawrence, KS (2002-present). With a partner, established "from scratch" and now manage a service station which has gained an excellent reputation for quality repairs and honest business dealings.

- *Accounting:* On my own initiative, created and implemented a computerized system which allows us to instantly track all work orders, inventory levels, and account balances; personally prepare all final work orders and initiate estimates for customer approval before work begins.
- *Customer Service:* Have become respected for my ability to clearly explain technical repair needs to customers; handle customer complaints and problems which occur.
- *Automotive Repairs:* Perform mechanical repairs and troubleshooting including engine replacement, cylinder head replacement, timing belts, brakes, and other jobs.
- *Finance and Purchasing*: Make all decisions regarding equipment/tools purchasing.
- *Advertising and Marketing:* Plan and implement advertising and special promotions designed to attract new customers and interest existing customers in our full line of services.
- *Special Skills:* Offer extensive experience related to these and other areas:
  Repair fuel and brake systems
  Operate tractor-trailers up to 10 tons
  Emergency dispatching and repairs
  Driving, troubleshooting, and repairing wheeled vehicles
  Operate five-ton wreckers, front-end loaders, buses,
  Troubleshoot and repair vehicles of all types and sizes
  Operate tire machine, brake lathe, wheel balancer
  Troubleshoot/repair vehicles of all types and sizes

**INDUSTRIAL MECHANIC.** Kelly Industries, Lawrence, KS (2001-03). In this large, state-of-the-art plant of a Fortune 500 company, solved numerous quality problems through my individual initiative while implementing changes which made machine setups more efficient.

**WELDER & FABRICATOR.** Melrose, Inc., Lawrence, KS (1998-01). Designed fixtures for some of the drilling processes while excelling in fabrication layout of materials used in building air control systems; performed final welding of systems frames and other devices.

**WELDER & AUTOMOTIVE MECHANIC.** U.S. Army, locations worldwide (1996-98). Became a welder and mechanic on wheeled and track vehicles.

**EDUCATION**      Studied Welding, Scarlet Oaks School, Sharonville, OH, 1993-96.
Completed U.S. Army training related to automotive repair/maintenance.

Date

Exact Name of Person
Title or Position
Name of Company
Address (number and street)
Address (city, state, and ZIP)

**STORE MANAGER**

Dear Exact Name of Person: (or Dear Sir or Madam if answering a blind ad.)

I would appreciate an opportunity to talk with you soon about how I could benefit your organization through my outstanding abilities gained in a multifunctional business where I oversaw activities ranging from training and supervision, to development of merchandising and promotional activities, to directing sales and customer service activities, to handling administrative and fiscal operations.

As the Store Manager of a Western Auto location which had $2.5 million in sales its last fiscal year, I have become very efficient at managing my time while dealing with three different operational areas — parts, tires and service, and automotive accessories. This store averages from 1,500 to 1,700 transactions a week with average weekly sales in the $40-60,000 range. In my five years as Store Manager I have achieved consistently high levels of productivity, sales, and customer satisfaction.

As you will see from my enclosed resume, before joining Western Auto I earned rapid advancement with Parts Plus. In my five years with this organization I was promoted to Store Manager after starting as a part-time sales person and then becoming a Merchandiser, a Parts Specialist, and Assistant Manager. As Store Manager I have been involved in making decisions concerning merchandising, computer operations and fiscal control, inventory control, and public relations, as well as internal employee counseling and supervision.

I am a very dedicated hard-working professional who can be counted on to find ways to ensure customer satisfaction and productivity while always impacting favorably on the organization's bottom line.

I hope you will welcome my call soon to arrange a brief meeting at your convenience to discuss your current and future needs and how I might serve them. Thank you in advance for your time.

Sincerely yours,


Chester Arthur Olaf


(Alternate last paragraph:
I hope you will call or write me soon to suggest a time convenient for us to meet and discuss your current and future needs and how I might serve them. Thank you in advance for your time.)

# CHESTER ARTHUR OLAF

1110½ Hay Street, Fayetteville, NC 28305   •   preppub@aol.com   •   (910) 483-6611

---

**OBJECTIVE**  To benefit an organization in need of an experienced manager with a strong background in inventory control/parts ordering, merchandising and sales, public relations, and fiscal operations along with specialized knowledge of the automotive parts business.

**EXPERIENCE**  **STORE MANAGER.** Western Auto, Jacksonville, FL (2002-present). Direct and oversee all phases of daily operations in an established store with 28 employees and with average weekly sales of from $40,000 to $60,000; motivate employees to achieve high levels of productivity, sales, and customer satisfaction.
- Played an important role in the success of a location with $2.5 million in annual sales and from 1,500 to 1,700 transactions a week.
- Received an Award of Excellence as an Auto Parts Specialist in recognition of my professionalism and knowledge of the inventory control aspect of the business.
- Received a Customer Service Award Pin recognizing my exceptional customer relations.
- Earned certification in tires and parts in recognition of my expertise in providing customer service in these areas).
- Was chosen to attend a corporate training program for store managers in 2003.
- Participated in setting up and running a job fair booth in order to recruit management trainees, Jacksonville University.
- Carried out interesting sales merchandising and promotional activities which helped to increase sales of additional services once customers entered the store.
- Became skilled in time management while overseeing the operation of distinctly different areas within one location — parts, tires and service, and automotive accessories.
- Contribute to successful customer relations efforts by monitoring employee performance and guiding them in the development of their sales and service skills.
- Handle administrative details such as scheduling, making bank deposits, taking care of personnel paperwork, and preparing various types of reports.

**STORE MANAGER.** Parts Plus, Tallahassee, FL (1996-02). Earned rapid promotion with this business and was placed in charge of overseeing all aspects of store operations from personnel, to sales, to inventory control.
- Advanced from a part-time sales position to Merchandiser, then to Parts Specialist and Assistant Manager, and in 2000 was promoted to Store Manager.
- Became familiar with management unique to the automotive parts industry involving public relations, computer operations/fiscal controls, and parts and inventory control.
- Manage 14 employees in a location which averaged from $15,000 to $18,000 in sales a week.

**EDUCATION**  Completed one semester of Business Administration, Jacksonville University, Jacksonville, FL, 1995. Studied Electronic Engineering and Business Management, Gulf Coast Community College, Panama City, FL.

**TRAINING**  Was selected for corporate-sponsored training including:
"Introduction to Management" — a part of the AutoZone Management School
Technical Electronic Ignition Course — Moxley Manufacturing Corp.

**CERTIFICATIONS**  Received ASE (Automotive Service Excellence) certification as a Parts Specialist and AutoZone certification as a Master Tire Specialist and Parts Specialist.

**PERSONAL**  Am a well-rounded professional with excellent communication skills in all areas — dealing with the public and with employees. Have a pleasant and friendly personality.

Date

Exact Name of Person
Title or Position
Name of Company
Address (number and street)
Address (city, state, and ZIP)

**STORE MANAGER** for a bike and motorcycle shop. This mid-level manager is seeking advancement with his current employer and is applying for a Sales Management position in the chain's largest store.

Dear Exact Name of Person: (or Dear Sir or Madam if answering a blind ad.)

With the enclosed resume, I would like to make you aware of my interest in the job of Sales Manager in the Columbus, OH area. As you know, we had the pleasure of working together when you were Events Coordinator. I can also provide an outstanding reference from Nathan Johnson. I believe you are already aware of my track record of outstanding performance as well as my demonstrated abilities related to operations management, sales management, customer service, and inventory control.

As you know, I have excelled as Store Manager in Kansas City. I began with Western as a Parts Clerk and gained expertise in that aspect of the business. I believe you are aware that I have excelled in my positions at Western while also working a full-time job as a Military Policeman. As an MP, I worked in jobs which included Investigator and United Nations Body Guard.

It is my desire to continue working to advance the profitability and growth of Western, and I wanted to formally ask you to consider me for the job of Sales Manager. I offer proven sales abilities and have trained employees at the Kansas City store in effective sales techniques. I believe solid product knowledge is a key to effectiveness in sales, and I certainly offer expert understanding of bikes and motorcycles. I am proud of the fact that I have hired and developed employees in the Kansas City store whom I have trained to utilize strong selling skills.

Let me know if you need any information other than what I have provided. I would enjoy the opportunity to talk with you by phone or in person about this position, and I feel certain I would further contribute to the company in that capacity. I send best wishes.

Sincerely,

Grif Wadleigh

# GRIF WADLEIGH

1110½ Hay Street, Fayetteville, NC 28305 • preppub@aol.com • (910) 483-6611

---

**OBJECTIVE**  To contribute to the Western company through my track record of outstanding performance which has demonstrated my abilities related to operations management, sales management, customer service, and inventory control.

**EDUCATION**  Completed numerous military training courses including Military Police School, Airborne School, as well as leadership and management training.
Graduated from Carter High School, Oakland, CA 1989.
Completed extensive on-the-job training with the Western company related to store operations, sales management, computerized inventory control, events management, personnel hiring and supervision, and service management.

**EXPERIENCE**  **Have progressed in the following track record of advancement with Western:**
**2002-present: STORE MANAGER.** Western, Kansas City, MO. Was promoted to manage the Kansas City store after excelling as a Parts Clerk; was responsible for interviewing, hiring, and managing new employees.
- Oversaw all areas of operation including the servicing of wreck estimates.
- Am known for my exceptional sales abilities, and have trained new employees in the most effective techniques of bike sales.
- Scheduled and coordinated special events including rallies, parties, and charity events; these events have greatly improved the store's visibility in the community.

**1997-02: PARTS CLERK.** Gained expert knowledge of Western's inventory while selling parts and accessories, using various catalogues to research the products of numerous parts distributors, and ordering parts for special orders.
- Learned to expertly handle the job as a Service Writer; became known for my persistence in locating sources for hard-to-find, custom, and high-performance parts.
- Advised customers on what repairs were needed on their bikes and motorcycles and coordinated the arrangements for scheduling and making the repairs.

**Military experience: Served my country with distinction in the following positions while simultaneously working at Western in my spare time:**
**MILITARY POLICEMAN.** U.S. Army, Ft. Nelson, MO (1995-97). Worked mostly at night as a Military Policeman and Team Leader.
- Developed an attitude of maintaining constant vigilance and attention-to-detail while controlling access in and out of a Top Secret compound.
- Played a vital role in rewriting a key Standard Operating Procedure.

**1994-95: INVESTIGATOR.** U.S. Army, Ft. Nelson, MO. Was specially selected for a special assignment to work as an Investigator with the Sheriff's Department.

**1993-94: MILITARY POLICEMAN.** U.S. Army, Ft. Nelson, MO. Maintained the peace and wrote traffic tickets while patrolling the Ft. Nelson military reservation.

**1990-92: UNITED NATIONS BODY GUARD.** U.S. Army. Worked in civilian clothes while acting as a Body Guard for United Nations personnel and driving security escort missions for Swiss and Swedish officers.

**PERSONAL**  Hobbies include western activities and golfing. In my limited spare time, volunteer to help Little League players. Will relocate.

# CAREER CHANGE: From military to civilian

Date

Exact Name of Person
Exact Title
Exact Name of Company
Address
City, State, Zip

**SUPERINTENDENT OF MAINTENANCE**

This distinguished military professional is leaving military service and attempting to enter the automotive field.

Dear Exact Name of Person (or Dear Sir or Madam if answering a blind ad):

With the enclosed resume, I would like to make you aware of my interest in exploring employment opportunities with your organization and introduce you to my background.

As you will see from my resume, I am an experienced supervisor who has served with distinction in the U.S. Navy while being promoted to the rank of Chief Warrant Officer 4 (CWO4). Although I was strongly encouraged to remain in military service and assured of continued advancement in rank, I have decided to leave the military and enter the civilian work force.

**Background in Safety and Quality Assurance:** In my most recent position supervising 98 people and managing a $185,000 budget, I was praised in writing for "always inspiring and producing superior results." Throughout my naval service, I was constantly in situations in which I was responsible for the safety of others in environments which were filled with hazards. I have learned that a relentless emphasis on training and safety is the key to operating safely in industrial situations.

**Technical expertise related to maintenance, production operations, and transportation:** In my most recent position, I planned and managed complex maintenance and renovation projects which involved supervising civilian contractors. I am knowledgeable of government contracting procedures, and I have technical expertise in all aspects of maintenance and transportation management.

**Strong problem-solving skills:** On numerous occasions I have taken on stubborn problems and figured out resourceful solutions that allowed deadlines and budgets to be met. I have earned a reputation as a resourceful and inspiring leader, and in one position I took over a poorly performing division and transformed personnel into a team which was praised for its "superb technicians with enormous confidence."

If my background and skills interest you, I hope you will contact me to suggest a time when we could meet in person to discuss your needs. I can provide outstanding references at the appropriate time. Thank you.

Yours sincerely,

Stanley C. Johnson

# STANLEY C. JOHNSON

1110½ Hay Street, Fayetteville, NC 28305 • preppub@aol.com • (910) 483-6611

---

**OBJECTIVE**  To benefit an organization that can use a skilled manager who offers an extensive background related to maintenance management, production supervision, quality and safety assurance, as well as the shipment of cargo of people and cargo including hazardous materials.

**SUMMARY OF EXPERIENCE**  Received numerous awards in recognition of my technical knowledge and management abilities while advancing to the rank of Chief Warrant Officer 4 (CWO 4) in the U.S. Navy.

**EXPERIENCE**  **SUPERINTENDENT OF MAINTENANCE.** U.S. Navy on board the USS Constellation, (2003-present). Received a prestigious medal for my results in this position which involved supervising 98 people and managing a budget of $185,000. Received praise in writing for "brilliant performance" and for "always inspiring and producing superior results" and was formally ranked as #1 of the 18 elite Chief Warrant Officers on board the USS Constellation.

- **Quality assurance:** Am commended for the "proactive leadership" I provided in coordinating preparations for an administrative and material inspection which found "no faults" and concluded that the condition of the department's training and material was "superior."
- **Maintenance management:** Plan and manage a complex maintenance and renovation program comprised of more than 115 separate maintenance projects; work closely with civilian contractors and assured quality and thoroughness of work performed.
- **Financial management and cost reduction:** Provide leadership in reducing costs of maintenance while improving quality results; also develop controls which assure meticulous oversight of the $185,000 budget. Am credited with saving the ship thousands of dollars through my "initiative and direct involvement."

**MAINTENANCE CHIEF.** U.S. Navy on board the USS John C Stennis, (2000-03). Managed numerous special projects related to maintenance operations, hazardous materials transportation, and safety management. Supervised between 60-105 employees and managed a $185,000 budget.

- **Maintenance management:** Managed projects including a preservation plan for 26,000 square feet of interior space.
- **Training management:** Instituted a computerized program to track qualifications and required training which ensured full qualified personnel.
- **Transportation management:** Organized the safe onload and offload of vehicles, thousands of tons of hazardous materials, and other materials.
- **Safety management:** On formal safety inspections, was commended for "the best safety results ever seen."

**MAINTENANCE CHIEF.** U.S. Navy on board the USS Lexington, (1994-00). Was handpicked for this job which involved taking control of a poorly functioning division; in just two months, retrained and turned around a poorly functioning division and transformed employees into a team praised as "superb technicians with enormous confidence."

- **Maintenance management:** Developed and implemented numerous refurbishments to existing facilities. On one occasion, coordinated preparations for a presidential visit for a special 4th of July ceremony, led my department to receive the coveted "Sailor of the Year Award for 1996," which a formal performance evaluation said was due to my "emphasis on impeccable material readiness and training."

**EDUCATION**  Completed 15 hours toward my Bachelor's degree and earned the equivalent of an **Associate's degree in Industrial Management** while earning more than 52 hours of college credit.

# CAREER CHANGE: from military to civilian

Date

Exact Name of Person
Exact Title
Exact Name of Company
Address
City, State, Zip

**TRANSPORTATION COMPANY MANAGER**

Dear Exact Name of Person (or Dear Sir or Madam if answering a blind ad):

With the enclosed resume, I would like to make you aware of my interest in exploring employment opportunities with your organization.

As you will see from my resume, I hold a Class A Commercial Driver's License (CDL) with Hazmat and doubles endorsement, and I have completed the Schneider International Truck Driver's Training Program. I also hold a Driver Badge and Mechanic Badge from the U.S. Army.

While serving my country in the U.S. Army, I earned a reputation as an outstanding communicator and motivator. I was handpicked for an assignment as Manager of a transportation company. I managed and trained 25 employees who included drivers and mechanics, and I also routinely supervised a 62-person maintenance section which processed thousands of maintenance requests with outstanding customer service.

As a Senior Training Manager, I was selected to train and manage individuals involved in training projects, and I supervised wheeled vehicle operators. I was commended by my supervisor as "a natural born leader who knows how to motivate ordinary people to accomplish extraordinary feats." You will notice from my resume that I have excelled in jobs which placed me in charge of training others. While stationed at Fort Stewart, I supervised seven other training managers while training 1,850 employees annually.

If you can use a hard worker known for the ability to produce the highest quality results under the pressure of long hours and tight deadlines, I hope you will contact me to suggest a time when we might meet to discuss your needs and goals. With an outstanding personal and professional reputation, I can provide superior references.

Sincerely,

Aaron B. Dennison

# AARON B. DENNISON

1110½ Hay Street, Fayetteville, NC 28305  •  preppub@aol.com  •  (910) 483-6611

---

**OBJECTIVE**  To contribute to an organization that can use a knowledgeable transportation industry professional with an outstanding safety record along with extensive management experience.

**LICENSES**  Completed two years (80 semester hours) of college coursework at St. Louis Community College, St. Louis, MO.
Completed Schneider International Truck Driver Training Center, St. Louis, MO, 2001.
Hold a Class A Commercial Driver's License (CDL) with Hazmat and doubles endorsement.
Hold Driver Badge and Mechanic Badge. Licensed to drive heavy trucks with 53' trailers.

**EXPERIENCE**  **TRANSPORTATION COMPANY MANAGER.** U.S. Army, Fort Knox, KY (2003-present). Manage a transportation company with 25 employees who included mechanics and drivers while directing the operations of a fleet of 17 six-ton cargo vehicles which supported the transportation needs of an infantry organization.
- Lead the organization in driving 59,000 accident-free and incident-free miles.
- Through my leadership and technical knowledge, the organization consistently maintain a fleet of 17 six-ton cargo vehicles above a 87% operational rate.
- Simultaneously perform as Shop Foreman and Maintenance Manager; supervise a 62-person maintenance section. Process thousands of maintenance requests efficiently and with outstanding customer service.
- During a special project was in charge of one of the largest transportation operation at Fort Hood, TX, and managed the organization's relocation there for a brief assignment.
- Managed a special project in which I was in charge of transporting 19 individuals and multimillion-dollar assets to national training centers without incident or loss of assets.
- Resourcefully figure out solutions when problems occurred because of hard-to-obtain parts.
- Maintain the fleet in an extremely high state of readiness above 97%.

**TRAINING MANAGER.** U.S. Army, Fort Wainwright, AK (2000). Was specially selected to plan and direct training activities for 270 people in Alaska.
- During a major training project, played a key role in the safe utilization of ammunition in live-fire training. Coordinated life support, ammunition issue, and inventory control for 90 personnel. Supervised eight wheeled vehicle convoys through the live fire training.
- Was commended in writing by my supervisor as "a natural born leader who knows how to motivate ordinary people to accomplish extraordinary feats."

**SENIOR TRAINING MANAGER.** U.S. Army, Fort Stewart, GA (1997-99). Was selected for this job as "Drill Sergeant," and was subsequently praised in writing as "the most reliable and capable Drill Sergeant in the company," and my platoon was described as "consistently outperforming all other platoons on all training activities."
- Supervised and mentored seven other company Training Managers; was cited for my outstanding leadership and mentoring skills. Trained more than 1,850 soldiers annually.
- Refined my ability to communicate effectively, and was commended for my success in motivating entry-level employees to take pride in their work.

**Highlights of other experience:** Was promoted ahead of my peers and commended for "strong initiative" and "outstanding performance" in the motor transport field.

**HONORS**  Received 18 awards, medals, ribbons, and letters of commendation for exemplary performance.

**PERSONAL**  Excellent references. Held Secret security clearance. Computer skills include Word and Excel.

Date

Exact Name of Person
Title or Position
Name of Company
Address (no., street)
Address (city, state, zip)

**VEHICLE MAINTENANCE MECHANIC**

Dear Exact Name of Person (or Dear Sir or Madam if answering a blind ad):

I would appreciate an opportunity to talk with you soon about how I could contribute to your organization through my technical expertise which includes experience in troubleshooting, maintaining, operating, programming, and repairing electronics systems.

My experience has included supervisory positions in organizations providing support for aircraft and vehicle communication, navigation, and electronic systems. I have consistently completed intensive on-the-job technical training ahead of my peers and been selected for supervisory roles as well as special duty assignments.

I earned commendation and achievement awards for "outstanding performance" and was officially recognized as Airborne Express's "best mechanic." Known as a quick learner, I have always been recognized for my adaptability and singled out for leadership roles in critical maintenance facilities.

I hope you will welcome my call soon to arrange a brief meeting at your convenience to discuss your current and future needs and how I might serve them. Thank you in advance for your time.

Sincerely yours,

Jeffrey C. Pelijash

(Alternate last paragraph:
I hope you will call or write soon to suggest a time convenient for us to meet and discuss your current and future needs and how I might serve them. Thank you in advance for your time.)

# JEFFREY C. PELIJASH

1110½ Hay Street, Fayetteville, NC 28305 • preppub@aol.com • (910) 483-6611

---

**OBJECTIVE**  To apply my technical electronics expertise for the benefit of an organization that can use a fast learner with proven abilities related to troubleshooting, maintenance, repair, programming, and operation.

**SPECIAL SKILLS**
- Troubleshoot, maintain, repair, operate, and program radar deception equipment and computer-operated test stations.
- Use test equipment including digital and analog volt meters, frequency counters, oscilloscopes, frequency generators, and watt meters.
- Am familiar with Westinghouse equipment including AN/ALQ-131, 119, 72, and 71 electronic countermeasure pods; AN/ALR-46 and AN/APR-38 radar warning and homing receivers; AN/ALE-46 and 38 chaff and flare dispensers; and all types of aerospace ground equipment (AGE).

**EXPERIENCE**  **VEHICLE MAINTENANCE MECHANIC.** Flint Airfield, Flint, MI (2003-present). Was placed in charge of special rebuilding projects while repairing and overhauling vehicles with both gas and diesel engines.
- Maintain equipment including aircraft tow vehicles and forklifts.
- Am qualified in snow removal and equipment repair after only two months of training.

**SPECIAL EQUIPMENT MECHANIC.** Airborne Express, Jackson, MI (2000-03). Completed special training in record time and became skilled in repairing equipment including towing vehicles and both electric and diesel forklifts. Attained a 96% vehicle availability rate and played a major part in the unit's recognition as "the best in the company."

**SUPERVISORY ELECTRONIC TECHNICIAN.** American Airlines, Indianapolis, IN (1998-99). Supervised one of three specialized repair crews while maintaining and overhauling equipment for the company's Boeing 747 and 767 aircraft. Maintained equipment including radar warning and homing receivers, chaff and flare dispensers, and self-protection jammers.

**ELECTRONICS TECHNICIAN.** NATO, Germany (1994-97). Was selected to train and test new employees on their job knowledge while troubleshooting, repairing, and maintaining electronic warfare equipment including jamming devices, radar warning systems, and test consoles. Was singled out to oversee quality control operations after completing training and earning qualification ahead of my peers.

*While serving my country in the U.S. Air Force, I excelled in the following positions:*
**SUPERVISORY ELECTRONICS TECHNICIAN.** U.S.A.F., Turkey (1993-94). Led employees in maintaining a 95% operational readiness rate while troubleshooting and repairing electronics problems in A-10A aircraft. Earned recognition as the only group to achieve rapid turn around of different types of aircraft during a major inspection.

**ELECTRONIC TECHNICIAN.** U.S.A.F., Beale AFB, CA (1990-92). Gained extensive experience in maintaining and repairing communication, navigation, and electronic warfare systems on T-33A aircraft while also becoming familiar with airframe and propulsion systems on other aircraft. Participated in load planning and providing supply support during numerous training operations.

**PERSONAL**  Hold a Top Secret security clearance with Background Investigation. Have studied electronics and vehicle maintenance at the community college level.

Date

Exact Name of Person
Exact Title
Exact Name of Company
Address
City, State, Zip

## VEHICLE MAINTENANCE SHOP FOREMAN

Dear Exact Name of Person (or Dear Sir or Madam if answering a blind ad):

With the enclosed resume, I would like to make you aware of my interest in exploring employment opportunities with your organization and introduce you to my mechanical and supervisory skills.

As you will see from my enclosed resume, I am serving with Hertz Rent-A-Car where I have become recognized as a hard-working young professional who is effective in prioritizing tasks, managing time effectively, and handling multiple simultaneous activities. I have been singled out for promotion to leadership roles ahead of my peers and have earned numerous awards and certificates of appreciation for my mechanical abilities as well as for my initiative, drive, and positive style of leadership.

In my present position in Germany, I was promoted to hold a supervisory job in a vehicle maintenance operation which supports the car rental service in Europe. I supervise and train three people while controlling and accounting for a $6 million inventory of vehicles, trailers, and generators. Highly regarded for my initiative and resourcefulness, I have frequently been cited for my problem-solving skills and my ability to make sound decisions under pressure.

I received extensive training as a Vehicle Mechanic, and I have attended other programs in leadership and supervisory skill development, hazardous materials, and waste handling and maintenance logistics support actions.

I am a hard worker who excels in dealing with people through my example of dedication and honesty and excel in troubleshooting problems and finding solutions. I work well independently or while contributing to the efforts of a team. If you can use an energetic and adaptable individual who offers a proven ability to work well with others, I hope you will contact me to suggest a time when we might discuss your needs.

Yours sincerely,

Terry W. Homer

# TERRY W. HOMER

1110½ Hay Street, Fayetteville, NC 28305  •  preppub@aol.com  •  (910) 483-6611

---

**OBJECTIVE**  To offer excellent mechanical skills and experience in vehicle maintenance to an organization that can use a dedicated and hard-working young professional with the ability to motivate and train others along with the ability to resourcefully resolve complex repair problems.

**EDUCATION**  Completed extensive leadership development and technical training programs such as:

| | |
|---|---|
| Vehicle Mechanic | Logistics Maintenance Supervisor |
| Vehicle Recovery Specialist | Heavy Wheeled Vehicle Mechanic |
| Oil Analysis Program (AOAP) Monitor | Physical Security Procedures |
| Mechanical Maintenance | Unit Level Maintenance |
| Driver's Training for Europe | School of Standards Orientation |
| Supervisor Development | Hazardous Materials Handling |

Emergency Program Manager (Emergency Preparedness and Disaster Assistance)
Completed the Basic Gas Welding course, Northwood University, 1996

**OVERVIEW OF EXPERIENCE**  Have extensive mechanical experience in the troubleshooting and repairing of electrical and mechanical components on light- and heavy-wheeled vehicles. Performed scheduled and unscheduled maintenance on a fleet of 255 vehicles, trailers, and generators valued in excess of $6 million. Have become skilled at utilizing schematics and technical manuals in order to troubleshoot complex repair problems according to strict regulatory procedures.

**EXPERIENCE**  *Refined my mechanical skills while serving with Hertz Rent-A-Car:*
**VEHICLE MAINTENANCE SHOP FOREMAN.** Germany (2002-present). Cited as a resourceful professional, physically and mentally tough under pressure, control the maintenance and operation of more than $6 million worth of facilities and equipment in a motor pool for this major car rental operation with 255 vehicles.
- Supervise three subordinates and coordinate scheduled/unscheduled maintenance and services as well as repair parts inventory support.
- Singled out for my resourcefulness and initiative, am known for my ability to maximize scarce resources while tackling and completing the tough jobs.
- Emphasize safety in all phases of training and work performance and am recognized as an effective and skilled trainer who produces knowledgeable personnel.

**VEHICLE MAINTENANCE SHOP FOREMAN.** London, England (2000-02). Promoted on the basis of a combination of my positive approach and energy as well as my mechanical skills and knowledge, trained and supervised four subordinates performing maintenance on the airline's vehicles and generators.
- Used test measuring and diagnostic equipment to troubleshoot malfunctions while also providing personnel with technical guidance and advice.
- Was officially evaluated as displaying "technical skills equivalent to a senior" supervisor and mechanic and as "best wheel mechanic" in my department.

**VEHICLE MECHANIC.** Germany (1996-00). Built a reputation for technical competence, attention to detail, and outstanding achievements as a mechanic.
- Displayed a high level of initiative and drive which on one occasion led me to travel to locate high-priority repair parts in order to ensure vehicle downtime was at a minimum.

**HONORS**  Earned Achievement Medals, Mechanic's Badge, Proficiency Award, and numerous Safety Award. Outstanding references on request.

Date

Exact Name of Person
Title or Position
Name of Company
Address (number and street)
Address (city, state, and zip)

**VEHICLE MAINTENANCE SUPERVISOR**

Dear Exact Name of Person (or Sir or Madam if answering a blind ad):

I would appreciate an opportunity to talk with you soon about how I could contribute to your organization through the application of my expertise in the field of fleet maintenance supervision as well as through my reputation as a self-motivated, articulate, and honest professional.

While serving as Vehicle Maintenance Supervisor at Towson Ford-Lincoln, Towson, MD, I have earned a reputation as a professional who can be depended on for personal integrity, resourcefulness, and dedication to excellence in everything I attempt. I train and supervise 18 people involved in automobile repair as well as maintain an inventory of spare parts and tools.

Throughout my career I have excelled in building productive teams of mechanically adept and knowledgeable professionals and have always achieved excellent safety records. I have emphasized compliance with EPA guidelines and all safety regulations and led one organization to a two-year accident-free record and another to three years of accident-free operations.

I am confident that through my ability to meet challenges head on and exceed expectations in all operational areas, I can contribute to any organization in need of a mature knowledgeable professional. With a reputation for high personal standards of integrity, self-confidence, and superior leadership and team building skills I can make important contributions to any organization.

I hope you will welcome my call soon to arrange a brief meeting to discuss your current and future needs and how I might serve them. Thank you in advance for your time.

Sincerely,

Federico M. Munoz

(Alternate last paragraph:
I hope you will call or write me soon to suggest a time convenient for us to meet and discuss your current and future needs and how I might serve them. Thank you in advance for your time.)

# FEDERICO M. MUNOZ

1110½ Hay Street, Fayetteville, NC 28305 • preppub@aol.com • (910) 483-6611

**OBJECTIVE**  To contribute my solid base of experience in fleet maintenance to an organization that can use a self-starter with outstanding motivational, leadership, and team-building skills who is always open to new ideas for making operations run more efficiently and effectively.

**EXPERIENCE**  **VEHICLE MAINTENANCE SUPERVISOR.** Towson Ford-Lincoln, Towson, MD (2003-present). Train and supervise 18 people involved in repair of automobiles; maintain an inventory of spare parts and tools while acting as supervisor on vehicle maintenance activities.
- Reduced the excess parts inventory by streamlining procedures as well as cutting repair time an impressive 21%. Use test measuring and diagnostic equipment to troubleshoot malfunctions while also providing personnel with technical guidance and advice.
- Oversee compliance with EPA (Environmental Protection Agency) guidelines.

**MAINTENANCE MANAGER.** Kern's Ambulance Service, Baltimore, MD (2000-02). Managed maintenance for an ambulance service, accounting for $3 million in equipment including 10 wheeled vehicles and 67 pieces of emergency equipment; oversaw maintenance of ambulances to ensure readiness at all times.
- Received, controlled, and accounted for repair parts. Supervised and trained 20 maintenance specialists while ensuring that activities were completed on schedule.
- Provided drivers with advice, guidance, and administrative support.
- Guided four of the ambulances to nearly perfect ratings in major inspections.
- Achieved a 95% equipment serviceability rate.
- Praised in formal evaluations for my strong leadership and for setting the standard for performance, was cited as a first-class instructor and expert at hands-on training.

**MAINTENANCE SUPERVISOR.** EATON Corporation, Southfield, MI (1997-99). Maintained inventory of materials and provided technical training to employees testing automotive products. Maintained 100% accountability of a million-dollar inventory.
- Supervised the recovery section which consisted of four tracked recovery vehicles and one wrecker; maintained a 98% readiness rate.
- Provided administrative and training support as supervisor of 31 employees.

**MAINTENANCE SUPERVISOR.** Clark Chevrolet, Joplin, MO (1993-96). Supervised a 16-person repair shop involved in maintenance of customers' autos and preparation of cars taken as trade-ins to ready for resale.
- Trained, supervised, and then inspected the performance of personnel as they maintained administrative records and followed repair parts procedures.
- Organized the work area for increased productivity and efficiency.
- Coached subordinates to a 100% pass rate during annual maintenance skills testing.

**MAINTENANCE TECHNICIAN.** Henley Toyota, Joplin, MO (1990-92). Worked on customers' autos brought in for repair; regarded as resident expert and advisor on maintenance. Received praise from my supervisor for my expertise in the areas of quality control and repair parts procedures.
- Became known as the mechanic who could handle the most difficult jobs.

**TRAINING**  Excelled in training programs which emphasized technical knowledge, troubleshooting, and professional leadership development.

**PERSONAL**  Am a team player who excels in motivating others and building productive teams.

Date

Exact Name of Person
Title or Position
Name of Company
Address (no., street)
Address (city, state, zip)

**VEHICLE MAINTENANCE SUPERVISOR**

Dear Exact Name of Person (or Dear Sir or Madam if answering a blind ad):

I would appreciate an opportunity to talk with you soon about how I could benefit your organization through my personnel management skills and my proven maintenance and inventory control expertise.

While serving as Vehicle Maintenance Supervisor at Star Truck Rentals, Moline, IL, I schedule and conduct training for 20 employees in the maintenance section. I ensure compliance with quality control guidelines and maintained a 90% equipment availability rate over a one-year period. My experience and knowledge extend to mechanical, supervisory, and inventory control expertise.

You would find me a reliable individual with a talent for motivating others and a desire to give "110 percent" in the performance of any task.

I hope you will welcome my call soon to arrange a brief meeting at your convenience to discuss your current and future needs and how I might serve them. Thank you in advance for your time.

Sincerely yours,


George Allen Sanford

(Alternate last paragraph:
I hope you will call or write me soon to suggest a time convenient for us to meet and discuss your current and future needs and how I might serve them. Thank you in advance for your time.)

# GEORGE ALLEN SANFORD

1110½ Hay Street, Fayetteville, NC 28305  •  preppub@aol.com  •  (910) 483-6611

---

**OBJECTIVE**  To apply my outstanding mechanical and supervisory abilities to an organization in need of a young professional who is knowledgeable of inventory control procedures, vehicle maintenance, and project planning.

**SPECIAL SKILLS**
- Through training and experience, have become skilled in operating a variety of equipment and wheeled and tracked vehicles including:

  | | |
  |---|---|
  | 1-1/2 and 2-1/2-ton trucks | 10-ton trucks |
  | 28-ton track vehicles | 3, 5, 10, and 15 kw generators |
  | 5-ton forklifts | |

- Proficient with computers using Word, Excel, and PowerPoint for record keeping and inventory control.
- Troubleshoot, maintain, and repair vehicles and generators.

**EXPERIENCE**  **VEHICLE MAINTENANCE SUPERVISOR.** Star Truck Rentals, Moline, IL (2002-present). Excel in a position usually reserved for a more experienced and higher-ranking professional; supervise 17 vehicle mechanics and two inventory control specialists while scheduling maintenance and repair activities.
- Prioritize and determine quantities for parts being ordered.
- Cited for my organizational skills and attention to detail.
- Maintained a 90% equipment availability rate over a one-year period.
- Ensure that quality control inspections were performed on time.

**SUPERVISORY VEHICLE MAINTENANCE SPECIALIST.** Allied Van Lines, Rock Island, IL (1999-01). Maintained 100% equipment readiness while supervising a team of 19 mechanics and inventory control specialists.
- Managed a one million-dollar parts inventory in addition to preparing regular readiness reports and overseeing calibration on all equipment.
- Initiated a new safety procedure that resulted in accident-free operations for one year.
- Earned an aware for "meritorious achievements" for improving repair turnaround time.

**VEHICLE MAINTENANCE SHOP FOREMAN.** RYDER/MLS, Peoria, IL (1996-98). Became known for my leadership ability as well as my mechanical skills as the supervisor of 12 employees involved in servicing 35 tractor trailer trucks.
- Conducted quality control inspections on vehicles and prepared necessary documentation.
- Maintained a 90% equipment availability rate.

**MOTOR POOL SUPERVISOR.** U.S. Army, Ft. Dix, NJ (1993-95). Earned promotion from Light Vehicle Maintenance Mechanic ahead of my peers to oversee vehicle maintenance and administrative support. "Turned around" an operation with a reputation for substandard performance and led it to consistently "superior" ratings.

**LIGHT VEHICLE MAINTENANCE MECHANIC.** U.S. Army, Ft. Ord, CA (1990-92). Was honored as the "Mechanic of the Quarter" for my high performance standards while servicing 23 track vehicles and ordering/replacing parts.

**TRAINING**  Excelled in almost 400 hours of leadership, counseling, and technical courses.
Have taken community college-level courses in auto mechanics, auto body work, and HVAC.

**PERSONAL**  Speak, read, and write Spanish.

Date

Exact Name of Person
Title or Position
Name of Company
Address (no., street)
Address (city, state, zip)

**WHEELED VEHICLE MECHANIC**

Dear Exact Name of Person (or Dear Sir or Madam if answering a blind ad):

I would appreciate an opportunity to talk with you soon about how I could contribute to your organization through my skills in troubleshooting, repairing, and maintaining heavy- and light-wheeled vehicles and power generation equipment.

As you will see from my resume, I am serving with the U.S. Postal Office with distinction while becoming known as a highly skilled troubleshooter who excels in repairing the stubborn mechanical problems that have baffled others. I am skilled in using diagnostic equipment, hand and power tools, and special tools for disassembly, repair, reassembly, and testing of components and major end items, and I am experienced in repairing/maintaining brake systems, hydraulic systems, pneumatic systems, electrical systems, as well as the clutch and transmission.

A self-motivated individual, I received more than 11 separate medals and awards while serving my country, and I am proud of my reputation as an extremely "quality-conscious, safety-first" individual. I can provide excellent personal and professional references, and I would be willing to relocate worldwide to suit your needs.

I hope you will write or call me soon to suggest a time when we might meet to discuss your needs and how I might serve them. Thank you in advance for your time.

Sincerely yours,


David C. Dante

(Alternate last paragraph:
I hope you will welcome my call soon to arrange a brief meeting at your convenience to discuss your current and future needs and how I might serve them. Thank you in advance for your time.)

# DAVID CHRISTOPHER DANTE

1110½ Hay Street, Fayetteville, NC 28305 • preppub@aol.com • (910) 483-6611

**OBJECTIVE**    To offer my mechanical skills and management potential to an organization that can use a seasoned troubleshooter who has earned a reputation for being able to solve difficult problems, often with limited resources.

**TECHNICAL SKILLS**
- Experienced in the repair and maintenance of heavy- and light-wheeled vehicles and generators.
- Skilled in diagnostic and repair procedures for drive train, hydraulic, electrical, and brake systems. Familiar with repair parts ordering procedures.
- Knowledgeable of the use of service and technical manuals, am experienced in reading electrical and hydraulic schemes as well as blueprints and diagrams.
- Troubleshoot and repair Detroit and Detroit Allison products, Cummins products, Caterpillar products, and Mercedes-Benz diesel products.
- Operate and repair forklifts; skilled in using diagnostic equipment, hand and power tools, and special tools including oxyacetylene welding for disassembly, repair, reassembly, and testing of components and major end items.
- Experienced in repairing/maintaining brake systems, hydraulic systems, pneumatic systems, electrical systems, as well as the clutch and transmissions.

**EXPERIENCE**    **WHEELED VEHICLE MECHANIC** and **ACTING SUPERVISOR.** U.S. Postal System, San Diego, CA (2003-present). Because of my reputation as a highly skilled mechanic with a knack for troubleshooting the most difficult diesel and mechanical problems, am sometimes put in charge of between six to 20 mechanics in the absence of the manager.
- Perform wheeled vehicle maintenance and repair on a multimillion-dollar fleet of vehicles; assured the highest standards of quality control and supervised road testing before equipment was returned to customers.
- Frequently train junior mechanics in mechanical techniques, use of tools, and analytical processes needed to diagnose and repair problems; assist and advise mechanics in the servicing and overhaul of drivetrains and hydraulic and electrical systems.
- Maintain a perfect safety record. Perform troubleshooting, repair, preventative maintenance, and modification of heavy-wheeled vehicles.

**WHEELED VEHICLE MECHANIC.** Carter Construction Company, Germany (2000-03). Serviced numerous makes and models of both light- and heavy-wheeled equipment as well as generators for an organization which had a fleet of 241 heavy-wheeled vehicles along with hundreds of other pieces of equipment, generators, and light-wheeled vehicles.
- Became experienced in all phases of gasoline, diesel, and electrically powered equipment ranging from preventative maintenance checks and services through complete service.
- Learned to make skillful repairs under tight deadlines, and assured conformity of all repairs, with schedules, time tables, as well as federal and local OSHA regulations.

**Other experience:** Learned mechanical skills as an adolescent and have been repairing mechanical components for several years; worked in construction prior to the U.S.P.O.

**EDUCATION**    At the St. Louis Vehicle School, excelled in the Heavy-Wheeled Vehicle Mechanic Course; graduated 1999. Also completed Wheeled Vehicle Recovery Specialist Course, Aug 1998. Completed the ICS Automotive Course, 1996.

**PERSONAL**    Am a self-motivated individual who prides myself on performing quality work at all times. Am extremely safety conscious. Enjoy teaching and training less experienced workers.

# PART THREE: APPLYING FOR FEDERAL GOVERNMENT JOBS

The position vacancy announcement which describes the position you wish to apply for will give you two or three alternative ways to apply for the position. One option you will probably be offered is to submit a resume. Submitting a resume for a federal job is different from submitting a resume for civilian jobs. More detail is required on a federal resume, and in order to illustrate what a federal resume looks like, we are showing you a federal resume on the following pages. The three-page federal resume on the next page is often called a "Resumix."

**ROGER C. JACOBS**
3789 Cambridge Avenue
Washington, DC 11111-1111
999-999-9999 Home
rogerjacobs@aol.com

**SSN:** 000-00-0000
**Country of Citizenship:** United States
**Veteran's Preference:**
**Contact current supervisor:** Yes
**Vacancy Announcement Number:** AR 0000-000
**Job Title:** Senior Transportation Manager, GS-00

**SENIOR TRANSPORTATION TERMINAL MANAGER**

**EXPERIENCE**

*Excelled in a track record of promotions with the Department of Defense in various locations:*
**SENIOR TRANSPORTATION TERMINAL MANAGER.**
**2004-present: Start and End Dates. Hours worked per week:** 40+. **Current Salary:** $42,000 per year. **Employer's Name and Address:** Department of Defense, 3876 7th Street, Washington, DC 11111-1111

**Supervisor's Name and Phone Number:** Walter Smalls, 888-888-8888. Because of my vast transportation knowledge and distinguished career, was handpicked and transferred to Washington as Senior Transportation Terminal Manager of the most diversified ocean terminal ordered to transship ammunitions, explosives, and sensitive cargo worldwide. Supervise the safety of 15 military, 195 civilian employees, and 120 contractor/longshoremen. Revitalized a stagnant training program and developed a training brief which became a model worldwide.

**OPERATIONS MANAGER.**
**2001-04: Start and End Dates. Hours worked per week:** 40+. **Salary:** $38,500. **Employer's Name and Address:** Department of Defense, 5127 Timber Lane, Miami, FL 33355. **Supervisor's Name and Phone Number:** Dennis Strickland, 777-777-7777. Commended for the success of the Armed Forces Identification and Evaluation organization methods and testing regiments by the Chief of Military Intelligence, Major General Frank D. Hoffman.

- Oversee the individual and group training for personnel in 18 different job specialties.
- Ensure the company is ready to respond with no notice and carry out support missions.
- Accountable for the readiness of 48 vehicles, ensure the quality of training, welfare, and readiness of imagery specialists operating and maintaining vehicles.
- Directly oversee the administrative and logistics support for 25 people operating and maintaining $12.5 million worth of imagery and intelligence equipment.

**VEHICLE PROCESSING CENTER & OPERATIONS MANAGER.**
**1997-01: Start and End Dates. Hours worked per week:** 40+. **Salary:** $35,000. **Employer's Name and Address:** Department of

Defense, 35347 Bishamon Avenue, Chicago, IL 45018. **Supervisor's Name and Phone Number:** Heather Wright, 666-666-6666. Operated two vehicle processing centers, a documentation section, and an administration section with 4 military bases and including, Fort Knox and Fort Campbell, KY; Fort Riley, KS and Fort Leonard Wood, MO. Accounted for $1.9 million in assets.

**BATTALION SERGEANT MAJOR & VEHICLE MAINTENANCE MANAGER.**
**1995-97: Start and End Dates. Hours worked per week:** 40+. **Salary:** $32,000. **Employer's Name and Address:** Department of Defense, 2436 Haywood Boulevard, Detroit, MI 45833 . **Supervisor's Name and Phone Number:** Jermaine Yarborough, 555-555-5555. Assured the rigorous training of 75 enlisted employees and 32 officers working in eleven different organizations. Was the organization's subject matter expert on all matters pertaining to the maintenance and management of vehicles as well as on coordinating and arranging transportation support. Provided aggressive leadership and training management which boosted soldier readiness from an unacceptable 58% to 88%. Played a key role in planning and executing transportation support for special operation in Central America.

**Other military experience:**
MOTOR TRANSPORTATION COMPANY MANAGER & FIRST SERGEANT.
**Start and End Dates:** June 1993-95. **Hours worked per week:** 40+. **Salary:** $28,900. **Employer's Name and Address:** US Army, 34th Motor Pool Division, Fort Drum, NY 10054 **Supervisor's Name and Phone Number:** SFC Mark Harris, 444-444-4444. Served as mentor and trainer for 62 employees while managing equipment valued at $8 million. Directed administrative and logistical support for a trucking company with a fleet of 115 wheeled and tracked vehicles. Developed new Vehicle Safety procedures which instilled in employees a new respect for safety and quality assurance and which resulted in more than 180,000 accident-free miles in an arctic environment.

**TRUCKING OPERATIONS COMMANDER.**
**Start and End Dates:** 1990-93. **Hours worked per week:** 40+. **Salary:** $25,000. **Employer's Name and Address:** US Army, 23rd ATC Maintenance Group, Fort Bliss, TX 73215-5940. **Supervisor's Name and Phone Number:** SFC Derrick Iverson, 333-333-3333. Managed operations of a medium truck company with a fleet of 85 vehicles, and directed long-haul transportation and distribution of cargo throughout Korea for an organization which accumulated 2 million driving miles annually. Managed 180 employees. Supervised operations of a driver's training academy, four trailer transfer points, and a trailer maintenance center. Developed new Vehicle Operation procedures which expedited the Department of Transportation cargo throughout Southwest Region. Solved complex problems during several combat mission exercises. Managed a dining facility in a remote location which earned us a Specialized Unit Award in 1992. Developed a driver's education course evaluated as "superb."

**Highlights of other military experience:** Began serving my country in 1983 as a Truck Driver; was promoted ahead of my peers and subsequently served in roles as a Chief Dispatcher, Light and Heavy Vehicle Operator, Transportation Company Squad Leader, Vehicle Operators Instructor, Vehicle Maintenance Manager, Truck Platoon Supervisor, and Senior Drill Sergeant.
- 1989. Was **Instructor** in the Vehicle Operating Course; trained and tested 36 students daily on coupling and decouping, backing into a simulated loading dock, and operations over open roads.
- 1988-89. As **Senior Drill Sergeant** in a training organization, oversaw the training of 1250 soldiers annually.

operations/maintenance of 25 vehicles ranging from ¼ ton to 5 tons annually. Also supervised the training of 190 individuals.

**SENIOR TRANSPORTATION TERMINAL MANAGER**

**EDUCATION** Completing **Master of Science (M.S.) in Management,** University of the District of Columbia, Washington, DC.
**Bachelor of Science (B.S.) in Management,** St. Thomas University, Miami, FL 2001.
**Bachelor of Science (B.S.) in Liberal Arts,** Northeastern Illinois University, Chicago, IL, 1998.
**Associate in Arts (A.A.),** Marygrove College, Detroit, MI, 1997.
**Associate of Science (A.S.) in Management,** Marygrove College, Detroit, MI, 1997.
**Associate of Arts (A.A.) in General Studies,** Watertown Community College, Watertown, NY, 1995.

**CLEARANCE** Secret Security Clearance

**HIGHLIGHTS OF MANAGEMENT AND TECHNICAL TRAINING**

Completed extensive executive-level training including the Leadership and Development Training Course, March 1995 and the Loadmasters Operation Course 1995; the Non-Commissioned Officer Training, 1995; Manager Development Course, 1994; the Defense Reutilization & Marketing System Course, 1994.

**Emergency Management Institute:** At this institute affiliated with the Health and Safety Management Course 1994, National Emergency Training Center, completed the Emergency Program Manager Course, 1994; the Hazardous Materials Course, 1993; and the Radiological Emergency Management Course, 1993; Guide to Disaster Assistance, 1993; Emergency Preparedness, 1993.

**Logistics Management College:** At the U.S. Army Logistics Management College, received diplomas for completing the Army Maintenance Management Course, 1994, and the SMPT-5 Hazardous Materials Handling Course, 1993.

**Army Institute for Professional Development:** At his famed institute which refines leadership and technical knowledge, completed the Weapons Specialist Course, 1992; Defense Financial Management Course, 1992; Supervisor Development Course, 1992; Defense Hazardous Materials/Waste Course, 1991; Manager Development Course, 1991; Intelligence/Operation Sergeant's Course, 1991; the Chemical Senior NCO Course, 1990; the NCO Logistics Program, 1990.

**Other training:** Lifesavers Course; Arabic Language Course; computer operations; light and heavy expanded mobility tactical trucks; drug and alcohol abuse prevention; Vehicle Operation Course.

**HONORS** Received 34 medals and awards during 25 years of military service.

**COMPUTERS** Proficient with software including Microsoft Word, PowerPoint, Access, and Excel; have utilized supply, inventory control, purchasing, and logistics software.

# About 612s & KSAs

The Optional Form 612 is probably the form used most extensively for applying for federal government jobs. A blank form 612 is shown on the next two pages. The first time you pick up a blank 612, you may be fooled into believing that the form is quick and easy to complete. Actually, very little of the information is typed onto the form. It is in your best interests to complete the form by using Continuation Sheets which contain your answers. Continuation Sheets allow you to be more detailed and thorough. Do **not** feel that you must fit your answers into the small blank spaces provided. Never hand write the form. Always type it.

In this section you will see the way in which you should complete the Form 612. The general rule you should follow is to be as thorough and comprehensive as possible in describing your experience and accomplishments. Remember that your 612 is "being graded" and will receive a numerical score which will determine your ranking among your competitors for the job. If you are applying for a specific job, read carefully the description of the job for which you are applying and make sure that you write your descriptions in such a way that you clearly "measure up" to the job requirements.

## Completing Questions 1-7

These questions are straightforward, and your answers to these questions should be typed onto the form. Make blank copies of the front page before you type in the answers to 1, 2, and 3, and you will be able to use the photocopied front page again and again, to apply for many different jobs, by simply typing in the Job Title, Grade, and Announcement number particular to the job for which you are applying.

## Completing Section 8 Work Experience

Section 8 is the "meat" of your 612. Normally, you are at a disadvantage if you "shrink" what you did in a job so that it fits into the small block of blank space which you are given. You should type "Please see Continuation Sheet for Job 8 (1)" in the blank space provided, and then use similar Continuation Sheets like the ones in this section to expand on your duties, responsibilities, and accomplishments in each job. For each job, use a separate Continuation Sheet. Notice that you are asked to describe paid and non-paid experience, so don't omit significant volunteer experience or non-paid positions you have held which helped you acquire knowledge, skills, and abilities.

## Completing Questions 9-12

Your answers to these questions should be typed onto the form. If you have more education than will fit on the form, use a Continuation Sheet for Item 12.

## Completing Question 13 Other Qualifications

The best way to complete Item 13 is to type "Please See Continuation Sheet for Item 13" in this section, and provide your extensive, detailed, and comprehensive responses to Other Qualifications on a separate page. You will find many excellent examples of Item 13 in this section.

## Completing Questions 14-18 General

Your answers to these questions can be typed onto the form. You must sign and date the form.

# GEOFFREY DAVID KEARNS

SSN: 000-00-0000

CONTINUATION SHEET FOR 612 ITEM 8 (1)

**Continuation Sheet For 612 Item 8 (1)**

**Job Title:** Highway Maintenance Worker/Equipment Operator
**From (MM/YY):** 03/2002
**To (MM/YY):** present
**Salary:** $7.53 to $12.00 per hour
**Hours per week:** 40+
**Employer's name and address:** Department of Transportation, 1110 Hay Street, Richmond, VA 28305
**Supervisor's name and phone number:** Francis Sweeney, (910) 483-6611

Drove a single-axle dump truck, eight wheeler, while hauling material for driveways and from shoulders and ditches. Utilized my expertise in operating chain saws, laying bricks, using bush axes, and mixing mortar and concrete while performing a variety of daily duties as the job required. I pulled a rubber tire backhoe, which I operated. We utilized a tilt-bed trailer to move the backhoe to the various jobs.

Was regarded as one of the Department of Transportation's most versatile workers because of my background in operating many types of heavy and light equipment used to excavate, backfill, or grade earth.

*This 612 was designed to help Geoff Kerns into an Equipment Operator job.*

Performed heavy, physical work which involved reaching, bending, turning, and moving my hands, arms, feet, and legs to handle different sets of controls that operated equipment and attachments. Performed this work outdoors, often in bad weather, in areas that were noisy, dusty, dirty, and smoky. Was exposed to fumes, heat, sparks, and glare.

Installed concrete drainage pipe in driveways and cross roads to ensure all roadways in Richmond County were safe from water standing or running across roadways. Cleaned brush to insure safety at intersections or shoulders of road clearances. Operated the air compressor and jack hammer to cut through roadways when installing new or replacing drainage pipe if it were damaged.

Also worked with an asphalt crew pouring tar in cracks in roads, which involved cutting out bad areas and replacing them with asphalt. Ran the roller to compact the asphalt and ran the 2 ½ cubic-yard scoop loader while loading trucks.

Safety was always our number one concern while operating the above equipment, and I had a perfect safety record. I learned to set up safe road construction signs, and insured that the person on the stop and go signs was trained properly to avoid all accidents. We had classes on excavating ditches and proper shoring to avoid cave-ins.

# GEOFFREY DAVID KEARNS

SSN: 000-00-0000

CONTINUATION SHEET FOR 612 ITEM 8 (2)

**Continuation Sheet**
For 612 Item 8 (2)

**Job Title:** Truck Driver/Equipment Operator
**From (MM/YY):** 04/1998
**To (MM/YY):** 02/2002
**Salary:** $8.00 hr.
**Hours per week:** 40+
**Employer's name and address:** Vulcan Ironworks, Inc., 1110 Hay Street, Hampton, VA 28305
**Supervisor's name and phone number:** Francis Lithe, (910) 483-6611

In all kinds of traffic and weather, drove an 18-wheeler with a roll-off trailer in order to deliver scrap metals from industries and to haul materials for recycling. Operated a 10,000-pound forklift and scoop loaders and a car crusher.

*Notice the extensive detail he gives. He really "sells" his ability to drive a truck and operate equipment.*

Maintained a perfect safety record while operating equipment to perform a variety of functions. Read and interpreted narrative specifications pertaining to the job to be accomplished.

Continuously was involved in heavy, physical work which involved constant bending, reaching, turning, and moving my hands, arms, feet, and legs. Frequently worked in awkward and strained positions. Often lifted and moved items heavier than 50 pounds with lifting devices such as jacks, truck excavators with magnet attachment, and hoists.

Worked in an environment in which I was constantly exposed to the possibility of injury. Utilized my extensive background in safety to maintain safety vigilance at all times and to exercise safety precautions constantly.

In rough terrain, operated a 10,000-pound forklift to load cars after they were crushed on a flatbed trailer and a 2 ½ cubic-yard scoop loader to land various metals, glass, cardboard, and paper for recycling.

Practiced the highest safety standards while preventing injury from sparks of metal from cutting torches and from the glare of arc welding.

Operated various types of heavy and light equipment used in small construction jobs. Equipment used included front-end loader and bulldozers to perform a variety of functions on rocky, soft, and uneven ground, on graded curves and shoulders, as well as on hills, steep slopes, and other surfaces with similar rough features. Frequently performed maintenance on such equipment. Operated vibratory roller for compaction of building foundations. Utilized bulldozer with brush rake attachment, 2 ½ cubic-yard track loader with 4-way bucket, and 15-ton tandem trucks to haul materials.

# GEOFFREY DAVID KEARNS

SSN: 000-00-0000

CONTINUATION SHEET FOR 612 ITEM 8 (3)

**Continuation Sheet For 612 Item 8 (3)**

**Job Title:** Construction Inspector
**From (MM/YY):** 10/1982
**To (MM/YY):** 04/1998
**Salary:** E7 to E8
**Hours per week:** 40+
**Employer's name and address:** HHC 28th MED BN, Ft. Sam Houston, TX 28305
**Supervisor's name and phone number:** CW3 F. Sweeney, (910) 483-6611

Managed 10 individuals who staffed the brigade sections specializing in survey, drafting, and soil analysis while providing quality assurance and quality control for all construction for an airborne engineer brigade. Managed and inspected all brigade construction projects to include major training exercises and deployments. Coordinated and advised the unit in proper construction and ground engineering techniques.

Continuously applied my expertise related to horizontal construction, specifically road and airfield construction. Operated heavy equipment including motor graders, dump trucks, front-end loaders, backhoes, and compactors.

Spent approximately 40% of my time insuring that my sections were on schedule and accomplishing their missions. Spent the other 60% of my time in coordinating, advising, inspecting, and managing the units in proper construction and sound engineering techniques.

Supervised individuals in operating light and heavy equipment to excavate, backfill, or grade earth. Supervised individuals using equipment fitted with front-end loaders and bulldozers to perform a variety of functions. Oversaw the construction of roads in rough features, and supervised the grading of terrain to prevent erosion. Oversaw individuals involved in the safe operation of motor vehicles to include wreckers, tilt-bed trailers, and tractor trailers capable of carrying up to 10 tons.

Performed a great deal of my work in the outdoors, frequently in bad weather in areas that were noisy, dusty, dirty, and smoky.

Was known for my emphasis on quality control and safety, and supervised the practice of strict precautions in order to avoid the possibility of injury.

During Operation Desert Storm, acted as Brigade S-3 NCOIC for five months in the absence of the Sergeant Major. Demonstrated my expertise in road construction, especially in a desert environment. Was awarded an **Army Commendation Medal** for "exceptionally meritorious achievement as the Brigade S-3 Section Sergeant Major during the Desert Storm Operation."

# GEOFFREY DAVID KEARNS
SSN: 000-00-0000
CONTINUATION SHEET FOR 612 ITEM 13

**Job-Related Training Courses:**
Brick Masonry, 1993
Carpentry, 1991
Supervisory Maintenance Course, 1991
Maintenance Management & Operations Course, 1985
NCO Academy, 1984
First Corps Support Command Leadership School, 1983
Battalion Training Management System, 1983
Roads and Airfields Course, 1982
Jungle Warfare Training Course, 1983
Jumpmaster Course, 1983
Air Movement Operations Course, 1982
Airlift Planners Course, 1982
Jump School, 1982
Army Infantry Company Amphibious Training Course, 1982
Maintenance and Operation of John Deere (JD 410) Backhoe Loader 1980

**Honors and Awards:**
- Army Commendation Medal (5)
- Army Achievement Medal (2)
- National Defense Service Medal with Bronze Service Star
- Kuwait Liberation Medal
- Non Commissioned Officer Professional Development Ribbon (3)
- Army Service Ribbon
- Meritorious Service Medal

**Safety Awards:**
Numerous safety awards

**Licenses:**
Commercial Drivers License Class A, X endorsement (licensed to pull tanker and hazardous materials)
NC Drivers License
Valid military forklift driver's license

**Security Clearance:**
Held a Secret security clearance

# KSAs--Knowledge, Skills, and Abilities
## GEORGE ROBERT ADAMS
SSN: 000-00-0000
AUTOMOTIVE WORKER, WG-08 ANNOUNCEMENT #XYZ123

**Automotive Worker, WG-08 Announcement #XYZ123 KSA #1**

On the following six pages, you will see examples of KSAs which are often required when applying for Federal Government positions. George Adams had to provide 10 separate KSAs in addition to his federal resume or form 612.

This KSA asks for evidence that someone can work with minimal supervision.

**KSA #1: Ability to perform the duties of an automotive worker without more than normal supervision**

**Overview of knowledge in this KSA:**
Over a period of 22 years in assignments with the U.S. Army, I have held responsible positions relating directly to automotive maintenance activities. I am thoroughly familiar with company-level maintenance on diesel powered vehicles and throughout my military career used a hands-on approach
during troubleshooting and parts replacement actions.

**Experience related to this KSA:**
From 1990-99, I was assigned as a Manager and Supervisor for the 7th Medical Group at Ft. Myers, VA, where I made the decisions based on my own judgment of what parts needed to be replaced and prioritized automotive work on three major types of diesel vehicles: the HMMMWV, 2 1/2-ton, and 5-ton trucks as well as occasionally working on forklifts. My knowledge of automotive work resulted in my selection as the person entrusted with several hundred thousand dollars worth of vehicles and equipment while transporting this equipment over a distance of several thousand miles in both military and civilian-leased vehicles.

From 1982-90, as an Instructor in a military training school at Ft. Leonard Wood, MO, I applied my knowledge of automotive work while teaching classes of up to 60 students and ensuring students were properly trained in the maintenance of transportation vehicles and equipment.

From 1977-82, I was a Maintenance Technician and Supervisor. In my first assignments in Germany I was a Maintenance Technician and learned to work independently while replacing parts in military diesel powered vehicles. My next assignment was at Ft. Bragg, NC, where I was soon selected to be a Maintenance Supervisor and became skilled in overseeing automotive workers while still continuing to gain hands-on experience. Additional experience in Korea gave me the opportunity to make decisions and do automotive work on diesel vehicles with no supervision.

**Education and training related to this KSA:**
Courses which helped me acquire or refine my knowledge of automotive work include the following:
- diploma — light wheel vehicle/power generator mechanic basic technical course
- training the instructor
- basic oxygen and acetylene welding
- mechanic supervision
- technical publications and logistics
- recovery vehicle operations
- operator and organizational maintenance
- automatic transmissions

# GEORGE ROBERT ADAMS
SSN: 000-00-0000
AUTOMOTIVE WORKER, WG-08 ANNOUNCEMENT #XYZ123

**KSA #2: Knowledge of automotive components and assemblies to include use of tools and test equipment**

**Overview of knowledge in this KSA:**
Over a period of 22 years in assignments with the U.S. Army, I have held responsible positions relating directly to automotive maintenance activities in which I have become thoroughly familiar with company-level maintenance on diesel powered vehicles. Throughout my military career I used a hands-on approach while troubleshooting and making determinations on which parts to replace while using basic tools including wrenches and screwdrivers and my own knowledge.

**Experience related to this KSA:**
From 1990-99, I was assigned as a Manager and Supervisor for the 7th Medical Group at Ft. Myer, VA, where I have used my knowledge of diesel powered vehicles along with the proper tools and equipment for each stage of the repair process. Through my many years of experience I am highly skilled in using my judgment to determine what parts needed to be replaced and prioritized automotive work on three major types of diesel vehicles: the HMMMWV, 2 1/2-ton, and 5-ton trucks as well as occasionally working on forklifts.

From 1982-90, as an Instructor in a military training school at Ft. Leonard Wood, MO, I applied my knowledge of automotive components, assemblies, and equipment while teaching classes of up to 60 students and ensuring students were properly trained in the maintenance of transportation vehicles and equipment.

From 1977-82, I was a Maintenance Technician and Supervisor. In my first assignments in Germany I was a Maintenance Technician and learned to work independently while replacing parts in military diesel powered vehicles. My next assignment was at Ft. Bragg, NC, where I was soon selected to be a Maintenance Supervisor and became skilled in overseeing automotive workers while still continuing to gain hands-on experience. Additional experience in Korea gave me the opportunity to make decisions and do automotive work on diesel vehicles with no supervision.

**Education and training related to this KSA:**
Courses which helped me acquire or refine my knowledge of automotive components, tools, and test equipment include the following:
- diploma — light wheel vehicle/power generation mechanic basic technical course
- training the instructor
- basic oxygen and acetylene welding
- mechanic supervision
- technical publications and logistics
- recovery vehicle operations
- operator and organizational maintenance
- automatic transmissions

---

*Automotive Worker, WG-08 Announcement #XYZ123 KSA #2*

*An "overview" of your knowledge may be a useful way to highlight an extensive background.*

# GEORGE ROBERT ADAMS

SSN: 000-00-0000
AUTOMOTIVE WORKER, WG-08 ANNOUNCEMENT #XYZ123

*Automotive Worker,
WG-08
Announcement #XYZ123
KSA #3*

**KSA #3: Ability to interpret instructions, specifications, reference manuals, and other regulatory guidance**

**Overview of knowledge in this KSA:**
During my 22 years with the U.S. Army, I have held responsible positions relating directly to automotive maintenance activities where the ability to use and understand parts manuals and other reference materials is an important factor while troubleshooting and repairing diesel powered vehicles.

**Experience related to this KSA:**
From 1990-99, as a Manager and Supervisor for the 7th Medical Group at Ft. Myer, VA, where I routinely used parts manuals and reference material while checking on the proper replacement parts to be used after making determinations on how to repair vehicles. In this unit I oversaw mechanics working on three major types of diesel vehicles: the HMMMWV, 2 1/2-ton, and 5-ton trucks as well as occasionally working on forklifts. As the military makes changes in its inventory of vehicles I have been required to keep up with the latest changes and aware of where to find the most up-to-date information. The varied types of technical publications I have had to interpret applied to such areas as inspections, troubleshooting, maintenance, repairs, modifications, calibration, and testing of vehicular equipment.

*Being detailed is important in this KSA.*

From 1982-90, as an Instructor in a military training school at Ft. Leonard Wood, MO, I applied my knowledge of automotive work while teaching classes of up to 60 students and ensuring students were properly trained in the maintenance of transportation vehicles and equipment.

From 1977-82, I was a Maintenance Technician and Supervisor. In my first assignments in Germany I was a Maintenance Technician and became familiar with using parts manuals and other technical reference material as I was learning to do parts replacements on military vehicles. My next assignment was at Ft. Bragg, NC, where I was soon selected to be a Maintenance Supervisor and became skilled in overseeing automotive workers while still continuing to gain hands-on experience. Additional experience in Korea gave me the opportunity to make decisions and do automotive work on diesel vehicles while constantly being aware of keeping informed of changes to the military's inventory of vehicles.

**Education and training related to this KSA:**
Courses which helped me acquire or refine my knowledge of how to interpret instructions, specifications, reference manuals and other regulatory guidance included the following:
    diploma — light wheel vehicle/power generation mechanic basic technical course
    mechanic supervision
    technical publications and logistics
    operator and organizational maintenance

# GEORGE S. ZANE
SSN: 000-00-0000
MAINTENANCE TECHNICIAN, WG-07/09 ANNOUNCEMENT #XYZ123

### KSA #1: Dexterity and Safety

During my years of service in the U.S. Air Force Reserves (1996 to present) as a Materials Expediter and Ordnance Equipment Mechanic, I have built an excellent safety record and have never been involved in an accident or received a work-related injury. I completed numerous safety-related courses such as AFOSH (the Air Force Occupational Safety and Health program), hazard reporting, and weapons safety which included missile and explosive handling techniques. I conduct safety training in such subjects as pretask safety and forward firing ordnance. The emphasis on safety while fulfilling mission goals and objectives has resulted in quicker response and delivery times for munitions. I have also received safety training and observe safety practices related to the safe storage of munitions such as which munitions can be stored near each other and how near.

In my full-time job with Service Merchandise, I have been the company's OSHA representative and a member of the safety committee. Since joining the company in 1985, I have suffered no work-related injuries.

My dexterity and fine motor skills are displayed on a day-to-day basis while accurately and rapidly using a ten-key calculator in both jobs and as a mechanic in the Air Force Reserves dealing with munitions and all associated munitions handling and support equipment. While troubleshooting I evaluate solid state circuits, electromechanical, pneumatic, hydraulic, and explosive components and systems using precision measuring tools and equipment. I interpret and apply information gained from blueprints, schematics, and technical drawings. I recondition, deliver, maintain, test, and assemble guided and unguided munitions. When controlling nuclear munitions, I handle, store, and transport them according to existing safety directives and operating procedures. Inventory control and documentation actions include conducting/documenting inventories and any discrepancies which may occur. Operate the Combat Ammunition System and Maintenance Classification programs.

### Education and Training Related to this KSA:
Attended courses including the Air Force Combat Ammunition Planning and Production Course, 80 hours, July 1999; a Total Quality Management (TQM) course; and the Munitions Supply Technical School, Schriever AFB, CO, 1996 (285 hours).

*Sidebar:*
**Maintenance Technician, WG-07/09 Announcement #XYZ123 KSA #1**

Don't let a vague KSA throw you; provide details.

# GEORGE S. ZANE
SSN: 000-00-0000
MAINTENANCE TECHNICIAN, WG-07/09 ANNOUNCEMENT #XYZ123

*Maintenance Technician, WG-07/09 Announcement #XYZ123 KSA #2*

**KSA #2: Ability to use and maintain tools and equipment**

In my capacity of Ordnance Equipment Mechanic with the U.S. Air Force Reserves since 1996, I have become qualified and certified to use the following test sets:

- DSM-151B for AIM-7E and F electronic, hydraulic function, performance, and operational use
- AN/DSM-162 for determining if AIM-7E, F, and M missile guidance units are functioning properly
- TS4044/D for determining if AIM-BE, J, M, and P missile guidance units are functioning properly
- GCU-26E for checking AIM missile coolant pressure tank recharging unit

My responsibilities extend to cover all associated munitions handling and support equipment for which I evaluate solid state circuits, electromechanical, pneumatic, hydraulic, and explosive components and systems using precision measuring tools and equipment. I interpret and apply information gained from blueprints, schematics, and technical drawings.

*Give specifics.*

I regularly and routinely use tools and equipment which include, but are not limited to, the following:

| | | |
|---|---|---|
| lineman's and common pliers | 3/8" ratchet drive | 7/16" socket |
| 6" and 8" adjustable wrench | 7" vise grips | flashlight |
| 3/8" and 5/16" box-end wrench | 1/4" t-handle wrench | 1/4" air fastener bit |
| 1/8" and 5/64" Allen wrench | 1/8", 7/32", 1/4" and 5/16" apex | |
| torque wrench | lanyard kits | sledge hammer |
| bomb lift adapter with hook | MK-82 slings | levels |
| bomb rotating tool | slings | nail can |
| claw hammer | banding cutter | crosscut saw |
| spanner wrenches | hydraulic jack | light cables |
| ATU-35 tool | swaging tool | air ratchet |
| alignment tool | adapter ratchet | adapter socket |
| safety wire | | |

4" common, 6" common, and 3" Phillips screwdrivers
ear plugs, safety glasses, hard hat, face shield, foam ear plugs, and safety glasses
**mobility equipment:** tie-down straps, rail assemblies, chock assemblies, trolley assemblies, ramps, boom adapters, load binders, load chains, and pallets
**communications equipment:** notebook computer, laser jet printer, hand-held radios, and control radio mobility box

*An extensive Education and Training section is best for this KSA.*

**Education and Training Related to this KSA:**
Attended courses including the Air Force Combat Ammunition Planning and Production Course, 80 hours, July 1999; a Total Quality Management (TQM) course; and the Munitions Supply Technical School, Schriever AFB, CO, 1996 (285 hours).

# GEORGE S. ZANE
SSN: 000-00-0000
MAINTENANCE TECHNICIAN, WG-07/09 ANNOUNCEMENT #XYZ123

### KSA #3: Ability to perform troubleshooting

As a Materials Expediter/Ordnance Equipment Mechanic in the U.S. Air Force Reserves since 1996, I manage, monitor, account for, identify, store, issue, distribute, deliver, procure, and dispose of Air Force munitions. These munitions include unguided bombs, dispensers, mines, rockets, aircraft systems, small arms ammunition, guided munitions, and chemical munitions. My unit's primary mission is to provide safe and timely delivery of nonnuclear munitions, training munitions, and components which support the F-16C and D Fighting Falcon combat training aircraft. My responsibilities extend to include all associated munitions handling and support equipment. While troubleshooting I evaluate solid state circuits, electromechanical, pneumatic, hydraulic, and explosive components and systems using precision measuring tools and equipment. I interpret and apply information gained from blueprints, schematics, and technical drawings. Inspect munitions for serviceability and apply all relative quality assurance procedures.

Made important contributions which led to the success of the team during two important OREs (Ordnance Readiness Exercises) and two ORIs (Ordnance Readiness Inspections) which consisted of EARFLAP (Emergency Action Reporting for Logistics Action Programming) reporting. Played an important role as a Munitions Systems Specialist on teams which deployed to locations throughout the world such as Italy, Hawaii, and Turkey as well as Nellis AFB, NV, and Miramar Naval Air Station, CA, for large-scale training exercises. Also served in Saudi Arabia for Operation Desert Storm and Operation Southern Watch as well as in Alaska during Operation Northern Watch.

Am certified to use the following test sets:
- DSM-151B for AIM-7E and F electronic, hydraulic function, performance and operational use
- AN/DSM-162 for determining if AIM-7E, F, and M missile guidance units are functioning properly
- TS4044/D for determining if AIM-BE, J, M, and P missile guidance units are functioning properly
- GCU-26E for checking AIM missile coolant pressure tank recharging unit

Received a Letter of Appreciation in recognition of my "dedication, superior efforts, and professionalism" and "some of the finest F-16 maintenance I've ever seen" and which contributed to the unit earning a coveted 1997 AFRC Maintenance Effectiveness Award.

### Education and Training Related to this KSA:
- Earned an Associate in Applied Science degree in Logistics Operations Management, Community College of the Air Force, Eglin AFB, FL, 1996.
- Attended courses including the Air Force Combat Ammunition Planning and Production Course, 80 hours, July 1999; a Total Quality Management (TQM) course; and the Munitions Supply Technical School, Schriever AFB, CO, 1996 (285 hours).

## ABOUT THE EDITOR

Anne McKinney holds an MBA from the Harvard Business School and a BA in English from the University of North Carolina at Chapel Hill. A noted public speaker, writer, and teacher, she is the senior editor for PREP's business and career imprint, which bears her name. Early titles in the Anne McKinney Career Series (now called the Real-Resumes Series) published by PREP include: *Resumes and Cover Letters That Have Worked, Resumes and Cover Letters That Have Worked for Military Professionals, Government Job Applications and Federal Resumes, Cover Letters That Blow Doors Open,* and *Letters for Special Situations.* Her career titles and how-to resume-and-cover-letter books are based on the expertise she has acquired in 20 years of working with job hunters. Her valuable career insights have appeared in publications of the "Wall Street Journal" and other prominent newspapers and magazines.

# PREP Publishing Order Form

You may purchase any of our titles from your favorite bookseller! Or send a check or money order or your credit card number for the total amount*, plus $4.00 postage and handling, to PREP, 1110 1/2 Hay Street, Fayetteville, NC 28305. You may also order our titles on our website at www.prep-pub.com and feel free to e-mail us at preppub@aol.com or call 910-483-6611 with your questions or concerns.

Name: _____

Phone #:_____

Address: _____

E-mail address:_____

Payment Type: ☐ Check/Money Order  ☐ Visa  ☐ MasterCard

Credit Card Number: _____ Expiration Date: _____

Put a check beside the items you are ordering:

☐ Free—Packet describing PREP's professional writing and editing services
☐ $16.95—REAL-RESUMES FOR RESTAURANT, FOOD SERVICE & HOTEL JOBS. Anne McKinney, Editor
☐ $16.95—REAL-RESUMES FOR MEDIA, NEWSPAPER, BROADCASTING & PUBLIC AFFAIRS JOBS. Anne McKinney, Editor
☐ $16.95—REAL-RESUMES FOR RETAILING, MODELING, FASHION & BEAUTY JOBS. Anne McKinney, Editor
☐ $16.95—REAL-RESUMES FOR HUMAN RESOURCES & PERSONNEL JOBS. Anne McKinney, Editor
☐ $16.95—REAL-RESUMES FOR MANUFACTURING JOBS. Anne McKinney, Editor
☐ $16.95—REAL-RESUMES FOR AVIATION & TRAVEL JOBS. Anne McKinney, Editor
☐ $16.95—REAL-RESUMES FOR POLICE, LAW ENFORCEMENT & SECURITY JOBS. Anne McKinney, Editor
☐ $16.95—REAL-RESUMES FOR SOCIAL WORK & COUNSELING JOBS. Anne McKinney, Editor
☐ $16.95—REAL-RESUMES FOR CONSTRUCTION JOBS. Anne McKinney, Editor
☐ $16.95—REAL-RESUMES FOR FINANCIAL JOBS. Anne McKinney, Editor
☐ $16.95—REAL-RESUMES FOR COMPUTER JOBS. Anne McKinney, Editor
☐ $16.95—REAL-RESUMES FOR MEDICAL JOBS. Anne McKinney, Editor
☐ $16.95—REAL-RESUMES FOR TEACHERS. Anne McKinney, Editor
☐ $16.95—REAL-RESUMES FOR CAREER CHANGERS. Anne McKinney, Editor
☐ $16.95—REAL-RESUMES FOR STUDENTS. Anne McKinney, Editor
☐ $16.95—REAL-RESUMES FOR SALES. Anne McKinney, Editor
☐ $16.95—REAL ESSAYS FOR COLLEGE AND GRAD SCHOOL. Anne McKinney, Editor
☐ $25.00—RESUMES AND COVER LETTERS THAT HAVE WORKED. McKinney. Editor
☐ $25.00—RESUMES AND COVER LETTERS THAT HAVE WORKED FOR MILITARY PROFESSIONALS. McKinney, Ed.
☐ $25.00—RESUMES AND COVER LETTERS FOR MANAGERS. McKinney, Editor
☐ $25.00—GOVERNMENT JOB APPLICATIONS AND FEDERAL RESUMES: Federal Resumes, KSAs, Forms 171 and 612, and Postal Applications. McKinney, Editor
☐ $25.00—COVER LETTERS THAT BLOW DOORS OPEN. McKinney, Editor
☐ $25.00—LETTERS FOR SPECIAL SITUATIONS. McKinney, Editor
☐ $16.95—REAL-RESUMES FOR NURSING JOBS.  McKinney, Editor
☐ $16.95—REAL-RESUMES FOR AUTO INDUSTRY JOBS. Patty Sleem
☐ $24.95—REAL KSAS--KNOWLEDGE, SKILLS & ABILITIES--FOR GOVERNMENT JOBS. McKinney, Editor
☐ $24.95—REAL RESUMIX AND OTHER RESUMES FOR FEDERAL GOVERNMENT JOBS. McKinney, Editor
☐ $24.95—REAL BUSINESS PLANS AND MARKETING TOOLS ... Samples to use in starting, growing, marketing, and selling your business

_____ TOTAL ORDERED

_____ (add $4.00 for shipping and handling)

_____ TOTAL INCLUDING SHIPPING

*PREP offers volume discounts on large orders. Call us at (910) 483-6611 for more information.

> THE MISSION OF PREP PUBLISHING IS TO PUBLISH BOOKS AND OTHER PRODUCTS WHICH ENRICH PEOPLE'S LIVES AND HELP THEM OPTIMIZE THE HUMAN EXPERIENCE. OUR STRONGEST LINES ARE OUR JUDEO-CHRISTIAN ETHICS SERIES AND OUR REAL-RESUMES SERIES.

Would you like to explore the possibility of having PREP's writing team create a resume for you similar to the ones in this book?

For a brief free consultation, call 910-483-6611
or send $4.00 to receive our Job Change Packet to
PREP, 1110 1/2 Hay Street, Fayetteville, NC 28305. Visit our
website to find valuable career resources: www.prep-pub.com!

**QUESTIONS OR COMMENTS? E-MAIL US AT PREPPUB@AOL.COM**